W9-BCU-742

Misunderstandings
of the Self

Cognitive Psychotherapy
and the Misconception Hypothesis

Victor Raimy

MISUNDERSTANDINGS OF THE SELF

Jossey-Bass Publishers
San Francisco • Washington • London • 1975

MISUNDERSTANDINGS OF THE SELF
Cognitive Psychotherapy and the Misconception Hypothesis
    by Victor Raimy

The Jossey-Bass
Behavioral Science Series

Preface

The approach to psychotherapy presented here specifies a particular cognitive variable—faulty beliefs or convictions, or, in our terminology, misconceptions—as responsible for psychological disturbances. The misconception hypothesis holds that if relevant misconceptions can be modified or eliminated, improved adjustment results. Because this approach does not depend on any given set of therapeutic methods or techniques, it can be used with almost any therapeutic procedures. In fact, most methods of treatment include, in some fashion and usually under different labels, the changing of misconceptions as one of their essential goals. This widespread interest in changing faulty beliefs has been obscured in most descriptions of psychotherapy by the attention paid to other variables—and by the historical popularity of characterizing psychological disturbances as emotional disorders or as the product of early conditionings or of unconscious conflicts. Only a few approaches have viewed cognitive change as the essential feature of psychotherapy. Although there has recently been a marked swing toward cognitive explanations in psychotherapy and in many fields of psychology that were previously dominated by noncognitive

explanations, these cognitive approaches to treatment have suffered
from the lack of a comprehensive rationale.

Therapists, students, and researchers interested in a cognitive approach to treatment can find in the first six chapters of
Misunderstandings of the Self a rationale for psychotherapy based
upon the misconception hypothesis. In Chapter One, the hypothesis
is explained and discussed in some detail within the framework of
the major approaches to psychotherapy today; the advantages of
applying the misconception hypothesis in therapy, as well as the
hazards (most of them, I hope, avoidable), are also listed and discussed. Chapter Two contains a study of the misconceptions of a
young woman treated by a colleague of mine. Chapter Three
enumerates four major techniques the therapist can use to help
clients locate major misconceptions: explanation, self-examination,
self-demonstration, and vicariation (modeling); then, in Chapter
Four, the task of the client or patient—namely, to change his misconceptions by means of repeated cognitive review of them—is
explored. Chapter Five, on affect and insight, emphasizes the role of
emotions and feelings in a cognitive approach ("Inappropiate
emotions and feelings are probably the best indication of the
presence of misconceptions") and provides a definition of insight in
accord with the misconception hypothesis ("Insight in psychotherapy is the individual's recognition that he has suffered from a
misconception"). Finally, Chapter Six demonstrates the presence of
clusters of misconceptions in psychoses; in the depressive, obsessive,
hysterical, and phobic neuroses; and in two types of misconceptions
that I have found in many of my clinical cases, the special-person
misconception (the individual's assumption of exaggerated self-
importance) and phrenophobia (the misconception that one is on
the verge of insanity).

I then turn to the use of misconceptions in particular
therapies. Chapter Seven discusses four well-known treatment approaches which concentrate explicitly upon changing faulty beliefs.
These four therapies were originally presented by Paul DuBois,
Alfred Adler, Arthur W. Combs and Donald Snygg, and Albert
Ellis. The eighth and ninth chapters discuss five approaches which
at first glance appear to be largely independent of the misconception hypothesis. I show, however, that even these therapies—

developed by Sigmund Freud, Eric Berne, Fritz Perls, John N. Rosen, and Albert Bandura—contain valuable contributions to a cognitive approach to treatment and the misconception hypothesis. The chapters devoted to particular therapies also outline some of the methods employed by their developers for discovering relevant misconceptions as well as for changing or eliminating those faulty beliefs. The final chapter draws together the major principles of the present approach.

Despite the fact that the changing of faulty beliefs or misconceptions has been a prominent feature of many therapies since the time of the early hypnotists, there is a curious paucity of research on this hypothesis. Although occasional studies have appeared which might be reinterpreted to throw light upon the role of misconceptions in treatment, objectively oriented investigators have paid little attention to such cognitive variables. The reasons for this oversight are not clear; there is certainly no historical warrant for ignoring patients' beliefs and convictions as important variables in their behavior. Granted that investigations in this realm are time consuming and difficult, much research conducted on other variables in therapy has been equally difficult and expensive. As the pendulum swings toward interest in cognitive factors in psychological treatment, this oversight may be rectified. This book, in fact, presents a rationale for locating misconceptions and tracing their fate throughout the course of treatment.

My interest in misconceptions as significant variables in therapy is a direct outgrowth of my long-term interest in the self-concept. For years I was baffled by the problem of devising appropriate operations for applying self-concept theory to treatment; the solution, however, turned out to be more simple than I had anticipated. It now seems obvious that the self-concept is composed of the more or less organized notions, beliefs, and convictions that constitute an individual's knowledge of himself and that influence his relationships with others. Even though beliefs and convictions about others which have no self-reference are important in adjustment, I doubt that they are as central as the beliefs about the self; the conceptions which define the self in relation to others not only are long enduring but also exercise almost continuous influence upon behavior. Hence misunderstandings of the self may be major hindrances to personal and social adjustment. The approach to treatment based upon the misconception hypothesis is thus an application of self-concept theory; this application emphasizes the role of specific and concrete faulty beliefs in therapy rather than the incomplete and often confusing theories of the self.

My friend Howard Jaques has amused us both by comparing my analyses of various therapies to the harbor raids of a buccaneer who cuts from their moorings only the ships he wishes for his own. Despite the accusation, I do not believe that I am engaged in intellectual imperialism by inspecting the works of noncognitive therapists for the help they provide to an approach based upon the misconception hypothesis. If eventually we are to have a good understanding of how psychotherapy works, we must also understand how similar successes are obtained by the most diverse procedures. Whether we like it or not, therapists now live in a pluralistic universe of methods and techniques. It is time to discover the common factors which reside in these diverse but successful treatment procedures.

I trust that no one will become too upset over the cavalier way in which I interchange the words *client* and *patient*. I have been forced into this indiscrimination by working in both a university and mental hospitals. Moreover, the writers on psychotherapy referred to in *Misunderstandings of the Self* have determined their own forms of reference to the individuals they treat. I suspect that psychoanalysts would be horrified to read that they treat clients, just as client-centered therapists would rebel against treating patients.

Over the past two decades various psychologists and psychiatrists at the Veterans Administration Hospital in Denver have permitted me to work much as I saw fit with their inpatients and outpatients. The opportunities thus afforded to compare relatively normal college student clients with severely disturbed mental patients have been invaluable for me in wrestling with general principles of therapy which might apply to both groups. I am grateful to the following members of the staff of that hospital: Fred H. Herring, Lawrence S. Rogers, George Katz, Edward P. Davis, David Starrett, and Irene Sanford.

At the University of Colorado, Gene V. Glass offered encouragement, criticism, and editorial help when I needed them most.

William A. Scott was particularly helpful in his reading and criticism of several chapters. Richard G. Ratliff enlightened me about some of the mysteries of various behavior therapies. Peter Bishop was the therapist of the young woman whose misconceptions are detailed in Chapter Two. Together we wrote the other material in that chapter. Edward S. Bordin of the University of Michigan and Hans H. Strupp of Vanderbilt University read critically an early version of the material on psychoanalysis. The suggestions of William E. Henry of the University of Chicago were exceptionally helpful in the final organization of the book.

Boulder, Colorado   VICTOR RAIMY
March 1975

Contents

Contents

Misunderstandings
of the Self

Cognitive Psychotherapy
and the Misconception Hypothesis

Chapter 1

Changing Misconceptions: The Goal of Treatment

Psychotherapists today are faced with an insistent, nagging problem: since widely diverse methods of treatment for similar problems have their successes as well as their failures, how can one defend a given set of treatment procedures as superior to others? Clearly, since quite different, even contradictory, methods of treatment produce similar results, explanations for the success of treatment must be sought outside the realm of method or technique. By now it is evident that successful treatment of psychological problems does not depend upon any of the following issues: focusing upon the past or focusing upon the present; treating individuals in private or treating them in groups; exploring unconscious impulses or attending to conscious motivations; employing directive procedures or practicing nondirective procedures; training therapists who radiate love and affection or training therapists to maintain a cool objectivity.

How, then, do we account for success in therapy? One popular trend has been to seek for unknown characteristics of the therapist which might be strongly influential in producing changes in the clients or patients under treatment. Despite some current research aimed at identifying therapist factors, or the goodness of fit between therapist and patient, the quest for influential therapist factors is still largely one of random conjecture, apart from the well-known requirement that the therapist should be skillful in communication. Still other efforts have been made to discover techniques which will solve the riddle of successful treatment. The most impressive recent research in this direction is found in the methods of the behavior therapists, who have concentrated upon externally observable behavior itself as the primary focus of treatment. Despite rather remarkable, documented successes in dealing with circumscribed fears and phobias, the behaviorally oriented techniques have not, at least as yet, been particularly successful in treating the more complex personality disturbances which afflict the vast majority of individuals seeking treatment. Even the circumscribed problems treated by the behavior therapists can now be dealt with by so many different techniques, such as systematic desensitization, implosive therapy, modeling, and hypnosis, that the behavioral approach is faced with an embarrassment of riches. Here also, quite different, even contradictory, methods seem to have similar successes with similar problems.

There is still another direction in which the search for crucial events in successful treatment can turn. One can logically seek for characteristics in the client or patient—namely, the convictions, beliefs, and notions that each individual has about himself and his world—which are open to modification by many different methods. To propose that there is only one way in which beliefs can be modified or eliminated is as absurd as the proposal that there is only one method for conducting successful psychotherapy. Beliefs, or cognitions, can be changed by effective explanations, by permitting the individual to discover his own mistakes, by allowing or encouraging him to engage in behavior which demonstrates to him his mistakes, or by showing him in real life that his premises are false. These are the methods traditionally employed to bring about change in unrealistic or undesirable cognitive structures. They are also methods that can be found in early and recent psychotherapies. Their goal is to change beliefs or other cognitions rather than to apply specific techniques in a more or less mechanical fashion with the hope that somehow behavior will change.

This approach, which constitutes the theoretical foundation of this book, depends upon a proposition as old as the formal practice of psychotherapy—that psychological disturbances are caused by "false ideas implanted in the mind" and that rooting out these false beliefs will bring about improved adjustment. Although that particular phrasing of the proposition is borrowed from the hypnotists of the previous century, it has many counterparts of more recent origin. These I have brought together under the still neutral term *the misconception hypothesis.*

Current Systems of Therapy

The number of brand-name treatments from which psychotherapists may select their own procedures does not permit an easy counting. In 1959, Harper identified thirty-six "systems" of psychotherapy; fourteen years later Jurjevich (1973) listed twenty-eight "directive" approaches alone. Even in the late 1950s, English and English (1958) sensed the flood when compiling their dictionary of psychology. Bemused, they included in the dictionary a new therapy, "psychosynthesis," the brainchild of Stephen Potter (1950), the celebrated exponent of oneupsmanship and gamesmanship. Faithful to Potter, the dictionary defined psychosynthesis as "a form of counter-psychiatry aimed at restoring useful inhibitions and putting the id back where it belongs." Shortly after publication, Horace English (1960) discovered that a therapy labeled psychosynthesis existed when he received a letter from an Italian psychiatrist enclosing several reprints on psychosynthesis from an Italian journal. The contents showed that Potter's definition of psychosynthesis was wide of the mark.

Not only has the number of supposedly distinct therapies multiplied, but also the confusion. Colby (1964) began his review of the state of psychotherapy with a two-word sentence: "Chaos prevails." There is, however, little cause for weeping, since most of the accretions to psychotherapy of the last two decades, except for the behavioral therapies, have been additions to technique rather than to theory, despite frequent pretensions to the contrary. If we can ignore, at least for the time being, the bewildering array of techniques, and concentrate on the psychological changes which take place in the client as a result of successful treatment, some order may be brought out of the current chaos.

At least four widely held hypotheses about the vital changes which take place in successful psychotherapy can be discerned both historically and in current practices. In presumed order of chronological appearance, they can be labeled as follows: the misconception hypothesis, the expression-of-emotion hypothesis, the redistribution-of-energy hypothesis, and the behavior-change hypothesis. Almost forty years ago, but in different terminology, Rosenzweig (1936) listed three of these four hypotheses among his "implicit common factors in diverse methods of psychotherapy." Instead of the misconception hypothesis, he wrote "providing alternative formulations of significant psychological events." He used the single word "catharsis" for the expression-of-emotion hypothesis. For the behavior-change hypothesis he wrote "implicit social conditioning." Another of Rosenzweig's common factors, the "therapist's personality," is out of place in our categories, since it refers to therapist influence rather than to presumed changes taking place in the patient. Although the labels for our four categories are almost self-explanatory, a few words about each may help to identify them more precisely.

The misconception hypothesis, from which this book draws its substance, is the basis for a particular kind of cognitive approach to psychotherapy. It proposes that successful psychological treatment occurs when faulty ideas or beliefs are modified or eliminated; ideas, beliefs, or conceptions are assumed to control maladjusted as well as adjusted behavior. The hypothesis has been suggested and applied in one form or another by a large group of therapists including Janet, DuBois, Breuer, Adler, Sullivan, Snygg and Combs, Kelly, Ellis, Frank, and Berne. It was probably introduced formally by Immanuel Kant.

The expression-of-emotion hypothesis is a proposal that psychotherapy should be directed toward the release of pent-up emotions or feelings. That hypothesis is largely responsible for the designation of psychological disturbances as "emotional" disorders.

Among its proponents one can list the early Freud, Moreno, and most of the relationship and some of the Gestalt therapists. Recent recruits include such radical approaches as Casriel's "scream therapy" and Janov's "primal therapy." Encounter-group advocates usually appear to subscribe to this hypothesis.

The expression-of-emotion hypothesis depends upon obscure mechanisms. I doubt that anyone seriously believes that the display of emotion rids the individual of his pent-up affect, any more than catharsis rids the individual of past emotional experiences. There is sometimes, however, a marked change in behavior after emotional outbursts. But is the outburst itself necessary and sufficient to produce such change? Must no other factors be present for such expression to be effective? Most therapists, I believe, suspect that the change in affect is only part of the picture. The behaviorists, who stress the role of peripheral conditioning and the mechanical extinction of learned emotional responses, do note the display of emotion; but for them severing the tie between stimulus and emotional response is the crucial consideration, not the catharsis which supposedly lowers the pressure of an impounded head of steam.

The expression-of-emotion hypothesis can also be reinterpreted (see Chapter Five) as referring to therapeutic events which can best be understood in cognitive terms. The principle invoked, generally referred to as the cognitive control of emotion, is that the meaning of what is perceived determines the emotion experienced. In other words, if the therapist can help the client change his perception or understanding of the significant events in an emotion-provoking situation, the affective response is also changed.

The redistribution-of-energy hypothesis is rather strictly limited to the writings of the later Freud and the classical analysts. That hypothesis is concerned with constructs which refer to psychic energies. When these energies are concentrated in or controlled by the id and the superego, symptoms of maladjustment are thought to result. When the balance of energy is controlled by the ego, good mental health presumably results. This classical psychoanalytic hypothesis depends upon a series of intricate inferences about an unobservable—psychic energy. I suspect that Freud had a sure instinct when he proposed the need for quantitative thinking about the changes brought about by treatment. Unfortunately, we are still groping for quantifiable variables which may throw light on behavior change. Ego strength, for example, is a fine device for understanding differences among individuals when it is brought into the cognitive realm by being defined as the number of satisfactions which the individual secures for himself. Such an accounting is, however, still a pseudo-quantification because we have yet to devise adequate measures of obtained satisfactions. For such reasons, I much prefer the nonquantified cognitive insights which psychoanalysts provide in great number, most of which can be viewed as sources of or statements about their patients' misconceptions.

The behavior-change hypothesis, originally based upon theories of classical and instrumental conditioning, is the latest arrival. Among its leading exponents are Wolpe, Eysenck, Ullmann, Krasner, Franks, and, in some fashion, Stampfl, Bandura, and Arnold Lazarus. In tune with the early behaviorists, proponents of this hypothesis assert that observable behavior is the only topic of interest to the therapist, since only external behavior can be reliably observed. They claim that therapists need be concerned only with observable maladaptive behaviors. If they can be modified or eliminated by conditioning techniques, the psychological difficulties disappear. That radical assumption has been changing in recent years and was, in fact, foredoomed when the first behavior therapist recognized self-report as "behavior." Observations of external behavior are only relatively objective, but language is famed for its ambiguity.

The behavior-change hypothesis is difficult to relate to the misconception hypothesis because the innumerable demonstrations of behavioral change by assertedly behavioral techniques have rarely been examined for the cognitive changes upon which the behavioral changes may depend. Systematic desensitization and modeling, as analyzed by Bandura (1969), are exceptions, since Bandura identifies cognitive factors in each. Lazarus (1971) also includes cognitive variables as necessary aspects of behavior therapy. And the use of imagery in implosive therapy, usually described as a behavioral procedure, inevitably opens the door to cognitive interpretations, since imagery is a hallowed cognitive variable. Many other behavioral procedures are also dependent upon complex and intense imaginings purposely produced by the therapist in the individuals treated. In fact, the behavioral therapies are almost completely confounded by prior, simultaneous, and subsequent cognitions, as their clients or patients are always awake and therefore aware of the events which affect them in treatment. Serious question can be raised as to what is effective in producing improvement. Nevertheless, the profound difficulty in distinguishing truly behavioral variables from cognitive variables, even in the laboratory, is a far-reaching dilemma in both research and therapy. Many behavior therapists recognize the dilemma when they refer to nonspecific variables which appear to influence the outcome of their treatment but which cannot be accounted for by their behavioral tenets.

The descriptions and listings above oversimplify practically everything. Thumbnail characterizations are unlikely to satisfy anyone; psychotherapists, like their patients, are usually uncharitable toward those who attempt to pigeonhole them. Many of the therapists listed above under a particular hypothesis might object to the classification, not only because (in their view) the hypothesis is incorrectly characterized but also because they subscribe to more than one hypothesis. We need not be vexed, however, by such difficulties; our immediate purpose is to highlight four major hypotheses about therapeutic change. The concern of this book is narrower still; we are, for the most part, engaged in an attempt to explicate the misconception hypothesis. The delineation of the other three must be left to others.

The Misconception Hypothesis

We can define the misconception hypothesis as follows: *If those ideas or conceptions of a client or patient which are relevant to his psychological problems can be changed in the direction of greater accuracy where his reality is concerned, his maladjustments are likely to be eliminated.* Note that in this definition "reality" is dependent upon the circumstances of a particular individual. Although we all share a similar reality, individual differences must be taken into account. Because of difficulties encountered in defining reality, many writers avoid use of the word, but all of them eventually succumb to euphemisms for it. Note also that the definition refers to "his reality" rather than to any assumed "objective reality" imposed by the therapist. The client's reality consists of *all* the information of which he has knowledge or of which he is aware. If the client ignores meaningful aspects of the reality of which he has knowledge, he suffers from a misconception because he omits part of his reality from consideration. He may ignore aspects of his knowledge for many reasons, ranging from simple failure to perceive relationships to all the devices for avoiding or twisting information found in repression, suppression, and other defensive measures (discussed later in this chapter, in the section on the neurotic paradox). Failure or refusal to integrate evidence of which one is aware distorts the client's own reality. Much time may be required in therapy to help a client or patient bring some of his obscure knowledge into focus, but that is part of the task of therapy. No one has ever asserted that all of one's knowledge is neatly arranged in ordered rows to be called up at will, and without error.

The definitional terms in the misconception hypothesis can be translated into different realms of discourse. For those who prefer the ordinary language of cognition, one could write that when the misconceptions of an individual become more rational, his adjustment improves. For the neobehaviorist, one might write that when centrally mediated processes become more appropriate to the available reinforcements, behavior becomes more adaptive. Regardless of the language employed, the cognitive core of the proposition can be discerned.

Do misconceptions exist? This question is analogous to such questions as "Do conceptions exist?" "Do faulty, mistaken, or erroneous conceptions exist?" If conceptions are subjective realities, then misconceptions are also real. Moreover, if misconceptions exist about the shape of the earth, or the size of an airplane, or the paternity of a child, then misconceptions also exist about one's social status, or one's sexual potency, or the danger presented by a harmless object. The question at issue is not the existence of misconceptions but the amount of influence they exert upon maladjusted behavior. In the present cognitive approach to psychology, relatively stable cognitions, particularly conceptions and misconceptions about the self, are assumed to be major influences which guide both normal and abnormal behavior.

Misconceptions about others and about the external world

undoubtedly influence our adjustment, but misconceptions about the self probably play a major role in our enduring maladjustments. The self-concept (or self-image, or empirical self) not only organizes and guides behavior but also requires significant modification for successful psychotherapy (Raimy, 1943, 1948). Because of its presence during all waking hours and its relative permanence, it defines the individual to himself, not only in long-term identity but also in day-to-day behavior. Misconceptions about the self may drastically and unrealistically limit the kinds of behavior an individual is willing to engage in, or they may relentlessly force him into unwise behavior which leads to perpetual defeat.

For many years I tried to apply self-concept principles to problems of psychotherapy, but concrete application was elusive despite the many available armchair descriptions of the self-concept, beginning with William James (1890). Not until I recognized that the self-concept's major components are the convictions, beliefs, and notions one has about oneself did I realize that some of these faulty components might account for faulty adjustment. For some years, while practicing therapy, I concentrated on trying to change the convictions and beliefs that were relevant to my patients' problems. I also discovered, through reading, that many other therapists had, for at least a century, been interested in the same proposition— that beliefs about the self that are consonant with reality lead to adjusted behavior, while inappropriate beliefs lead to maladjusted behavior.

Only a few of the other therapists had chanced upon or felt it necessary to postulate an organizing superstructure of self-concept. They had also employed different terminology, and often embedded the proposition in complex theories of personality. Nonetheless, the misconception hypothesis, with faulty beliefs about the self occupying a prominent role, has been one of the central, but often implicit, themes in the history of psychotherapy for the past hundred years. The tracing of that history in detail must be left to another time; only its highlights are touched on here.

Proponents. Among those who have emphasized the centrality of the misconception hypothesis, regardless of the terminology and labels employed, one can cite the following individuals. Late in the eighteenth century, according to Ansbacher (1965), Immanuel Kant proposed that mental illness occurs when a person fails to correct his "private sense" with "common sense." More than a century later, Alfred Adler also contrasted "private sense" and "common sense"; he used "private sense" as a synonym for "mistaken opinions," which he viewed as the source of neurosis. Almost thirty years later, H. S. Sullivan transformed "common sense" into a sophisticated synonym, "consensual validation," which Sullivan regarded as essential for maturity and mental health.

During the years between Kant and Adler, the hypnotists of the nineteenth century believed that "morbid ideas" implanted in the mind are responsible for psychological disturbances. Using direct or indirect suggestion while the patient was hypnotized, they attempted to expunge these morbid ideas, or misconceptions. Although he practiced and wrote while the hypnotists were at their peak, Paul Charles DuBois (1909), best remembered for his emphasis upon persuasion and his opposition to suggestion and hypnosis, believed that "incorrect ideas" produce psychological distress. Pierre Janet (1907), who practiced hypnosis, believed that "fixed ideas" dissociated from awareness are responsible for the psychological problems of hysterics.

A decade after Janet published his first case studies emphasizing the role of fixed ideas, Breuer (Breuer and Freud, 1957) wrote that he was in essential agreement with Janet but preferred to write of "unconscious pathogenic ideas." Although Freud was most interested in unconscious emotions, at least early in his career, he agreed with Breuer that pathogenic ideas along with "strangulated affect" are responsible for hysteria (Breuer and Freud, 1957). Freud can hardly be regarded as a direct contributor to the misconception hypothesis, since later in his career he emphasized poorly distributed psychic energies as the underlying cause of neurosis. Nonetheless, in practice he recognized that he was forced to deal with cognitions, and many of his ideas about therapy can be translated into the misconception hypothesis (see Chapter Eight).

Near the middle of the present century, when theories of psychotherapy began to multiply, Sullivan (Perry and Gawel, 1953) emphasized the role of "parataxic distortions" in mental illness. These can be regarded as synonymous with misconceptions. At about the same time, Snygg and Combs (1949) developed a phenomenological theory of personality and psychotherapy in which "inadequate differentiations" of the phenomenal field account for psychological disturbances. Inadequate differentiations are synonymous with misconceptions, since both refer primarily to distortions of reality. Rotter's (1954) learning-based theory of personality emphasizes "erroneous expectations" which are at least partially synonymous with misconceptions, while George Kelly (1955) devised a system of personality and psychotherapy in which "disordered constructs" are posited as the source of maladjustment. Still other therapists have incorporated the misconception hypothesis, but under different terms, in their systems of therapy. Ellis (1962) is perhaps the best-known proponent, since his system of psychotherapy aims single-mindedly at changing patients' "irrational ideas." Frank (1961) views therapy as an attempt to correct "erroneous assumptions," which are the equivalent of misconceptions, in the patients' "assumptive worlds." Horney's (1950) "idealized self-image" can readily be viewed as a cluster of organized misconceptions about the self which conflict with the "real self." In Berne's (1961) view, two primary "relics of the past" interfere with rational functioning. One of the relics, the "Child," is composed of a cluster of "prelogical, poorly differentiated perceptions"; the other cluster, the "Parent," is made up of uncorrected "imitative judgments" learned early in life from parents.

These are only a few of the bewildering number of terms which are synonymous with misconception, and the varying theories of personality and psychotherapy in which they play a large role. In each instance, the cognitive core of the misconception hypothesis can be found.

Neurotic paradox. We know that the vast majority of misconceptions acquired by individuals tend to be corrected by further experience, and the associated behaviors are thereby modified. Whether learning is formal or informal, it is ordinarily effective in helping the individual to grasp reality. Abnormal behavior, however, often appears immune to the usual processes of training and education. At one time or another, almost all persons suffering from neurotic or other psychological disturbances have been given corrective information by well-meaning friends, relatives, and psychotherapists. Yet the misconceptions persist, creating havoc in the personal lives of the disturbed individuals. Without an explanation for the tenacity of faulty conceptions which persist in the face of corrective evidence, the misconception hypothesis is an exercise in naive rationalism. A naive rationalism implies that simple reasoning based on the available evidence should correct an individual's misconceptions. Yet we know that clients and patients often fail to correct their faulty ideas even when they have more than sufficient evidence to do so, and continue in their self-defeating behavior. Therefore, the misconception hypothesis needs to be supplemented with another principle to avoid any implication that therapists face a simple task when trying to correct faulty beliefs.

The failure to profit from experience can be labeled the *neurotic paradox*. In cognitive terms, we can say that conceptions that have been persistently disproved by experience may still be retained as trustworthy guides for action. The paradox lies in the disconcerting discovery that adequate evidence may not dispel a mistaken belief. Mowrer (1948, p. 571) coined the term *neurotic paradox* when he proclaimed its significance in behavioral language. "I invite you to consider what, in many respects, is the absolutely central problem in neurosis and therapy. Most simply formulated, it is a paradox—the paradox of behavior which is at one and the same time self-perpetuating and self-defeating." Translating Mowrer's behavioral terminology into the cognitive framework permits us to utilize the many explanations which have been advanced for the paradox to explain the surprising tenacity of many misconceptions.

Many reasons have been advanced for a patient's failure to correct his faulty thinking when more valid conclusions are available to him. The most frequent explanation emphasizes the patient's avoidance of thoughts, situations, or information which might correct his misconceptions. Mowrer (1948) proposed the general principle that situations which produce self-defeating behavior are avoided because of the anxiety they arouse. White (1964) translated Mowrer's avoidance principle into the cognitive framework by suggesting that avoidance due to unbearable anxiety prevents "reappraisal of the threat." Even before Mowrer's formalizing of the neurotic paradox, Sullivan (Perry and Gawel, 1953) regarded selective inattention as "the classical means by which we do not profit from experience"; because of selective inattention, "we don't *have* the experience from which we might profit."

The most prominent explanation for such avoidance assumes that misconceptions can be isolated from awareness, so that corrective experience cannot be associated with them. One or another doctrine of the "unconscious" is usually invoked to account for the isolating process. Janet (1907), for example, thought that fixed ideas (misconceptions) are "subconscious" "dissociated" trends of thought. Breuer and Freud (1957) believed that "pathogenic ideas" are repressed into the "unconscious." Although Adler wrote that "mistaken opinions" are "unconscious," his usage of that term is best understood as meaning the "dimly envisaged." Sullivan preferred to speak of the "unformulated," for he regarded "unconscious" as an "old-fashioned word." Regardless of terminology, isolating a misconception from conscious awareness is the central core of these explanations for the neurotic paradox.

Although Freud was interested in explaining faulty impulses rather than faulty cognitions, his thinking produced a number of well-known mechanisms, in addition to repression, which can be used to explain the neurotic paradox. An early explanation was his proposal that "fixation" of certain impulses occurs during early stages of the individual's development. Fixation can also be regarded as the result of overlearning based upon such overwhelming evidence that later evidence which might correct the misconception is insufficient to contradict the faulty conviction. The other traditional defense mechanisms of the Freudians can also be viewed as illogical efforts to support misconceptions against attack. Rationalization, for example, is a twisting of the available evidence to avoid recognition of an unpleasant reality. Projection can be viewed as an improper conclusion about the locus of rejected aspects of the self. Denial can be viewed as the conscious avoidance of a misconception to prevent its reappraisal.

Frank (1973) proposed a novel explanation for the neurotic paradox. He suggested that many patients engage in self-fulfilling prophecies by continuing to manifest their disturbed behavior in the presence of others. When others respond reciprocally, by treating the patients in a fashion appropriate for the disturbed behavior, the misconceptions are reconfirmed.

In view of the variety of explanations proposed for solving the conundrum of the neurotic paradox, we might ask which of them are likely to be most valid and most useful in understanding why individuals in treatment have failed to profit from experience. At the present time, there appears to be only one answer to such a question. The known ingenuity of human beings in creating an amazing number of different ways to solve complex problems argues against the exclusion of any of the explanations proposed. Even if we accept them all as methods which are employed often or occasionally to escape from reality, we may be only touching the surface of what Mowrer termed "the absolutely central problem in neurosis and therapy."

For the practicing therapist, failure to reckon with the neurotic paradox often leads to what might be termed the "teacher's fallacy." That is, once the therapist has carefully explained a client's error to him, the therapist may believe that the misconception has been corrected. The client may even dutifully verbalize his apparent insight. But no experienced therapist is surprised to discover that his own insights have failed to penetrate the client's thinking. The necessity of repeated cognitive review to overcome the effects of the neurotic paradox is a central theme in many therapies. That topic is discussed further in Chapter Four.

In order to round out our discussion of the workings of the neurotic paradox, it is helpful to consider it from a slightly different standpoint. When misconceptions are avoided, denied, or repressed, they are often kept inaccessible to correction by still other misconceptions, which can be termed "defensive misconceptions." Like all conceptions or misconceptions, defensive misconceptions are dependent upon evidence, faulty though it may be. A defensive misconception protects the individual from having to recognize an alternative misconception which is more threatening than the defensive misconception. The threat posed by the alternative misconception is part of the evidence perceived by the individual when he rejects it in favor of the defensive misconception. For example, one patient who was extremely dependent upon his wife, despite his very successful efforts to make her miserable, attributed her cavalier treatment of him to the fact that she was always exhausted from her full-time job. He refused to consider the obvious fact, confirmed by an interview with the wife, that she was ready to divorce him. To have recognized her intention to break up the marriage would have forced him to abandon his misconception of himself as the indulgent, protective husband. Thus, he preferred the defensive misconception that her rejection of him was due to her constant fatigue.

When the neurotic paradox is at work, the individual often appears to be acting out of ignorance, just as the husband in the case cited above appeared to be ignorant of his own responsibility for his wife's rejection. In therapy, however, we are practically never dealing with sheer ignorance. Ignorance by itself is not a misconception, nor does it ordinarily require psychotherapy; it can best be treated by education or training. Therapists are usually struggling with a patient's *partial* ignorance, much of it produced by his avoidance of the experiences he does not "have," as Sullivan phrased it.

In discussing the effects of the neurotic paradox, we have also been dealing with the suspension of reality testing. Misconceptions are not tested against reality because of the avoidance of corrective evidence, the twisting and distorting of such evidence, and the interference of defensive misconceptions. The patient appears to be ignorant, but his lack of understanding is only partial. When the reduction in reality testing as a result of these mechanisms is taken into account, misconceptions emerge as exceedingly sturdy and persistent false beliefs and false convictions. Instead of being superficial targets unworthy of the therapist's skill, they not only control and maintain maladjusted behavior but also require considerable skill to modify or eliminate.

Advantages. There are a number of advantages in adopting a therapeutic strategy devoted to detecting and changing relevant misconceptions. In listing these advantages I am not implying that the misconception hypothesis provides the therapist with an established set of specific principles which can be applied in a cut-and-dried fashion. And more's the pity. Therapists must still be highly skillful in finding and changing misconceptions.

1. A large number of common misconceptions thought to be of significance in producing and controlling psychological disturbances are already known to most therapists. The list is certainly not complete, and there are contradictory points of view about

many of the misconceptions. Nonetheless, therapists have available a rich store of specific hypotheses which they can utilize whenever they deem them appropriate. A few examples taken at random illustrate this contention. Alfred Adler (Ansbacher and Ansbacher, 1956) proposed that neurosis is produced by the patient's mistaken belief that he must achieve personal superiority without regard for the common good. Freud's explorations of his patients' histories convinced him that unconscious, distorted beliefs—mostly about sex and aggression—acquired in early childhood are the chief villains in neurosis. Among other examples of maladjusting self-perceptions, or inadequate differentiations, Combs and Snygg (1959) cite the retention of beliefs about the self which were appropriate for an earlier period of life but which become inappropriate later. Ellis (1962) lists ten "irrational ideas" commonly encountered in his patients—for example, the conviction that one must be loved or approved of by all important persons. Rotter (1970) discusses six "generalized expectancies," each of which can be viewed as a misconception; the best known is the patient's faulty belief that his behavior is not under his own control and therefore that he cannot control his own positive reinforcements. Finally, in Chapter Six, I discuss two misconceptions commonly encountered in psychotherapy: the special-person misconception and phrenophobia—the false belief that one is losing his mind.

Practicing therapists need not, however, depend only upon the proposals of their predecessors. Since therapists have experiences in common with most of their clients and patients, they are able to recognize many of their distortions of reality. In treatment, therefore, therapists frequently depend upon their intuitive discoveries of the misconceptions by which their patients are possessed. In addition, some statements of misconceptions, such as Adler's proposal that neurosis is controlled by strivings for personal superiority, are quite broad and thus are thought to be responsible for large areas of maladjustment.

2. Procedures for discovering misconceptions have been proposed by many therapists. Among such procedures we might include free association, nondirective interviewing, Gestalt therapy techniques for analyzing nonverbal behavior, dream interpretation,

and simple history taking. Many of these procedures are standard in the therapeutic armamentarium. Chapter Three groups most of the procedures currently being used into four categories: explanation, self-examination, self-demonstration, and vicariation (or modeling)'. In locating and changing misconceptions, the therapist is not limited to a particular approach but may use any method he prefers, ranging from rational discussion (exemplified by the Adlerians and Ellis) to intensive self-exploration (exemplified by the analysts and Rogers) to hypnotic procedures and even to the behavior therapies. Such flexibility permits the therapist to adapt readily to the particular needs of the individual he is dealing with while maintaining his own orientation to the central task of therapy.

3. Misconceptions provide a relatively specific and concrete focus for treatment. They may be hidden in masses of verbiage, but once they become salient, they sharpen the therapist's understanding of the difficulties faced by the client or patient. They are largely inferred from self-report during the course of therapy, but observations of affect and other nonverbal behavior may be used to supplement self-report.

4. Both therapist and patient have had lifelong practice in detecting mistakes in thinking—sometimes in their own, invariably in that of others. When therapy focuses on misconceptions, its procedures and rationale are thus readily understood. The client's self-knowledge is not isolated from the therapeutic endeavor but becomes integrated with it. And self-observations need not be translated into an artificial language which may have meaning only for the therapist. Both therapist and client become friendly detectives working in the client's interest. Such self-discovery by the client promotes learning and performance. Analysts and client-centered therapists emphasize this principle.

5. Therapists and patients already have considerable skill in changing their own misconceptions as well as those of others. They are not faced with a novel task but with old procedures applied in novel settings.

6. The misconception hypothesis provides the therapist with a consistent orientation toward everything that happens in treatment; all is grist for the mill. When client histories are obtained, the content can be examined for misconceptions which might result

from patterns of past experiences. If diagnostic tests are used, much
of their content, particularly from the Thematic Apperception Test
(TAT) and the Minnesota Multiphasic Personality Inventory
(MMPI), may reveal relevant misconceptions. Initial and subsequent structuring of therapy to orient the client can be employed to
clear up his misconceptions about therapy. The therapist-client relationship can also be helpful in searching for and changing misconceptions. Transference reactions, for example, can be examined for
the light they throw on characteristic misconceptions of the client in
his intimate relationships. Emotional displays often alert the therapist to the presence of significant misconceptions. Defenses can be
understood as faulty explanations which clients devise to explain
their puzzling behavior to themselves. Termination of treatment
can often reveal client misconceptions about life without the support
of the therapist.

7. Changes in relevant misconceptions can often reorganize
behavior far more rapidly and radically than can changes which
occur through other approaches. We are not surprised when major
changes in self-perception following religious conversion, falling in
love, and important job promotions produce far-reaching behavior
changes. Perceptions which are central to the self govern large areas
of behavior. Such self-perceptions may penetrate many seemingly
unrelated activities. The religious convert, for example, often reor-
ganizes much of his life in terms of his new perception of himself.

8. The therapist need not swear allegiance to any dictum
regarding the proper time focus in therapy. Past, present, and the
imagined future are all useful arenas in which evidence about misconceptions can be obtained. Working on current misconceptions
usually appeals to the person in treatment who knows that his misery
is also current, although some patients are likely to flee into the past
to avoid current stresses. The therapist's recognition of such flights
provides him with clues to another misconception of his patient.

9. The misconception hypothesis is basically a pragmatic approach to psychotherapy. As a pragmatic hypothesis, it does not
rule out more fundamental processes, such as conditioning and
other forms of learning, which may explain how conceptions are
acquired and dissipated. It does, however, focus on those products

of learning which can be observed and which account for maladjusted behavior.

Hazards. Psychotherapists who attempt to find and change relevant misconceptions in their clients and patients encounter the usual hazards common to all psychological treatment, such as poor motivation, faulty diagnoses, difficulties in establishing satisfactory relationships, and lack of personal and social resources. In addition to these general difficulties, specific hazards are inherent in the finding and changing of relevant misconceptions. The formula for using misconceptions can be easily encapsulated in the slogan "Locate the misconceptions and root them out," but application of the formula is anything but mechanical. All the skills of the experienced clinician are required. Sometimes they are not sufficient.

1. Lack of insight by the client (that is, the client's recognition that he suffers from one or more relevant misconceptions) is the most immediate hazard faced by the therapist (see Chapter Five). Clients often do not recognize their conclusions and judgments as faulty, even though they may be willing to agree in the abstract that they are seriously mistaken about many things. Direct interrogation in the search for misconceptions is, therefore, usually a fruitless task, since patients, along with everyone else, have reasons to defend their concepts of themselves and of significant others. They believe that they have drawn the best conclusions they can from the information they possess. Questioning anyone's major assumptions is hazardous, regardless of his apparent cooperation.

Although the therapist cannot expect the client to present him with prepackaged, relevant misconceptions, most clients can usually discuss problem areas, such as too much anxiety or difficulties with authority figures or conflicts with significant individuals or disturbances in family, sex, or vocation. These offerings of the client can indicate areas where misconceptions may lurk. They are not, however, specifications of the concrete misconceptions themselves. These must be inferred by the therapist with the help of the client; they must be checked against available evidence, checked again when further evidence appears, and then either discarded or retained for further examination and treatment. Locating the misconceptions which are relevant to a specific disturbance is always open to error. Nonetheless, even those attempts which turn out to be abortive may still provide both therapist and client with information useful for further explorations of relevant misconceptions. Ruling out possible misconceptions can be as important as locating the relevant ones.

2. The client's protest that the therapist interested in misconceptions is "too rational" sometimes hinders treatment if the client becomes exasperated over lack of progress or is frustrated by being unable to solve a knotty personal problem. The search for a logical explanation in the client's faulty cognitions often produces a strong outburst such as "Well, it's not a problem that can be solved with logic. It's emotional!" Such outbursts motivated by frustration are usually abetted by clients' notions that psychotherapy should be a highly emotional affair in which great insights are achieved with dramatic suddenness. Misled by such fantasies, they ignore their own emotionally charged behavior and falsely blame a "too logical" approach for the difficulties they experience in trying to understand themselves.

Many therapists, particularly those interested in the expression-of-emotion hypothesis, also regard a cognitive approach as sterile because it is "too intellectual." I have difficulty in understanding that point of view. In or out of therapy a challenge directed at one's fundamental assumptions invariably leads to intense ego involvement, coupled with emotional displays—witness the reactions of therapists when they are closely questioned about their beliefs concerning psychotherapy. Clients' misconceptions usually concern perceptions of themselves, or of themselves in relation to others, which when threatened evoke emotional reactions. A good relationship is usually necessary before a therapist can be too free with his guesses and hunches about the appropriate target misconceptions. Threat from a stranger may result in too much anxiety and hostility for the patient to handle.

3. Suspected misconceptions can be phrased in such an abstract fashion that they lack personal, concrete meaning for the client. The futility of allowing clients to engage in prolonged discussion of abstractions is well recognized by experienced therapists. Such "intellectualizing" is a defensive maneuver which protects because it lacks personal relevance. It should not, however, be confused with discussions of concrete, personal misconceptions.

4. There is a timing hazard in dealing with misconceptions. This hazard is similar to the timing problem in the making of interpretations and confrontations—and for a good reason. Interpretations and confrontations are usually attempts to emphasize faulty thinking or to refine misconceptions already under consideration. Significant misconceptions spotted early in treatment are often rejected by the patient because he is unable at that point to follow the therapist's reasoning or evidence. One patient, for example, indirectly revealed early in treatment that his concerns about his approaching middle age led to a prolonged depression at the end of what he was sure was his last love affair. He was also insistent that he harbored no resentment toward his lost love. Although his conceptions that his future lacked hope and that he retained no hostility were pointed out as false during the third interview, he was unable to consider them as misconceptions for several months. Then he was able to recognize that his love affair had not been as ecstatic as he had thought, that he was strongly ambivalent toward the woman, and that he had been overly concerned about the future. As in the case of interpretations initially rejected by the patient, experienced therapists usually file rejected misconceptions away for future reference if they are suspected to have some validity. Even rejected misconceptions may serve the purpose of planting a seed which the patient may consider at a later time when his thinking has changed.

5. The relevance hazard is probably the most difficult problem faced by therapist and client in locating those misconceptions which are responsible for the problem behavior. Sorting out significant misconceptions from the welter of information available to therapist and client is likely to be a major task. At the present time, the client's reactions, including any reported or observed changes in behavior, furnish the best clues for deciding whether a significant or relevant misconception is being considered. In this respect, psychotherapy is still a pragmatic undertaking. Pursuit of the wrong set of misconceptions is therefore frequent. Lacking any hard and fast procedures for determining in advance those misconceptions which are relevant, therapists and clients may spend weeks and months on wild goose chases. A therapist may, for example, work diligently on a presenting sexual problem only to discover that the primary prob-

lem is due to unrevealed social difficulties in forming interpersonal relationships.

6. Pet hypotheses held by therapists present other hazards in treatment. The belief that a particular kind of misconception must be responsible for a given kind of behavior often blinds the therapist to other possibilities. This error may apply to isolated, idiosyncratic hypotheses of the therapist or to indiscriminate application of an entire therapeutic ideology. Franz Alexander (1961, p. 555) makes a similar observation when he comments on "the trend toward losing sight of the gap between theoretical generalizations and the individual patient, whose uniqueness of necessity requires a flexible application of general principles." Misconceptions favored by a therapist often obscure other misconceptions which may be more central to the patient's problems.

7. There is also a semantic hazard in application of the misconception hypothesis. Clients, as well as therapists, have their own meanings for the words they employ or hear from others. This problem in communication is likely to imperil the appropriate phrasing of a misconception, whether it is first suggested by the client or by the therapist. For example, a patient who tended to sink into a gloomy but satisfying reverie about a recent loss refused all interpretations of this tendency which did not emphasize the "pain" he felt on such occasions. One day in exasperation he burst out that he felt "exquisite pain" in his reveries. After this revealing phrase was discussed, he was then quite content to agree that he did obtain some perverse satisfaction from his reveries. The semantic hazard is most readily observed in beginning therapists who have not learned to employ short, graphic statements which vividly capture the misconception. Although they may grasp the client's meaning, their rambling attempts to describe the misconception to the client are often more confusing than helpful.

8. Once relevant misconceptions have been detected, innumerable hazards are encountered in trying to bring about cognitive change. Here we must rest content with a look at only one such hazard, the tenacity of convictions. Misconceptions which have been in existence for many years assume the status of full-fledged convictions. Clients and patients are prepared to defend them with evidence which may extend back for several decades. Neuroses of

long standing, character disturbances, and psychological aspects of chronic psychoses present almost insuperable barriers to effective treatment. The misconceptions which control such maladjusted behavior are supported by mountains of evidence. Less chronic maladjustment may also be maintained by strong convictions. The hazard to the therapist is failing to realize that he is struggling with a strongly reinforced conviction rather than with some immutable hereditary or physiological defect. He may give up too soon on the grounds that the difficulty is not open to correction. The obverse error is to refuse to terminate treatment when all indications point to the hopelessness of attempted change because of a lack of psychological or environmental resources available to the client or patient. The mysteries of good clinical judgment in such matters must be left for future solutions.

Another hazard, of a different order from those listed above, may confront the therapist who is appalled by the number of misconceptions harbored by any given individual. The task of treatment, however, is not as great as one might fear. Three saving considerations help to limit the number of misconceptions which must be dealt with.

First, not all of a client's misconceptions are related to his maladjustment. A distinction can be made between "benign" and "malignant" misconceptions. Those which do not produce maladjusted behavior of any consequence can be viewed as benign; those which produce psychological maladjustment are malignant (also referred to as *relevant, responsible,* or *controlling misconceptions*). Misconceptions held in common by one's reference group are likely to be benign. For example, certain bizarre religious practices based upon superstitious notions are examples of benign misconceptions which have little if any maladjusting effect. Idiosyncratic misconceptions which are unrelated to an individual's behavior are also benign. For example, I once knew a girl who believed that cheese grew on low trees or bushes. Each of us undoubtedly has many misconceptions which do not interfere with our adjustment except under highly unusual circumstances. Even among malignant misconceptions, those which produce minor or unimportant limitations can be distinguished from those which produce disturbed or distorted behavior in need of treatment. For example, if an individ-

ual believes that spiders are dangerous and that he would collapse
if he had to give a public speech, the misconceptions are of little
moment provided he is required neither to come into frequent contact with spiders nor to engage in public speaking.

The second saving consideration is the client's tendency to
discuss symptoms and problems with which he is gravely concerned.
Freud made use of this principle when he stated that in free association "all roads lead to Rome." While not all client talking leads
directly to key misconceptions, much of it may lead to them indirectly. If the therapist and the client are continually alert to indicators of misconceptions, attempts to detect and define the relevant
ones can often be made early in treatment. In general, the therapist
often can identify misconceptions simply by recognizing inconsistencies and illogic in the client's discussions. The therapist can then
ask himself what misconception is likely to produce this faulty
thinking. Attending to unusual or inappropriate affect is another
aid to narrowing down the responsible misconceptions, since misconceptions which have been challenged in the past may acquire
associated emotional reactions.

The third factor which reduces the number of misconceptions
requiring attention in treatment is the likelihood that misconceptions are clustered in some hierarchical fashion. If the most central
misconception is modified or eliminated, then the subordinate misconceptions can also be expected to change. The clustering of
misconceptions is probably the rule except for isolated problems
which have little significance in overall adjustment.

To illustrate such a hierarchical arrangement, a forty-year-
old man with a disabling fear that he might become insane was
positive that he could not resume his occupation as a lawyer because
his mind was badly affected. Thrown into a visible sweat if he had
to ride in an elevator with other people, he became greatly flustered
if he had to ask a clerk for an article he wanted to buy in a store.
These were only two of the many consequences of his faulty belief
that psychosis would be precipitated if he came into close contact
with strangers. Theoretically he could have been desensitized to
each of his fears, which depended upon a specific misconception;
but all were dependent upon his superordinate misconception that
social stress would result in mental collapse. When he was led to

question the reality of his impending breakdown and was persuaded to resume part-time work, at which he did well, his fear of insanity was greatly reduced, and the other disturbing symptoms disappeared without direct treatment.

Despite the fact that only a small portion of an individual's misconceptions need attention during psychotherapy, the task of the therapist remains difficult. Usually the effectiveness of the treatment procedures can be gauged only by the outcomes which occur. Not all of the burden rests upon the therapist, however; clients and patients, when well motivated, can also participate in the search for and the changing of malignant misconceptions.

Before we explore other aspects of the misconception hypothesis, the fairly obvious faulty beliefs of an illustrative case might help to reduce the abstractness with which misconceptions have been discussed so far.

Chapter 2

Case Study of a Young Woman

The following analysis of the treatment of twenty-three-year-old Mrs. Bin illustrates within a relatively brief compass the misconceptions underlying the difficulties which brought her to treatment. All case material can be interpreted in various frames of reference; but here we have attempted to demonstrate how misconceptions play significant roles in treatment, even though the therapist was not consciously aware at the time that he was dealing with them. The case report was written by her therapist, Peter D. Bishop, who was a graduate student in clinical psychology when he saw Mrs. Bin. The therapy was supervised by another faculty member. The misconception analysis is the joint product of the author and Bishop, written about two years after the termination of treatment. All identifying content has been removed or altered, and some of the material has been rearranged. Italicized phrases provide clues to Mrs. Bin's misconceptions; the various misconceptions are numbered and discussed in the bracketed portions of the case report.

Presenting Problem

Mrs. Bin is an attractive, intense, intelligent, open, and introspective young woman with a college degree who is locally employed in a business office. Her husband, to whom she has recently been married, is a graduate student. Mrs. Bin came to the clinic for help in dealing with what she describes as *"free-floating anxiety."* [Misc. 1: "I am anxious without reason." In Chapter Five, free-floating anxiety is viewed as a misnomer. Persons who report anxiety symptoms without an apparent source will usually supply the clinician with many statements about feared psychological disintegration. They often use such phrases as "I'm falling apart" or "I'm coming loose at the seams." They do not ordinarily view these feelings as explanations for their anxiety, since such explanations are not in accord with their concepts of anxiety. Mrs. Bin's perception of her fear of disintegration, a misconception, is a current reality for her even though its likelihood of occurrence is objectively remote. One of its immediate sources, as we shall see later, is her concern over her husband's love for her and her negative reactions toward him. She covers up those concerns with the less threatening Misc. 1, and Misc. 2 which follows.]

Mrs. Bin states that she has been planning to obtain therapy for a long time in order to help her gain insight into her problems, which she sees as *centering on an extreme dependency relationship with her parents.* [Misc. 2: "My current problems are due to my extreme dependence upon my parents." As we shall see later, although she may at times feel the lack of her parents in her present life, she faces more pressing current difficulties.]

Mrs. Bin put off seeking help until she was faced with anxiety attacks for which she could find no reason. In addition to her expressed concern over anxiety, she complains of being bothered by hypochondria, feelings of insecurity and inadequacy, irrational jealousy, *fear of losing control or going crazy, fears of death and being left alone,* and always searching for and finding something to worry about. [Misc. 3: "I am likely to lose control of myself, go crazy, die." In this misconception, Mrs. Bin is providing specific content for her "free-floating" anxiety. Anxiety symptoms are often construed as evidence for impending insanity. Fear of death is often a confused response to one's fear of madness; insanity and death are often equated. Most persons with anxiety do not become psychotic. The discussion of phrenophobia in Chapter Six expands this point of view.]

Mrs. Bin has considerable phrenophobia. She is definitely concerned about the possibility of madness, although intellectually she believes she is strong enough to avoid it. She recalls that in childhood she once saw a television program about a young girl who was going insane. She strongly identified with the girl and became so frightened that she asked to sleep in her parents' bedroom. She also describes how fearful she was as a child—she was unable to close her eyes before falling asleep, she was afraid that someone was watching her from her closet, and she was afraid to look in a mirror for fear that she had been transformed or had vanished.

She is reluctant to delve into her childhood for fear that she may uncover a dark mystery about herself. Frequently, she discusses her concern about control. If she should lose control, she fears that she may learn something terrible about herself. Her concern about control is also manifested in her fear that she may become hooked on the tranquilizers which she is taking on her physician's prescription. Although she has smoked marijuana, she claims that she has never "let go" because she is afraid to lose control and learn about her real self. [Comment: Her phrenophobic fear of loss of control evidently has a long history, extending back to her childhood.]

In a relatively short time, Mrs. Bin was able to connect her anxiety to feelings of abandonment by her parents. [Comment: Here she is building a misconception upon Misc. 2, her supposed dependence on her parents, although we cannot ignore the historical possibility that at one time she may have been overdependent on them.] She says that she had always had a very close relationship with her parents, particularly with her father. Now she is separated from them by great distance. She mentions her ambivalence about a forthcoming visit by her parents. She cannot get excited about their coming. She is caught in the trap of wanting things to be the same with them, telling herself that they can be the same, and simultaneously fighting off feelings of jealousy toward her brother, who still has a close, dependent relationship with her parents; although she has labeled this kind of relationship as bad, she had thrived on it while she was at home, and she still wants it.

Mrs. Bin remarks with some bitterness, that her parents had been her security and now offer none. She has, however, come to the healthy realization that she must make a life for herself without her parents. She has also come to realize that *she is not alone, because her relationship with her husband is good and improving.* [Misc. 4: "My relationship with my husband is good and improving." This statement about her marriage is probably the most basic misconception which could account for her current symptoms. Contrary to this idealization of the marriage, later events in therapy indicate that she is beset with resentments, fears, and jealousy toward her husband.]

Early History

Mrs. Bin says that she came from a very close-knit liberal family. The oldest of three children, she has one brother three years younger and another twelve years younger. She entered therapy *protecting an idealized image of both parents.* [Misc. 5: "I am the daughter of ideal parents." Idealized images are misconceptions by definition.] She had idolized her father since she was very young. He had been her confessor and therapist. She sees herself as extremely dependent, with many fears and feelings of inadequacy, but *she wants to take the blame alone.* [Misc. 6: "I blame only myself for my dependency, my fears, and my feelings of inadequacy." Later, she turns out to be quite willing to blame her parents.]

Mrs. Bin describes her family as warm, loving, open, and permissive. Yet she had gone to a child-guidance clinic for emotional problems. The psychologist at the clinic, where she had received brief treatment when in third grade, reported that her insecurity came from her parents' failing to provide her with a sufficiently structured environment. Her parents had always given her a choice, rarely placing demands upon her. To Mrs. Bin, their permissiveness was actually an implicit demand to "make up your own mind, even if you are just a young child." She feels that she has always had to make decisions. Today she really struggles with them. [Comment: Her interpretation of this bit of her history was reported to her therapist at about the same time that she told him she could not blame her parents for her difficulties. Misconceptions can be in conflict with misconceptions as well as with more valid conceptions. Mrs. Bin was blaming her parents for their over-permissiveness at the same time that she was idealizing them. Their permissiveness may actually have resulted in the development of a special-person misconception (See Chapter Six), which requires the person always to be right. Such a demand upon oneself creates great difficulties in making decisions. There is considerable evidence that Mrs. Bin is something of a "special person" who was mildly unsuccessful in her relationship to her husband.]

Mrs. Bin describes her relationship with her parents as extremely loving; yet she also remembers that she always competed with her brother, who is three years younger, for her father's attention. A possible clue to why she felt a need to fight to win love and attention in a loving family can be found in her statement that for the first three years of her life she was the center of attention. She also related a very dramatic episode in which her grandfather callously shifted his attention to her brother. That provided Mrs. Bin with an intense feeling of loss of love.

Mrs. Bin describes her early school years as very uncomfortable because she was forced to lead a double life. Her parents were working with communists, and the children had to be very careful about what they said in school. She claims that she was very successful as a member of the popular crowd at school, but this was accomplished at a price: when very young, she became highly aware of *the necessity of playing a role in relations with others.* [Misc. 7: "I must play a role in order to be accepted by others." Mrs. Bin evidently believes that she engaged in role playing, rather than forming genuine relationships, solely because she had to conceal from her schoolmates her family's political interests. This, of course, is an easy and dramatic and possibly valid explanation, but another plausible explanation should probably be given more weight. Children who yearn to be the center of attention frequently discover that they must hide these desires to avoid rejection. Hiding one's genuine motives leads to the playing of artificial roles. One might surmise that Mrs. Bin, as a young child, had many more occasions to cover up her desire for attention than to cover up her parents' politics.]

Mrs. Bin is insistent that the primary message she received from both parents was that they loved her as someone very special. *She does not understand how she is the way she is, since she had such loving, accepting parents.* [Misc. 8: "A child who is given complete love and acceptance must automatically grow up well adjusted." Here Mrs. Bin shares a common misconception. Although her therapist senses that Mrs. Bin's early treatment by her parents may well have led her to develop a special-person misconception, Mrs. Bin is totally unaware that her difficulties might be traced to her insistent and overriding need to be treated as someone who is highly special.]

Mrs. Bin describes herself as having been a fearful child. She recalls that on one occasion she was unable to close her eyes before falling asleep and was afraid that someone was watching her from the closet. [Comment: Here she is dredging up evidence from her childhood to support her fearful belief that she may be going mad—Misc. 3.]

She has characteristically had difficulty in examining any negative feelings she may have had toward her father. Her blocking also seems to be influencing her present life, since she reacts to her husband's overcriticalness as if his criticism were always justified (as if her husband were her father disapproving of her). [Comment: Mrs. Bin evidently idealizes her husband just as she had idealized her father; she ignores negative evidence concerning father and husband by selective perception, thus maintaining the misconceptions of ideal father and ideal marriage.] She reacts emotionally to her husband's horseplay in which he pretends to be a monster, as if he really were one. She is very jealous of anything her husband does which does not include her. *She reacts to his report of a casual conversation with an attractive girl as if he no longer loved her,* as if he were her father showing love to her brother. [Misc. 9: "If

my husband shows interest in anyone else, that means he is less interested in me; I must have all of his love and attention." If the
therapist is correct, Mrs. Bin perceives her husband as though he
were her father. But this is a complex misconception, which includes
her belief that any interest her husband shows in others thereby
diminishes his love for her—the common misconception of the
jealous person.]

The recurring themes of Mrs. Bin's case seem to derive from
the *childhood which she resists examining.* [Misc. 10: "If I dare
to examine my childhood memories, I shall get worse." This misconception is part of a common belief that examination of unpleasant memories imperils one's stability, whereas avoiding such thoughts
eliminates them.]

Social Relationships

Mrs. Bin fears that in some ways she may be unacceptable
to others, but she also obtains reassurance from the fact that her
anxiety attacks occur only when she is alone. She states positively
that she can and does form very good relationships with people; yet
she also says, "I must act in certain ways to get people to like me,"
implying that she is likely to lose friends if she does not play a role.
When she was in a sensitivity group in college, she learned from
others that she had a habit of qualifying anything important she
had to say. *She cannot lay herself on the line, because she fears
being rejected.* [Misc. 11: "If people get to know me well, I shall
be disliked." This misconception is the basis for Misc. 7, "I must
play a role to be accepted by others," the widely held misconception of the maladjusted that intimate self-revelation must result in
his being disliked and rejected by others. We cannot, however, be
too dogmatic about its always being a misconception; completely
spontaneous displays of one's genuine feelings may sometimes be
offensive to others. God simply failed to guarantee that all of one's
spontaneous feelings and reactions will be respected.]

Mrs. Bin sees herself as too ingratiating. She feels that she
must work to win love. She has trouble accepting the idea that
anyone could love her for herself. She is amazed that her husband

chose her as his wife. She is worried about scaring her husband away by appearing to be too demanding.

Mrs. Bin reports a long history of what she sees as successful yet frequently empty social adaptability. In the past, she wanted to be accepted so badly that she would play whatever role was required of her. She is frequently passive, dependent, and even weak in close relationships in order to get attention. Although she has been quite successful when relating in her "sick" role, she is afraid that her husband will not take too much of her while she acts that role; yet she questions whether he really wants her to be more independent, since they seem to complement each other now. [Comment: This passage catapults us into the intricacies of the marriage relationship, about which we have very little information. We know neither what her husband wants of her nor what he will be willing to accept. She seems to have the same difficulty, much amplified, of course, by the fact that she herself is one of the two central characters in that drama. In addition, we have very little information about her actual social relationships with persons other than her husband and her parents. Was she as successful in other social relationships as she claims? As in all case histories, much always remains for speculation, even after prolonged contacts in psychotherapy.]

Mrs. Bin reacts very strongly to her husband's constant criticisms of her. Although *intellectually she accepts the fact that his criticizing is his hangup, emotionally she reacts as though his criticisms were valid. She denies becoming angry with him on this issue.* [Misc. 12: "I understand and can accept my husband's criticisms of me." This defensive misconception covers up Mrs. Bin's true reactions to her husband's critical attitude toward her. If his criticisms are as frequent as she implies, there must be considerable reaction of anger and frustration on her part which she refuses to face and deal with, because she is fearful of upsetting the positive aspects of her marriage. Misc. 13: "I do not get angry even when criticized by my husband." Misc. 12 and 13 permit her to ignore her difficulties with her husband as the immediate and efficient source of her current anxieties, and to proffer a less threatening explanation— Misc. 2: "My current problems are due to my extreme dependency on my parents." Historically, her preferred explanation probably has some validity, since many of her patterns of interpersonal reaction probably do trace back to her parents. As usual, however, one must ask: If her early relationships with her parents produced problems for her, why did she come to therapy at this particular time? We must also recognize that having had several undergraduate courses in child psychology, she had learned some easy and conventional answers for the causes of current maladjustments.]

Five-Month Report

Mrs. Bin has not been bothered by acute anxiety attacks since the beginning of the school year, about three months after beginning treatment. She thinks that her busy new schedule involving work, school, and new friends accounts for her reduced anxiety. Her time is filled, and she is not often left alone with her thoughts. She says, however, that she does not want to depend on crutches like tranquilizers or time fillers to protect her from anxiety.

One area in which she is progressing is her attempt to become more independent in her relationship with her husband. She believes that she has become more assertive. She is realistically ambivalent about this change, because her husband is uncertain whether he approves of her new behavior. She is afraid that if she becomes too assertive, the relationship may be in peril.

Near the middle of the fourth month of treatment, she made a giant step forward. Unlike most of her soul searching, in which she found herself up a blind alley, she finally confronted directly her feelings of jealousy. She came in very upset and jealous because her husband had described to her a conversation he had had with a very attractive girl at work. Because she was fearful of scaring her husband away if she let him know about her jealousy, she guarded her feelings very closely.

In describing her reactions to the incident, she said that if her husband shows even a casual interest in someone, she feels that their relationship has somehow been negated. [See Misc. 9, "If my husband shows interest in anyone else, that means he is less interested in me." In the following passage, Mrs. Bin reports some of the evidence from her early history which still supports her misconception.] When I asked her if she had ever had similar feelings with other people, she talked about a former boyfriend who began to pay attention to one of her close girl friends, and the two ended up excluding her. This time she also remembered her feelings about her brother's birth, which seemed to threaten her close relationship with her father. When she recalled this, she began to cry. She had cried before in therapy, but it had usually been a form of emotional release without insight. She saw now, she said, that she was still acting like a child; that she had to be the center of attention or she felt she was not loved. [Comment: The two sentences preceding illustrate insight as defined in this book—the recognition of a misconception.]

Six-Month Report

I am presently quite frustrated about Mrs. Bin's progress. In some ways she is moving much closer to some basic issues, and in other ways she is quite resistant. I am encouraged about her increasing awareness of hostility toward her parents and her husband [see Misc. 6, "I blame only myself for my dependency, my fears, and my feelings of inadequacy," and Misc. 4, "My relationship with my husband is good and improving"]. Although she still backs away from examining the source of her anger, at least she is more aware of it. A clue to the source of her anger is seen in the ironic, almost sarcastic way she recently said, "It's nice to know that my husband will accept me the way I am." She has doubts whether her husband does accept her the way she is.

A couple of weeks ago, Mrs. Bin began telling me again about how she overreacts to news about world crises. When I mentioned that what seemed to frighten her most was not knowing what was going to happen, she responded by talking about her general fear of the future and the unknown. She then began to talk about John, her steady boyfriend in high school. Even after going steady with him for two years, she was always uneasy until definite plans were made for a date. Sometimes she would call John when she became upset over not hearing from him. She could not tolerate indefiniteness in their relationship. In another session, she talked quite thoughtfully about her fear of the future and her need to gain control over it. She went beyond the abstract fear to speak of her fear that if she does not manipulate people, she will not have control over them and they will "disappear." She went so far as to say, "If I don't actively engage with people or manipulate them, somehow they'll never come around again." Related to her concern over being accepted is the feeling she had as a child that she had to please her parents. She does not know exactly how she got the message that she had to do well, but she felt she had to. She still does. While visiting her parents over Christmas vacation, she felt great pressure to be on time for a meeting with them. She does not know what would happen if she let them down.

In a recent session, Mrs. Bin discussed her fears that her husband does not accept her for what she is. She has also mentioned her husband's increasing annoyance over her hypochondria. She has serious doubts about whether she will ever change her constant concern with her health.

She has also expressed the feeling that she is a phony who must please others by pretending to be something she is not. Related to this is her report that she played the role of a boy in fantasy when she was a child, which can be interpreted as her feeling that she had lost her father's love when her brother was born. She has also mentioned several things which point to her having competed with her mother, as well as with her brother, for her father's attention. Recently, she dreamed she was having sex with her father. She also recalled an incident when, as a little girl, she had been seductive toward him.

Mrs. Bin is certainly pulling her parents off the pedestal on which she had placed them [see Misc. 5, "I am the daughter of ideal parents," and Misc. 6, "I blame only myself for my dependency, my fears, and my feelings of inadequacy"]. The recent visit to her parents showed how much she is still affected by them. Her husband remarked how different she was around them. He particularly noticed her constant efforts to put her mother down. She would argue with her mother about anything, even taking a position she did not strongly believe for the sake of argument. Her hostility could be the result of her resentment toward implied demands from both parents. I suspect that both parents communicated implied demands that she should be strong, intelligent, obedient, liberal, atheistic. She felt these demands and became the obedient little girl. Now she is still not free of parental demands, but she is becoming openly resentful of her mother's attempts to make her feel guilty and of her father's "knowing all the answers."

Final Report

We are now terminating after eight months because her husband has finished his graduate work and is accepting a job elsewhere. She plans to resume therapy in a couple of years in order to learn more about herself, but both she and I agree that she is now well able to cope with her situation without more immediate therapy.

She has been free of her "free-floating anxiety" over a period of months, and is now more in touch with her feelings and understands herself better. Our focus during her final sessions has been on her awakened awareness of her anger. When she first began to experience it, she stated that it was a "revelation" to her to see herself as an angry person. She came to realize that her fear of losing control was directly related to her repressed anger. Even now, she is afraid to have the fear confirmed that she is "demonic." [Comment: It seems evident that as Mrs. Bin came to recognize that she was very angry at her husband and also to some extent at her parents (Misc. 13 and 6), her anxieties began to lessen and her "free-floating anxiety" disappeared. Some of her phrenophobia (Misc. 3) seems to persist; she is somewhat fearful of seeing herself as "demonic," an ambiguous word which can mean either a sinister person or one who is possessed by demons—psychotic.]

I talked with Mrs. Bin at length about the relation of her anger to the demands she felt were made on her by other people— her parents, her husband, and some of the people where she worked. I talked about being more direct in expressing anger, but also about using judgment. She was able to see that she was overreacting to the demands made upon her, although she could also appreciate that some of her anger was appropriate. Seemingly as a consequence, she was better able to cope with the people at work as well as with her husband, toward whom she began to be more open in expressing her anger. After she exploded at him recently, he did not with-draw but comforted her and gave her the needed message that she was still loved in spite of her explosion. She could then talk with him more about her problem with anger. She has also stood up to her mother, who recently made a request which would, if fulfilled, have been a direct contradiction of what Mrs. Bin wanted to do.

Although I feel that much more could have been done in therapy, both she and I feel that much has been accomplished.

Discussion

The misconception hypothesis proposes that when miscon-ceptions are modified or eliminated, the individual's adjustment will improve. The reader must judge for himself whether Mrs. Bin's ad-justment improved, since therapists have many different criteria for making this assessment. As the therapist indicated, Mrs. Bin still had problems at the termination of treatment. We are here attempting only to illustrate that misconceptions can be inferred rather directly and that changes in them during treatment can be detected.

At the end of Chapter One, we mentioned the tendency of misconceptions to appear in clusters. On the basis of four themes, twelve of Mrs. Bin's thirteen misconceptions can be assigned to four somewhat independent clusters: fear of madness (phrenophobia), influence of parents, relationship with husband, and playing a role.

Three of her misconceptions fall into the *fear-of-madness* cluster: Misc. 1, "I am anxious without reason"; Misc. 3, "I am likely to lose control of myself, go crazy, die"; and Misc. 10, "If I dare to examine my childhood memories, I shall get worse." As the report indicates, Misc. 1, her free-floating anxiety, was rather quickly modified during treatment when she came to see that there were concrete reasons for her anxiety, most of which appeared to relate to her husband. Misc. 3, her explicit concern over going mad, seems to have been much reduced during treatment, but still per-sisted at the end of the contacts. Even though Mrs. Bin, according to the therapist, "came to realize that her fear of losing control was directly related to her repressed anger," the therapist had to add,

"Even now, she is afraid to have the fear confirmed that she is 'demonic.' " The reduction in phrenophobia without complete eradication is a common event in successful treatment. If the fear of going mad has persisted over many years, as was probably true in the case of Mrs. Bin, partial insight into it as a misconception often occurs, but its extirpation is difficult unless it is dealt with directly and intensively. The fate of Misc. 10, "If I dare to examine my childhood memories, I shall get worse," is ignored in the therapist's report. Because he was not consciously looking for and reporting on misconceptions, his lack of reference to it after its initial appearance is not surprising. However, her fear that she may be "demonic" suggests that Mrs. Bin is still afraid of the skeletons buried in her childhood closet.

Three of Mrs. Bin's misconceptions fall into the cluster labeled *influence of parents:* Misc. 2, "My current problems are due to my extreme dependence upon my parents"; Misc. 5, "I am the daughter of ideal parents"; and Misc. 8, "A child who is given complete love and acceptance must automatically grow up well adjusted." As therapy progressed, Misc. 2 was modified when she came to see that many of her problems related to her husband rather than to her parents. Mrs. Bin was undoubtedly aware that she was less endangered by ascribing her difficulties to her parents than to her husband, if only because her parents were a thousand miles away while her husband was at hand. Furthermore, when she came to realize that her parents made her angry by their demands, she could not readily ascribe her problems to her dependence upon them. Mrs. Bin's "dependence" upon her parents may actually have been her attempts to control them through "weakness," a ploy which is often confused with true dependence. Her description of herself as manipulating her husband and others by being "passive, dependent, and even weak" seems to reinforce this supposition. Misc. 2, then, seems to have been altered in two ways: Mrs. Bin came to see that her parents were not responsible for her current difficulties; she also began to realize that her dependence was not a simple need to be protected but a method she employed for manipulating others. Misc. 5 was probably a defensive misconception in the first place. There is considerable evidence throughout the report that Mrs. Bin had always been highly ambivalent toward her parents. Misc. 8 seems also to have been a defensive misconception, possibly sparked by her courses in child psychology.

Four misconceptions make up the cluster labeled *relationship with husband:* Misc. 4, "My relationship with my husband is good and improving"; Misc. 9, "If my husband shows interest in anyone else, that means he is less interested in me; I must have all of his love and attention"; Misc. 12, "I understand and can accept my husband's criticisms of me"; and Misc. 13, "I do not get angry when criticized by my husband." These misconceptions appear to have undergone the greatest changes. Misc. 4 was consistently contradicted by the evidence that Mrs. Bin's relationship with her husband was the primary reason for her interest in therapy, even though she was only dimly aware that she had difficulties in that quarter. She evidently learned that her need to have all of her husband's attention (Misc. 9) was motivated by irrational jealousy. Misc. 12 and Misc. 13 disappeared when she realized that she did not accept his criticisms and that she became angry when criticized by him.

Only two misconceptions make up the cluster labeled *playing a role:* Misc. 7, "I must play a role in order to be accepted by others," and Misc. 11, "If people get to know me well, I shall be disliked." The two could even be combined into a single misconception, phrased "If people get to know me well I shall be disliked, so I must play a role in order to be accepted by others." The change in Misc. 7 was evidenced in the six-month progress report when the therapist stated, "She has also expressed the feeling that she is a phony who has to please others by pretending to be something she is not." There are other indications that Misc. 11 was at least modified when she became less fearful over letting other people know about her more negative side, particularly when she argued with her mother and became openly angry with her husband.

The last of the thirteen misconceptions still unaccounted for is Misc. 6, "I blame only myself for my dependence, my fears, and my feelings of inadequacy." This misconception contradicts Misc. 2, in which she blamed her current problems on her parents. Misc. 2 and 6 represent an interesting layering of defensive misconceptions, for blaming herself was less threatening than blaming the parents whom she professed to idealize. Misc. 6, which does not seem to fit readily into any of the four clusters, was eliminated fairly early in treatment, when she came to see that she was blaming her parents rather than herself. Her mistake about her parents' influence on her current difficulties was corrected when she realized how much she was upset about her husband. In the end she may have returned to "blaming herself," although such self-blame at the end of therapy would have been based upon quite different grounds than the blame she initially claimed as a sanctimonious defense. At the end of treatment she probably came to see that she was responsible for many of her difficulties because of her suppressed anger, her playing of the "sick role," and her manipulation of others.

The obscure fate of some of Mrs. Bin's misconceptions is not entirely due to the incompleteness of the report. Incompleteness characterizes any report of interviews that have extended over many months. Therapists have traditionally recognized that as clients and patients improve, the exact source of improvement is often hidden from view. In Mrs. Bin's case, there seems to be good reason to suspect that those misconceptions which underwent observable change during treatment were largely responsible for her difficulties when she entered treatment. Her anxiety and confusion about herself were manifested in her free-floating anxiety and her phrenophobia. The phrenophobia was considerably reduced in intensity, whereas the free-floating anxiety was eliminated. The specific sources of her anxieties were uncovered when she cleared up her faulty understandings about her interactions with her husband. To do so, she had to make a detour to explore her misconceptions about the current role played by her parents. The examination of her misconceptions about her parents and her husband provided her with additional therapeutic gains when she discovered that role playing and manipulation of others were unnecessary.

Chapter 3

Therapist's Task: Presenting Evidence

One of the major contentions of this book is that misconceptions of the client or patient are established and can be changed by evidence. When attempting to change misconceptions, the therapist must therefore find ways to present evidence or information which the client can utilize to correct his misconceptions. The process of making such evidence available is not necessarily a straightforward presentation of corrective information, since the neurotic paradox (discussed in Chapter One) often interferes with what might otherwise be a teaching situation in which the therapist presents information to the client to correct misconceptions singled out for change. Inasmuch as the manifestations of the neurotic paradox are usually themselves based upon misconceptions (for instance, the client's belief that he must avoid even thinking about matters which evoke in him feelings of fear or shame), treatment for these defensive beliefs still consists of making corrective evidence available to the client. The process of therapy is, therefore, a cognitive one which attempts to bring the patient closer to reality by rational methods, even though it deals much of the time with the irrationalities of the patient.

There is always a danger that the term *cognition* will be interpreted as referring only to coldly rational, systematic, and highly intellectualized thinking. In this book, however, *cognition* is used in a much broader sense, such as that given by English and English (1958): "A generic term for any process whereby an organism becomes aware or obtains knowledge of an object." This is the traditional meaning of the word *cognition*, which by subtle corruptions is now often limited to the strictly systematic. The definition does not refer to the obtaining of *correct* knowledge. How an individual gains accurate knowledge of himself and the world is one of the major mysteries of cognition, but accuracy of perception or of concept formation is not implied in the definition of the word.

The term *evidence*, as used in this book, refers to sudden untested insights (or the cognitive component of an emotional outburst, or of a "feeling") as well as to carefully analyzed data. The systematic gathering, sifting, and testing of evidence is probably a fairly unusual accomplishment for most persons; nonetheless, they are still engaged in cognitive appraisals even when they use haphazard and untested data. Nonsystematic thinking makes use of many different sources of evidence, thereby escaping the rigidities of formal systems which specify what should be thought about. In a court of law, highly standardized rules supposedly govern the kinds and sources of information considered as evidence. Jurors, however, are usually willing to apply far less rigid principles than those prescribed by the formal rules of the court. Lawyers know only too well how difficult, if not impossible, it is to keep jurors from being swayed by any kind of information they obtain about a case at issue. Much the same can be said for the ways in which all of us, including clients and patients, reach conclusions about ourselves and our worlds.

Although many psychologists are likely to speak of feelings, attitudes, emotions, and experiences as some kind of spontaneous behavior *without cognitive precursors or cognitive consequences,* there is little doubt that individuals are quite aware of their affective experiences and make use of these cognitive data in trying to understand themselves. Spontaneous affective reactions are certainly influenced by cognition and also have cognitive consequences. One consequence is that they are often recalled and reviewed by the person who experiences them. In such review he is also likely to evaluate what they mean to him and to use such affective experiences to categorize himself. Self-evaluation and self-categorization are preoccupations of most human beings. Feelings and emotions are scrutinized for the evidence they provide; and the individual uses this evidence to establish beliefs about himself and also to change them.

We are, I believe, doing cognition and psychology a great disservice when we perpetuate the fiction that thinking and cognition occur only under the rules of evidence or the rules of logic. In adhering to such fictions, we have been forced to dichotomize reason and emotion as though they were two quite different and opposed guides for behavior. Such statements as "He was ruled by his emotions" or "He was not emotionally convinced" have been interpreted so literally that our clients and patients are often portrayed as creatures governed by unpredictable and unanalyzable surges of "feeling." In the present view, clients and patients are seen as imperfect data processors who often assign undue weight to evidence which has vivid demand characteristics because it is accompanied by emotion and feeling.

The methods utilized by psychotherapists to present evidence to their clients and patients can be divided into four categories: self-examination, explanation, self-demonstration, and vicariation (or modeling). It is difficult to correlate particular approaches to therapy with any one of these four methods, because most treatment approaches employ more than one. Only a brief description of each of these four methods will be presented here, since the remainder of the chapter is devoted to a more detailed discussion of each.

In *self-examination* the client or patient is encouraged to talk and think about himself and his problems in the hope that he can locate his misconceptions and find more adequate evidence which will modify or eliminate them. The client-centered approach is perhaps the best example of the self-examination method, although other approaches, such as psychoanalysis in some respects and the Adlerian approach in other respects, also employ the self-examination procedure, at least part of the time. *Explanation* is probably the most widely used procedure for presenting evidence in therapy. Its essence consists of explaining in some fashion the evidence or information which is more valid than that upon which the misconception is based. *Self-demonstration* is a procedure whereby the client is maneuvered into a situation where he can observe for himself that he has a misconception and can change it. Group therapy makes considerable use of self-demonstration, particularly when members of the group discover that they have had faulty ideas about their ability to behave appropriately in social situations. In the *vicariation* (or modeling or imitation) procedure, the client observes a model performing behavior which the client cannot perform because of lack of information or distorted information.

To some extent, all four of these methods of making evidence available to the client or patient overlap in actual practice. Explanations by the therapist may stimulate the client to engage in self-examination. Verbalizations by the client resulting from self-examination may elicit explanations from the therapist. When the therapist maneuvers clients into self-demonstration, explanations are often used before and after the self-demonstration. Explanations may encourage clients to participate in demonstrations as well as in vicariation. These four methods of presenting evidence must therefore be viewed as categories of convenience which describe *how the therapist is proceeding* at any given moment in his effort to detect or to correct one or more misconceptions. All four methods promote cognitive review. They are sometimes difficult to distinguish, since the flexible therapist may switch rapidly from one to another as he maneuvers the client into considering evidence.

During the course of therapy, clients and patients are often required to think and act in ways which are foreign to them or which they may resist for a variety of reasons. All methods of presenting evidence may evoke such resistances. Persuading a client or patient to engage in such activities is an important therapeutic skill to which relatively little attention has been paid in the literature. The therapist who lacks such skills is prone to develop considerable frustration, which often leads to unnecessary hostility or discouragement on his part. Therapists can, however, become quite skilled in *maneuvering* clients and patients into the desired activities. Maneuvering is to be distinguished from *manipulating*. In maneuvering, the therapist provides a clear and frank explanation of his purpose; in manipulating, the therapist's intent is concealed. There is no reason why individuals in treatment cannot be fully informed of the procedures which the therapist believes are beneficial. Maneuvering by the therapist is essential not only when he presents evidence to correct misconceptions but also in many other aspects of therapy.

Self-Examination

When a therapist encourages a client or patient to engage in self-exploration, the therapist is not directly providing the individual with evidence or information. He is, however, structuring the therapeutic situation so that the individual may discover for himself the information necessary for locating and changing one or more misconceptions. In this sense, self-examination can be regarded as a procedure in which the therapist indirectly makes evidence available to the client or patient.

Client-centered therapists have developed self-examination in its purest form. The client is given no instructions or interpretations as he discusses his problems. The therapist facilitates the client's thinking only by using "reflections" to paraphrase and sharpen the meanings in the client's discussion. Thus in this approach the client is left largely on his own as he tries to find the evidence which will help him to identify and change his misconceptions. The therapist simply follows the train of thought, interfering as little as possible with the self-examination process. In reading client-centered protocols, one is struck by the frequency of clients' references to misconceptions they have detected in their self-explorations. For example, one client suddenly exclaimed after only a few interviews, "I can see now that my trouble lies in thinking that I am smarter than anyone else. As a result, I have been manipulating people who are important to me and ending up feeling depressed without knowing all along that I was the one who was producing my own problems." In this brief statement, the client has revealed three related misconceptions which he has just discovered: (1) He believed falsely that he was smarter than others. (2) He believed falsely that he was interacting honestly with others. (3) He had failed to recognize that he was responsible for his own difficulties.

The therapist's task is not a minor one in self-examination. Even though he does not directly provide the client with evidence, he must provide encouragement; for most clients have strong tendencies to avoid thinking and talking about disturbing aspects of their problems. In addition, the therapist's reflections or clarifications of meaning help the client to perceive more precisely what he has been discussing; verbalized thoughts that have been responded to by a therapist often become more concrete and tangible to the thinker. Reflections can also provide subtle guides for the client, because they often emphasize particular verbal contents whose significance may have escaped the client's attention.

How does self-examination bring about change in misconceptions if the therapist gives no new evidence or information to the client? An experienced therapist can make useful observations and guesses about the conceptions and misconceptions of the persons he works with, but he inevitably lacks the full knowledge which the client possesses about the meanings he attaches to his own experiences. As the client reviews his experiences, he can often discard the defensive misconceptions which he has customarily employed to avoid the real issues he faces. He is then enabled to perceive relationships that had previously escaped his attention, and to discover things about himself and others that had gone undetected.

What are the limitations of the self-examination approach? Only conjecture can be used to answer this question, although certain suggestions appear plausible. Where highly technical information constitutes the basis of a misconception, the client is ill prepared to locate a misconception. For example, if he restricts his physical activity because he falsely believes that he suffers from a defective heart, he can hardly depend upon self-examination for a more adequate diagnosis of his physical condition. In the realm of psychology similar technical problems can arise, as when a patient has been inadvertently and incorrectly informed that he suffers from "schizophrenia," or that he is a "sociopath," or that he is a victim of some form of mental disorder which he does not understand.

Another limitation of the self-examination procedure may

relate to its efficiency. Granted that a client may, after many months
of self-examination, locate some of his major misconceptions, is it
fair to the client if the therapist does not at least hold up for consideration some of the misconceptions which the client has failed
to recognize? The answer is not as simple as it might first appear.
One of the goals of the self-examination approach, as is true for
most other forms of therapy, is to enable the client to solve his own
problems without returning constantly for treatment. But the notion
that therapy is primarily a training procedure for teaching clients
how to solve their problems can be overdone, and treatment can
be unnecessarily prolonged if the therapist refrains from helping the
client to find and change his misconceptions. Such a contention
seems particularly appropriate for clients who are in the throes of
highly disturbing anxiety reactions which not only impede their rational thinking but also interfere markedly with their everyday responsibilities. There is, however, some validity to the observation
that highly skilled, aggressive therapists too often provide the client
or patient with direct instructions on how to overcome specific psychological disturbances. Such instructions may be temporarily successful but may also ignore underlying misconceptions which produced the more superficial symptoms. The thoughtful therapist is
frequently caught in the dilemma of having to choose between the
putting out of fires or engaging in more lengthy training procedures
which may have more favorable long-term effects. Happily, our
clients and patients often resolve this dilemma for us.

Self-examination is practiced extensively in everyday life
when problems develop which interfere with living. If we suspect
that we may be at fault, we customarily examine our behavior and
our conceptions in the hope of discovering our faulty conceptions.
If self-examination fails to provide us with suitable alternatives, we
may then seek the advice of others.

Explanation

In trying to provide clients and patients with evidence to
change misconceptions, therapists have traditionally employed verbal procedures. Words, however, can also be used for other purposes

in treatment, such as locating misconceptions and maneuvering patients into self-examination, self-demonstration, and vicariation. Knowing the intent of the therapist is, therefore, critical for determining when verbal procedures are used for explanation to correct misconceptions. A number of different ways in which a therapist employs explanation can be distinguished.

In *interpretation* and *confrontation,* the therapist proffers information which the patient supposedly does not have, or which he does not recognize as relevant. When interpreting, the therapist may make use of any information he has about the patient, although ordinarily interpretations are regarded as most helpful when the patient himself is almost ready to recognize them. Such "shallow" interpretations are usually thought to be preferable to "deeper" interpretations, which draw upon information somewhat remote from the patient's immediate preoccupations. In confrontation, the therapist more forcefully calls the patient's attention to expressed or implied inconsistencies whose significance the patient has failed to recognize.

Originally defined and elaborated in the client-centered approach, *reflections of feeling* are subtle ways of emphasizing significant meanings in the client's most recent utterance in the interview. Therapist reflections are often thought to emphasize only the affect or feelings detected in the client's responses—hence the appellation "reflection of feeling." Examination of verbatim interviews reveals, however, that although reflections are sometimes based upon the singling out of affect, more frequently the therapist is attempting to restate the personal meaning or personal significance of the client's utterance. Colloquial English employs "I feel" for emoting, thinking, believing, and other kinds of self-references. "I feel," "I think," and "I believe" may all be employed to indicate uncertainty or a cognition or an emotion. Reflections which underscore client meanings, with or without attached affect, presumably convey information to the client which he either did not have or failed to emphasize sufficiently. In some cases, of course, reflections may simply inform the client that the therapist understands what is being said. In such a case, reflections encourage the client to continue his self-examination.

The emphasizing and labeling that occur in reflections provide the client with more information about himself, which may lead to a change in his misconceptions. Combs and Snygg (1959) refer to this process as one which produces better differentiations in the client's perceptions. Better differentiation not only produces more accurate self-knowledge but also may support more adequate self-perceptions and induce the correction of misconceptions.

A common type of subtle explanation is found in the use of *questions* that call the client's attention to evidence which he has ignored or does not recognize. Reflections and interpretations are often phrased in the form of questions. Questions are thus often used in therapy to convey information to the patient by emphasizing meanings which the therapist may regard as significant. Of course, questions may also encourage the client to search for additional information.

Evidence can be conveyed without subtlety by the therapist when he uses *suggestion* and *exhortation*. Both contrast with the presumably uninvolved stance of the therapist when he interprets, confronts, reflects, and questions. Both depend upon the implicit rational authority of the therapist as an expert. He uses suggestions to inform a less knowledgeable client of more appropriate ways of thinking and acting. When he resorts to exhortation, he usually represents himself as the vicar of those who have an unassailable body of knowledge; that is, a psychotherapist may invoke supposedly accepted principles of mental health or social mores, just as a physician may enunciate the collective wisdom of medicine or a parent may invoke the principle of what is "right" or "good." The information offered in suggestions and exhortations is ordinarily presented in such a fashion that the recipient is denied any opportunity to engage in critical consideration of the proffered "advice."

Finally, and without exhausting the list of classes of explanation, more or less detailed *therapeutic frames of reference* may be taught by therapists in order to lay the groundwork for the correcting of misconceptions by presenting a system wherein misconceptions become more salient. A minor form of providing a frame of reference occurs whenever the therapist uses *structuring* to explain the role the patient is expected to play in treatment. In psychoanalysis the patient is trained in free association; in client-centered therapy he is informed that talking about himself however he wishes is likely to produce the desired results; in systematic desensitization he is told that relaxing and imagining items in his hierarchies is effective. Structuring, in the present context, is therefore a form of explanation intended to disabuse the patient or client of the misconceptions he may have about psychotherapy and, at the same time, to inform him of the presumably correct procedures. Another example of the use of a frame of reference in psychotherapy is found in Berne's (1961) transactional analysis when patients are taught about their tripartite personalities—the Parent, the Adult, and the Child. This instruction is clearly intended to inform patients that they are under the sway of internal forces of which they have been unaware. In essence, Berne's procedure in this respect is similar to the analyst's informing his patients that they are governed by unconscious forces and can become aware of these forces through free association. The desired goal of such explanations is to clear up the patient's misunderstandings and to lay the groundwork for a system in which more specific misconceptions can be recognized.

Although explanation has been the traditional method of changing misconceptions in psychotherapy as well as in education, in recent years many psychotherapists have rejected this procedure as ineffective and inefficient. Some therapists believe, for instance, that recent behavioral approaches are preferable because they are more "active" than the traditional explanatory procedures in psychotherapy. Such a contention may be plausible at first glance, although it turns out to be nebulous when one considers that at least two behavioral approaches, systematic desensitization and implosive therapy, both depend upon the client's imagining or thinking. The preference for an "activity" approach to treatment traces back ultimately to the general principle that learning is likely to be facilitated when the learner is "active." Gross muscular activity cannot, however, be equated with activity in learning. Individuals can become highly proficient learners when they are galvanized by ideas; they may display very little muscular activity when "deep in thought." Where learning is concerned, the requisite "activity" is primarily psychological involvement with the material to be mastered. Explanation as a therapeutic technique cannot, therefore, be dismissed on the grounds that it produces less "activity" in the patient, since it may be highly effective when the evidence being considered deeply involves the client.

For a number of reasons, however, explanations may be less effective than one might hope. For instance, when the therapist attends to irrelevant misconceptions which pertain to his own ideology but not the patient's problem, such explanation is irrelevant. Failure to deal with relevant misconceptions, however, does not reduce the usefulness of explanation. More systematic attention by therapists to significant misconceptions might well produce better therapeutic results when explanation is employed.

Explanation also may be weak and ineffective for misconceptions which are historically and psychologically remote from the patient's problem. Psychoanalytic preference for early-childhood problems as the source of current difficulties may be at issue here. Such a contention is not new; it was foreshadowed by a 1923 paper by Ferenczi and Rank (1956) which emphasized, heretically for that time, the necessity of dealing with present intrapsychic and interpersonal "conflicts" at the expense of dredging up infantile and childhood disturbances. Alfred Adler, of course, was emphasizing patients' current "mistakes" long before Ferenczi and Rank wrote their paper.

The prohibition against permitting the therapist to intervene when he recognizes relevant misconceptions may account for the prolongation of client-centered treatment. In psychoanalysis, the concentration on historically remote misconceptions may account for the similar prolongation of treatment. Both approaches perhaps became encrusted by their need to validate their publicly announced doctrines, which turned out to be half-truths. If, as the misconception hypothesis proposes, the primary task of the therapist is to change misconceptions, then explanations aimed directly at relevant misconceptions can be one of the effective methods for changing them.

Self-Demonstration

As employed here, self-demonstration is *not* intended to refer to situations in which the client can observe other persons working out the same kind of problem from which he suffers. That meaning of demonstration is more appropriate for vicariation. Self-demonstration refers to any procedure whereby a therapist encourages a patient to participate in a situation in which he can observe his own behavior, so that he may locate his own misconceptions or obtain direct evidence from self-observation that he can change his misconceptions. This definition can also be extended to the imagining of situations. In real and imagined situations, the therapist maneuvers the patient into experiencing his false convictions or beliefs about himself, or about himself in relations to others. The same procedures can be employed for helping patients to discover that they can change their thinking and acting. When, for example, a therapist places a socially fearful person in a receptive group, the therapist is hoping that the patient will obtain evidence that he is capable of interacting comfortably with others.

There is nothing novel psychologically about self-demonstrations; they are therapeutic applications of everyday "experiments" which are conducted universally from early childhood through old age. The process consists essentially of trying oneself out to determine what happens. Such experiments start early in childhood play with others, or they can be enacted by a lone child using toys or other materials to accompany his fantasies. In later life, similar experiments are employed in reality settings, or reality-oriented daydreaming can serve as a substitute. In daydreams the individual usually imagines himself engaged in activities related to the problems that he senses in himself and in his interactions with others. *Role sharing,* another commonly employed term, also pertains to everyday experiments of this kind.

In psychoanalysis, the analyst may take advantage of naturally occurring self-demonstrations to provide the patient with opportunities to recognize and change his misconceptions about a particular person—the analyst. The analysis of transference reactions constitutes a self-demonstration, since the patient can observe for himself how he reacts. When he discovers these misconceptions, either by himself or with the help of explanations (interpretations) from the analyst, he can also experiment with modifying these misconceptions in the interview. There is also the hope that he will generalize his new knowledge about himself to social interaction outside of the treatment situation. (See also Chapter Eight.) In addition, a number of subtle and immediate self-demonstrations have become acceptable in many forms of traditional therapy. In the use of countertransference, verbalized reactions of the therapist are intended to demonstrate to the patient how he affects others. The same is true when a therapist displays "genuineness," particularly when he openly discloses some of his own "feelings" about his client's behavior. Social workers who discuss "using the self as a tool" in treatment are to some extent referring to self-demonstration procedures similar to those found in manifest countertransference and manifest genuineness.

Prohibited by doctrine from employing many explanations for presenting clients with evidence, client-centered therapists nonetheless make ample use of subtle self-demonstrations. They may sometimes interpret, but more often they reflect transference reactions if they are discussed by the client. In addition, the therapist's insistence that the client must take responsibility for the hour forces the client to recognize that he is able to explore himself and his social interactions and to make his own decisions. Since the hallmark of most persons in need of psychotherapy is confusion and self-diagnosed inability to break out of endlessly frustrating circular thinking, the client-centered therapist tactfully employs his nondirectiveness to show clients that they are not hopelessly enmeshed in their own confusions. In a very real sense, the nondirective structure of client-centered therapy provides an hour-long self-demonstration procedure.

Combs and Snygg (1959) also utilize another form of self-demonstration when they advocate that the client should be treated as though he is "lovable, likeable, acceptable, and able." They believe that most persons coming for treatment suffer from a false belief in their own inadequacies and deficiencies. The therapist's behavior should therefore provide evidence during treatment intended to contradict such misconceptions in the client. (See also Chapter Seven.)

In Gestalt therapy, at least that variety practiced by its founder, Fritz Perls, self-demonstration consumes a large portion of treatment time. Clients are frequently maneuvered into performing many different kinds of demonstrations, such as frequent playing of different roles accompanied by interpretations from the therapist and reinforcements provided by the audience. In the behavior therapies that utilize imagination (for instance, systematic desensitization and implosive therapy), imaginary roles are played intensively and for long durations by the clients.

Although many kinds of group therapy may utilize mostly verbal explanations in much the same fashion as in individual treatment, more recent group approaches, including encounter groups, rely heavily upon self-demonstrations. These may be initiated by the therapist or simply permitted to develop as interactions multiply within the group. Encounter-group leaders have been particularly innovative in encouraging what they usually describe as strictly nonverbal activities, such as having silent partners lead a blindfolded person around a room or an outside space. These activities can hardly be regarded as explanation-free, however, since explanations are customarily employed to orient participants to what is happening and to subsequent analysis of the events.

Psychodrama, a special form of group therapy, provides one of the most explicit methods for presenting evidence by self-demonstration. The therapist organizes the events in such a fashion that the patient has an audience to which he is constantly playing the role structured for him by the therapist. The audience can be used in many different ways, depending upon the preferences of the therapist, but its continuing presence establishes for the patient a constant background for reality orientation. Most groups intent upon behaving therapeutically are likely to adopt the stereotyped constructive attitudes exemplified by approval of realistic, normal behavior and disapproval of unrealistic, abnormal behavior. As they become more sophisticated, they come to approve of open expression of "feelings" and disapprove of the holding back of "feelings." Resolution of conflict, sloughing off of hostile attitudes which have been vented, and discovery of hitherto hidden motives to explain idiosyncratic behavior are generally approved of by therapy groups. In psychodrama, therefore, the audience acts as a standard against which the patient can obtain evidence for the social adequacy of his own reactions.

Self-demonstrations can be destructive as well as constructive, for misconceptions may be intensified, as well as eliminated,
by evidence. Custodial mental hospitals, for example, frequently
facilitate the deterioration of patients rather than helping them to
recover from their disturbances. A major source of such deterioration can be traced to the multiple ways in which regimented, constricting hospital atmospheres and regimens add to the patient's
beliefs in his "illness" and incapability. But hospitals do not have to
operate in this way; many modern hospitals, in fact, are effectively
providing evidence to patients that they can think adequately and
can engage in appropriate social interactions with other human
beings. Hospital staffs have sometimes been pleasantly surprised
when they have set up situations in which patients can demonstrate
to themselves that they can behave normally. At Hawaii State Hospital, patients from many wards were routinely taken on picnics to
bathing beaches. At these picnics, even fairly disturbed patients
acted quite normally at the beach, even though they often reverted
to psychotic behavior upon return to their wards. Some years ago
at New Mexico State Hospital, a dayroom was completely refur-
nished with wall-to-wall carpeting and comfortable modern fur-
niture. To the surprise of the staff, patients who had been accustomed
to throwing cigarettes on the floor, spitting, and generally littering
their former dayroom now took good care of the new "parlor." The
expectancies provided by the refurbished dayroom gave the patients
opportunities to engage in self-demonstration.

Many additional examples could be given of the ways in
which environmental treatments can often be helpful in changing
misconceptions by means of self-demonstrations. Summer camps for
problem children, as well as foster homes for both children and
adults should be mentioned here as self-demonstration procedures.
Although to date there has been relatively little systematic attention
to utilizing environmental settings for self-demonstration purposes,
many psychologists interested in operant procedures in behavior
modification have been working in hospitals and schools to convince
individuals that they can behave more normally. These procedures
are not ordinarily recognized as demonstrations intended to change
misconceptions, but there is no reason why they cannot be so in-

terpreted. Systematic, graduated situations for the presentation of evidence should facilitate self-demonstrations.

Vicariation

As yet, psychologists have only dimly appreciated the process by which vicarious experiencing (vicariation) takes place, although a number of words subsumed by *vicariation* have been in uneasy use for some time: imitation, empathy, identification, and, more recently, modeling. For many years, the horror expressed by behaviorists, when confronted with any of these terms, stunted their growth and probably our knowledge of the processes involved. Now that even the behaviorists have relented in their downgrading of "imitation" and "imagery," there is a revival of interest in these psychological processes.

Kelly's (1955) fixed-role therapy, an early application of vicariation to psychotherapy, employs an imaginary or artificial model. Although Kelly did not explicitly consider vicariation in his treatment procedures, its presence can be readily established in them if it is agreed that imitating an imaginary model is one form of vicariation. There is no necessity for a model to be real rather than imaginary. In fact, much of our experience in reference to others comes from our empathizing with fictitious characters in novels, stories, plays, movies, and television. Kelly's own initial recognition of the possibilities of fixed-role therapy stemmed in part from his observations of friends and students in amateur dramatics. Although the roles they played were quite different from their customary behavior, several of them underwent lasting personality changes after their theatrical experiences.

In fixed-role therapy, the client is asked to write a character sketch of himself. Then the therapist, with the help of the client, writes another personality sketch, in which desirable characteristics are substituted for the undesirable characteristics in the original sketch. After the new sketch is role-played by therapist and the client several times, the client is advised to try out his new role in everyday life. The instructions by the therapist are always given with a playful attitude of "let's see what happens," rather than with constricting solemnity. For a trial period of two or three weeks, the therapist sees the client on alternative days to discuss with him the vicissitudes of his role playing. Kelly describes the trial period as one of "cutting and fitting" the role to the client. No research reports have been found for this approach to treatment, but Kelly and his students found it useful in treating college students.

The presence of vicariation in this treatment approach is obvious; the sketch prepared by therapist and client is intended to create a verbal model which contrasts with the customary behavior of the client. Verbal models may have considerable depth and subtlety, depending upon the skills of the persons who compose them. There may, in fact, be more depth and subtlety in a well-written sketch than in an insensitive client's perception of himself or in his perception of live models with whom he may be confronted. (Of course, if the client tries out his sketch and is successful, he is also demonstrating to himself that he is capable of behaving in a different, more appropriate way. Furthermore, as he and the therapist discuss his experiences with the sketch, he is likely to obtain from the therapist verbal information about his customary behavior, his new behavior, and the reactions of others toward him. Thus, explanation, demonstration, and vicariation are all employed to present evidence in fixed-role therapy, as is likely to be the case in most therapy techniques.)

Much of the work on modeling as a treatment procedure has been done by Bandura (1969, 1971) with his students and colleagues. Bandura's theory of modeling is a complex explanation which includes the reduction of the emotional avoidance reaction by vicarious extinction, so that approach to the feared object can take place. As the client watches the model, he imagines himself performing the same activities, thereby acquiring coded images and verbal responses by stimulus contiguity. Actual performance of the new responses is elicited and guided by environmental reinforcements. An analysis of the cognitive aspects of Bandura's approach appears in Chapter Nine. In the usual modeling paradigm, a child or an adult who displays fear or inability to perform a common activity, such as handling snakes or playing with dogs, is maneuvered into observing a peer or a therapist performing the normal activity without difficulty. Various procedures can be added, such as "guided participation," in which the therapist physically participates with the client in joint performances with the feared object. Bandura has found that guided participation with live models is a very effective method for overcoming fears. In fact, for the treatment of snake fears, Bandura (1969, pp. 182–191) found that live modeling with participation was more successful than was systematic desensitization. Bandura also notes that his procedure is most useful for treating problems which are readily observable in external behavior.

Examination of the procedures employed in modeling treatments for common fear responses indicates that they provide clients with evidence in regard to three of their misconceptions. The first is the misconception that the feared object is far more dangerous or harmful or loathsome than it is in reality. The client's conclusion can be shown to be unrealistic by the modeling performed by therapist or peers. He is given visible proof that at least *this* snake or *this* dog does not bite under *these* circumstances. At this point vicariation enters: the client, who is participating of his own accord, imagines himself handling the dog or snake. That, after all, is the purpose of treatment. He thus obtains evidence from two sources that he suffers from a misconception; the model is not harmed, and in his imagination he is not harmed either.

The second misconception of the client, developed from earlier emotional reactions, is the anticipation of collapse: "If I were to undergo the horrible experience of touching that object, I would be overwhelmed and suffer severe collapse." In one study, for instance (Horowitz, 1970), some subjects being treated for common phobias indicated that they feared being overwhelmed or suffering collapse if they were to touch spiders or snakes. This second misconception is also likely to be dispelled in modeling treatments as the client obtains evidence that the model does not collapse, nor does the client himself faint when he imagines himself performing the same activities as the model. Furthermore, when he responds to the demands of the situation by actually touching or handling the animal, the most feared consequences do not occur.

The third misconception is the client's belief that he is incapable of overcoming his fear. This is clearly a misconception, since evidence from many sources indicates that such fears can be over-come in many different ways other than by modeling. In examin-ing the modeling treatment, however, we find that it contains considerable evidence presented to the client that he can overcome his fear. He is undoubtedly told that by the therapist. If the client is not informed explicitly, he can infer it from the mere fact that he is present of his own accord for treatment intended to overcome his fear.

The four methods employed by therapists to provide evi-dence to change misconceptions accomplish nothing unless they bring about cognitive changes in the client or patient. These changes, which are vital for the success of therapy, are discussed in the next chapter.

Chapter 4

Patient's Task: Cognitive Review

The process within the client which brings about changes in misconceptions is here referred to as *cognitive review*. Even though we know little about it, we can assert that it is the same process which occurs in the forming and changing of concepts, since misconceptions are simply faulty conceptions. The principle of cognitive review can be stated most simply as follows: For an individual to change a concept of any kind, he must ordinarily be afforded opportunities to examine and reexamine all available evidence that is relevant to the concept. The word *ordinarily* is inserted to exclude those unusual situations in which one-trial learning of a concept occurs. Complex misconceptions in psychotherapy rarely yield to a single reexamination of the pertinent evidence.

Cognitive review is as commonly encountered in everyday life and in therapy as are the four methods for presenting evidence. Most of the time we are only vaguely aware that we are engaged in such a process when we ruminate about problems we are facing.

Over and over again we may examine all facets of a problem, until eventually we see a better solution or discard the problem as unsolvable, at least for the time being. The same process occurs in therapy, although most therapists refer to it under different labels, such as working through, or the need for more time, or the requirement of patience on the part of the therapist. Behavior therapists have developed systematic procedures for cognitive review, particularly when they repeatedly present the same or similar stimulus patterns to their clients, as in systematic desensitization or in implosive therapy.

The review process is not coldly mechanical and appropriate only for highly intellectual, scholarly, scientific, or judicial purposes. These are extreme instances in which systematic efforts are made, usually without complete success, to exclude affective elements. Cognitive review must include consideration of the cognitive aspects of affective responses (see Chapter Five).

Must a therapist be present for cognitive review to be effective? Not necessarily—although talking things over with another person may be helpful in a number of ways. Communicating problems to another person requires some organization of the problem, which is not required in solitary thinking. The necessary use of language sharpens the content presented. The troubled person is also likely to adopt a more objective attitude toward his difficulties in the presence of another. Finally, the listener may make truly helpful comments by pointing out errors, indicating relationships within the content which have escaped attention, and suggesting alternative concepts which may not have been available to the individual. Since all of these matters, except the content supplied by the listener, are also available to the solitary thinker, there seems to be no inherent need for another person during cognitive review. If we conclude from reports of its failure that solitary cognitive review is relatively useless, we ignore a most important aspect of the issue: that most personal problems of most people are solved by solitary cognitive review. Successful instances are not ordinarily reported to therapists.

There is still a second question to be answered: Why is cognitive review not always effective? There are several plausible answers.

1. Naive introspection may fail to reveal the pivotal misconceptions. If one believes, for example, that most of one's problems are due to sexual difficulties, one acquires a set to ignore the misconceptions which are not sexually related. Another example can be found in the analysis of phobias. Although the phobic tends to have a distorted concept of the fearful object, the pivotal misconception is not the innocuous object but the phobic's misconception that if he permits himself to remain in the presence of the feared object, he will be precipitated uncontrollably into intense fear and possible collapse.

2. One's misconceptions are frequently much more difficult to recognize as misconceptions than are those of other individuals. The personal evidence one has gathered for one's own concepts appears so conclusive that it seems impossible to question their validity. A provocative sidelight on this issue has been commented on by many observers of group therapy. Neurotics or even psychotics who have complete lack of insight into their own mistakes in thinking can frequently display acute insight into the mistakes of other patients.

3. The effects of the neurotic paradox can be detected in that emotionally toned misconceptions, with much negative affect, produce avoidance reactions during introspection. The individual may, therefore, never come to consider his pivotal misconception. Analysts believe that these avoidance reactions are the result of repression; other therapists have laid the blame on the establishment of "emotional sets"; behavior therapists attribute them to conditioning.

4. Learned avoidance reactions may not yield to repeated cognitive review without some kind of systematic intervention, such as extinction or counterconditioning. This claim, however, must be examined carefully; for if some conditioned-avoidance reactions yield to cognitive review, there is reason to suspect that most or all of them would also yield to cognitive review if we knew how to establish the proper conditions. The question becomes an empirical one which requires more evidence than is now available. As a practical matter, there is no reason why a therapist should not utilize extinction or counterconditioning if his attempts to employ only cognitive review fail.

5. Patients may fail to verbalize with sufficient precision their misconceptions and the supporting evidence, thus failing to make the relevant misconceptions salient. They may also fail to alter their style of self-examination, thus remaining trapped in their own vicious circles.

Illustrative Cases

Although the principle of cognitive review may sound complex when it is described, the following short case of Freud's (Breuer and Freud, 1957) illustrates how simple it may be in actual practice, once the therapist discovers and focuses upon the relevant misconceptions. Freud reported his findings on this case in 1895.

While on a hiking trip, Freud was approached by the eighteen-year-old Katharina, who told him that she had seen his name and medical title in the visitors' book of the small inn run by her mother. She asked his help, saying, "The truth is, my nerves are bad. I went to see a doctor in L—— about them and he gave me something for them; but I'm not well yet." Her two-year illness had begun with vomiting, later supplanted by shortness of breath, pressures on the eyes and chest, feelings of dizziness, choking sensations, and a hammering in the head.

Recognizing her symptoms as anxiety attacks, Freud guessed a sexual etiology, and suggested to Katharina that the attacks first began when she had seen or heard something that greatly embarrassed her. The girl readily agreed, stating that two years earlier she had unexpectedly observed her father having sexual relations with their servant girl. Further questioning revealed that the father had attempted intercourse with Katharina when she was fourteen and also fifteen years old. She had not told her mother about the incestuous attempts, but she had told her about the servant. When the wife confronted her husband with the daughter's story, he was enraged and blamed Katharina for the subsequent divorce. He also threatened "to do something" to her. After the brief interview, in which she evidently perceived the psychological explanation for her symptoms, Katharina became, in Freud's words, "like someone transformed. The sulky unhappy face had grown lively, her eyes were bright, she was lightened and exalted."

Freud's explanation of Katharina's anxiety attacks was based on his early hypothesis that any exposure to sex in "virginal individuals" during their "presexual period" produces anxiety. In Katharina, he claimed, the anxiety produced by her father's attempted seduction, plus her observation of him in bed with the servant, "isolated" the group of sexual memories from her ego, thereby producing her symptoms. Freud's talking with her, he thought, brought about "an associative connection between this separated group of memories and the ego." Freud later abandoned this early description of cognitive review in favor of another theory, based upon expression of affect. We can, however, examine his therapy in this case as an example of cognitive review which changed some of Katharina's misconceptions.

We must begin with her major misconception that she suffered from a physical illness due to her nerves. This mistaken idea was strengthened by her visit to a doctor in L——, who had reinforced the misconception by giving her medicine for her nerves. She still adhered to the misconception when she approached Freud. Instead of questioning Katharina about her physical symptoms, Freud asked her about the psychological events which preceded their development. There is no evidence in Freud's account that the girl had seen a relationship between her symptoms and her observations of her father's sexual behavior. But Freud's questions about those observations implied to Katharina that Dr. Freud was telling her that her symptoms were related not to her nerves but to the frightening experiences with her father. When the girl was able to perceive the relation between her anxiety symptoms and the frightening events related to her father, the misconception was eliminated and the symptoms apparently vanished. The evidence she obtained during this review was sufficient to convince her that she did not suffer from a physical illness.

Katharina probably had a second misconception: that her sexual responsiveness to her father, although suppressed, was actually fear. This misconception can only be inferred, but it probably kept her from examining (reviewing) too closely her own role in her father's attempted seduction. We are indebted to Freud for recognizing by 1905, when he published *Three Essays on the Theory of Sexuality*, that sexual attempts on children often result in their sexual arousal, which may then evoke considerable guilt. At the time of the Katharina report, however, Freud attributed all of her anxiety to the trauma produced in a virgin by "the mere suspicion of sexual relations." Thus, both Katharina and her therapist suffered from the same misconception.

Freud took almost a decade to correct his misconception, as evidenced by his 1905 book on sexuality, but Katharina required a much shorter period of time to correct hers. It would appear that the girl recognized her sexual responsiveness to her father when Freud asked her at the end of the interview, "What part of his body was it that you felt that night?" He described her response. "But she gave me no more definite answer. She smiled in an embarrassed way, as though she had been found out." That it took longer for Freud than Katharina to dissipate the misconception about sexual responsiveness in young females can probably be attributed to the girl's having more corrective evidence available than he did at the time.

The following example (one of my own cases) illustrates not only the use of cognitive review of a misconception but also the problem faced by the therapist when the patient presents a number of possibly crucial misconceptions at the same time. In emergency situations, the therapist faces the dilemma of choosing a misconception to serve as the focus of immediate treatment. When there is no emergency, the therapist often gains by allowing the patient to select the topic of most interest, thereby saving the therapist from having to make a decision for which he has insufficient knowledge. Sometimes, however, the therapist must intervene as quickly as possible, either to save the patient from fruitless self-explorations or to resolve an immediate crisis. The following illustration relates to the latter problem.

A thirty-eight-year-old chemist was recovering from a depression precipitated by an extremely unhappy love affair. After three hospitalizations, he was beginning to resume his normal activities. Unexpectedly, he was thrust into an encounter with the woman whose loss had had much to do with his initial depression.

Considerably shaken by the encounter, he made an emergency appointment for the following day. When he appeared, he was obviously agitated despite his apparent superficial control, and soon he began to sob. The gist of his disconnected, spasmodic efforts to talk centered around the resurgence of his great feeling of loss when he saw the woman, interlarded with fears about being thrust back into depression and into another hospitalization, "which I can't possibly go through again; the only thing is suicide."

On several previous occasions, I had warned him that, as he gradually recovered, he might misinterpret strong emotional reactions of a normal nature as the return of the feared depression. We had discussed these warnings, and he had seemed to understand them. On the day of the emergency, however, he had only a hazy recollection of them. He was convinced that his relapse was entirely due to the emotional impact of the unexpected encounter on a "sick mind." Rather than concentrating on his reawakened feelings of enormous loss, I decided to work directly on his expressed fear of needing further hospitalization, which he associated with being "on the verge of insanity" (during his longest hospitalization he had been told by a resident that he was suffering from psychosis).

For almost an hour, we discussed his confusion over his current emotional reactions and the experiences he recalled during the depths of his depression while in the hospital. Similarities and differences between the two sets of events were analyzed to help him perceive his mistake in thinking that he was doomed to repeat the depression. After another hour, he left the office in a much better frame of mind. On the following day, despite considerable exhaustion, he was able to return to work and carry on his activities.

Although I had pointed out in our earlier discussions that a strong emotion during recovery might unnecessarily precipitate his fear of another depression, my assumption that I had thereby prevented such a fear was incorrect. A statement he made at the beginning of the emergency interview alerted me to the possible need to work on his fear rather than his feeling of loss. In an aside while sobbing, he said, "I guess I'm more afraid of becoming insane than I thought. I originally denied to you that I had any such fear."

This case illustrates the need for repeated cognitive review of misconceptions, which have many sources of evidence to support them; it also suggests that this principle applies particularly to the treatment of phrenophobia. In working with patients who suffer from that common misconception, I am continually impressed with its tenacity. By now I have learned that a patient's apparent insight into it as a misconception is usually accompanied by reservations which are difficult to root out, because they often depend upon vague but crucial feelings of disruption and disorganization. Because internal feelings of disruption and disorganization are strongly associated by laymen with psychosis, they have difficulty in accepting the fact that anxiety may produce the same sensations in a normal individual; hence the need for repeated cognitive review.

Repeated Cognitive Review in Various Psychotherapies

Most if not all approaches to therapy utilize the principle of repeated cognitive review, either explicitly in theory or implicitly in practice. So widespread is the tendency of experienced therapists to help patients review their misconceptions repeatedly, on either a systematic or a nonsystematic basis, that sufficient warrant exists to establish it as a general principle of psychotherapy. In the practice of psychoanalysis, for instance, the patient's task in *working through* clearly involves cognitive review of his misconceptions. Fenichel (1945, p. 31) defines working through as "a chronic process which shows the patient again and again the same conflicts and his usual way of reacting to them, but from new angles and in new connections." In a 1914 paper Freud (1950a, p. 376) describes the process of working through as "the part of the work that effects the greatest changes in the patient and that distinguishes analytic treatment from every kind of suggestive treatment." Such working through, in Freud's view, will occur in the course of treatment when the patient is ready; the analyst therefore should "let things take their course, a course which cannot be avoided or hastened." Menninger (1958, p. 38) refers to the product of working through as ridding the patient of his misconceptions (although Menninger uses the term *illusions*): "For it is an empirical fact that the same general type of material and the same general type of resistance reappears in the analysis time after time, to the considerable dismay of the young analyst, who feels that, having accepted everything [that is, the analyst's interpretations], the patient has relinquished his insight for the same old illusions." Fromm-Reichmann (1950, p. 141) comes to a similar conclusion: "Any understanding, any new piece of awareness which has been gained by interpretive clarification, has to be reconquered and tested time and again in new connections and contacts with other interlocking experiences, which may or may not have to be subsequently approached interpretively in their own right. That is the process to which psychoanalysts refer when speaking of the necessity of repeatedly 'working through.' "

Fromm-Reichmann illustrates the complexity of the interlocking experiences, which must be repeatedly reviewed in working through, with the case of a female patient who evidently had the misconception that she *had* to be both submissive and superior in her love relationships. The woman had had four unhappy love affairs. The analyst discovered that the patient displayed both hero worship and submissiveness, combined with an attitude of superiority toward all significant persons in her life. The analyst showed the patient how this pattern operated in her relationships with her parents, her four lovers, and her analyst, as well as in her "dissociated" childhood experiences. Despite these explanations, the patient failed to integrate the understanding until it had been repeatedly worked through in the transference situation with the analyst.

The great importance of working through is also recognized in brief analytic psychotherapy, although Alexander and French (1946, p. 88), for example, stress the advisability of avoiding the working through of infantile experiences. Instead, they advocate the working through of current problems and the transference relationship. In accord with their principle of flexibility, Alexander and French also appear more likely than classical analysts to take a direct hand in encouraging repeated reviews of the same theme by the patient, rather than waiting for nature to take its course. They even advocate ending interviews with a clearly defined problem on which the patient is expected to do his "homework" before the next interview.

In summary, psychoanalysts are well aware of the significance of repeated cognitive review, although they may explain its effectiveness in somewhat different terminology. There is also a difference in opinion among analysts as to how active the therapist should be, both in directing the process of working through and in selecting problems which should be the focus of the patient's attention.

The Viennese psychiatrist Viktor Frankl (1967) developed a technique called *paradoxical intention* as part of his more general treatment approach, called *logotherapy*. In paradoxical intention, the therapist repeatedly urges the patient to produce consciously those symptoms which he fears the most, such as collapsing or losing other forms of control; this technique allegedly produces "a reversal of the patient's attitude toward his symptom" (p. 163). Frankl believes that the technique is most effective with phobias and obsessive-compulsive symptoms. One woman, for example, with a twenty-four-year history of severe claustrophobia was cured in five months; during that period, she was instructed to attempt to pass out and to become as fearful as possible whenever she was in enclosed places. Repeated review appears to be an integral part of paradoxical intention, although some simpler cases seem to yield in one treatment session.

The principle of repeated review is quite apparent in the verbatim reports of Gestalt therapy, although I have been unable to locate any explicit statement concerning it. In reading reports of Fritz Perls's therapy, I have been struck by the frequency with which he repeatedly instructed his patients to act out their "feelings" about one of their misconceptions in a variety of ways. He not only asked for repeated display, but he returned to the same theme time and again until the patient said he had changed, or until Perls decided that no change was possible in that session. Unlike the analysts who expect that patients will return of their own accord to the same misconceptions, Perls quite directly took charge and taught the patient how to talk about and act out his reactions to the theme which Perls identified.

The following example is my analysis of one episode (lasting twenty or thirty minutes) in the case of Liz, who was treated by Perls before an audience in one of his Dreamwork Seminars (Perls, 1969, pp. 82–89). When asked for a dream, Liz said only, "I dream of tarantulas and spiders crawling on me. And it's pretty consistent."

Because Perls believed that every item in a reported dream represents some aspect of the dreamer, he immediately asked her how it would feel to be a spider. Her response indicated that she perceived a spider as something which covers up someone who is "inanimate" and unaggressive. Further questioning by Perls indicated that Liz consciously described herself as being inanimate, unaggressive, having only two legs, and lacking in color. Following more instructions, she played her revealed self talking to a spider, during which it turned out that she could not view herself as important because she was not perfect. Here she provided Perls with one of his favorite themes (or, in my terms, misconceptions): "I can only be important if I am perfect."

For the remainder of this episode, Perls had Liz repeatedly review her misconception that she could not be important if she was not perfect. He had her approach it from many angles and with many techniques while trying to convince her that she was wrong. I have been able to detect twenty-six sorties in his prolonged attack on this one misconception: (1) After telling Liz to conduct a dialogue between herself and the spider, Perls criticized her dutiful statement that it is mentally healthy to "feel self-important and worthy" [deriding a compliant intellectualization]. (2) He instructed her to play the role of a spider who wishes to be beautiful [exploring the patient's conception of the spider]. (3) He instructed her to give reasons why the spider is important [further exploration of the meaning of *spider*]. (4) He had the spider compliment Liz [exploring Liz's conception of herself]. (5) He announced to the audience that Liz unnecessarily lacked self-confidence [enlisting group support for his attack upon Liz's misconception]. (6) He again instructed the spider to give Liz appreciation [exploring Liz's reaction to the group's agreement that she had a misconception about herself]. (7) He accused Liz of suffering from "the curse of perfectionism" [labeling the misconception in negative terms]. (8) He explored her willingness to change her misconception. (9) He rewarded a positive self-reference made by Liz. (10) He presented verbal evidence of her misconception. (11) He explained how misconceptions are maintained. (12) He pointed out that impossibly high standards produce self-devaluation. (13) He publicly derided her perfectionism. (14) He emphasized that her perfectionism inhibited her enjoyment. (15) He tried to get Liz to reject her perfectionism publicly. (16) He explored the historical source of the misconception. (17) He explored the historical influence of the misconception. (18) He publicly derided perfectionism and its history. (19) He tried to get Liz to shake off undesirable associations. (20) He tried to evoke uninhibited reactions in Liz. (21) He tried to get Liz to reject publicly her perfectionism. (22) Recognizing her unwillingness to change, he suggested private consultations and again emphasized the desirability of changing her misconception. (23) He elicited support from the audience for his point of view about the undesirability of perfectionism. (24) He pointed out the negative consequences of the misconception. (25) He again pointed out the negative consequences of the misconception. (26) He personalized the negative consequences of the misconception. These twenty-six sorties illustrate the many ways in which at least one Gestalt therapist repeatedly helped his patient to review her misconception as he attempted to explore and change it.

The originator of implosive therapy, T. G. Stampfl, regards it as a procedure whereby an anxiety response to an ordinarily harmless aversive stimulus is extinguished when the response is repeated without reinforcement. In Stampfl's (1970) procedure, the therapist repeatedly gives vivid verbal descriptions of the aversive situation, which the client imagines as thoroughly as possible. The therapist attempts to produce as much peak anxiety in the patient as he can, and relaxation is never included. Since the aversive stimulus is essentially harmless, and since the patient's anxiety is therefore clearly unrealistic and uncalled for, Stampfl's procedure can be considered a review of a misconception. The repetition principle is followed methodically until extinction (or cognitive reorganization) occurs. Although Stampfl reports that implosive therapy may be effective for a circumscribed emotional reaction in only one session, many more ninety-minute sessions are ordinarily required. Repeated review is, therefore, likely to occur over a considerable period of time. In addition, Stampfl customarily requires "homework" of his clients as a routine aspect of treatment. At the end of each session, the client is instructed to implode himself, using the same scenes that have been presented to him by the therapist dur ing the treatment session. Such instructions, when carried out, further assure repeated review of the misconception.

Of all approaches to psychological treatment, the behavior therapies are most systematic in arranging the necessary conditions for repeated cognitive review. In their rationale, changes in behavior are the product of a learning or conditioning process. Repeated presentation of a stimulus situation, in order to evoke a desired response or to extinguish an undesired response, is the customary procedure employed in conditioning paradigms. Although the proponents of systematic desensitization are unlikely to agree that cognitive review of a misconception is an essential part of their treatment, their procedures ensure that cognitive review must take place repeatedly. Their patients and clients are provided with a precise understanding of the problem being treated; that is, more specifically than in other treatment approaches, the patients are told *what* they are being treated for, *what* is wrong with their behavior, and *what* are the criteria for improvement.

The best known of the behavioral techniques, Wolpe's (1969) systematic desensitization, ensures repeated review of the patient's misconceptions about the harmfulness of the phobic object and the inappropriateness of his own reactions to it. Systematic and repeated review of these misconceptions occurs throughout treatment as the patient, previously trained in relaxation, imagines himself coming into contact with the feared object. Other writers, particularly Bandura (1969, p. 473), Wilkins (1971), and Locke (1971), have also commented on the heavy reliance in Wolpe's methods upon the cognitive processes which occur in repeated review.

There has been a growing tendency within the behavior-therapy movement to make use of the client's cognitive capabilities. These efforts have not yet developed into formal treatment approaches, but they are frequently reported as being successful adjuncts to treatment. Among the earliest treatment adjuncts which appear to depend for the most part on cognitive principles is the technique of *assertiveness training,* which has been interpreted by Salter (1949) as "excitatory" and by Wolpe (1969) as an inhibitor of anxiety. In assertiveness training, a patient is explicitly taught (through role playing or through performing tasks of graded difficulty) how to assert his own rights as a human being. Logical arguments are directed against the irrationality of the patient's submissiveness, and the advantages of assertiveness are advanced in such phases as "You are making a mistake in not asserting yourself; if you follow the procedures you are being taught, you can expect improvement in your problems." Repeated review—induced by explanation and assisted by the self-demonstrations inherent in role playing and homework assignments—seems to be the most parsimonious explanation of the success of training in assertiveness. It is essentially a coaching procedure. Confirmation of this explanation has been reported by McFall and Twentyman (1973), who concluded after four experiments that behavior rehearsal and coaching are the significant ingredients in assertion training; "symbolic modeling added little to the effects of rehearsal alone or rehearsal plus coaching."

Peterson and London (1965) report success in three treatment sessions with a three-year-old child who had difficulty with bowel training. The treatment consisted in stroking the child's forehead while he was reclining, and monotonously repeating to him that he would feel "real good" when he moved his bowels. In an earlier era such a procedure would have been interpreted as suggestion; and, in fact, the writers originally had attempted to use hypnosis without success. Peterson and London, however, interpret their success in a fashion that readily squares with cognitive review of a misconception: "To the extent that a therapist can show a patient that the latter's previous cognitions were inaccurate and that more correct explanations are possible, just to that extent will the patient modify his behavior" (p. 294).

A form of role playing, termed *behavior rehearsal* (Lazarus, 1966) is used by many therapists to help a patient review repeatedly his faulty conceptions of himself in troublesome situations. The therapist partially controls the patient's successes and failures as he acts out a variety of scenes with the patient in which the roles may be frequently reversed. In the vocabulary of the previous chapter, one can propose that behavior rehearsal is largely a prearranged self-demonstration, with some modeling, to help the patient perceive that he can behave in a fashion more constructive than is his wont.

In a procedure called *covert sensitization* or *aversive imagery,* an imaginary event with an aversive consequence is presented to the client when he is also imagining or in the presence of the undesirable activity which is to be suppressed. This procedure contrasts with traditional aversion therapy, in which an external aversive stimulus, such as an electric shock, is administered when the client is thinking about or actively engaged in the undesirable activity. Cautela (1966), who introduced the term *covert sensitization,* believes that cues associated with the imagined noxious stimulation, such as the imagined nausea and vomiting described to the alcoholic patient, become discriminatory stimuli for avoidance behavior. Rachman and Teasdale (1969) regard aversive imagery as "the most promising alternative" to the traditional aversion therapies. Moreover, according to Rachman (1968), "Covert sensitization and aversive imagery are techniques which emphasize the effects of cognitive manipulations on behavior. " He goes on to cite evidence that cognitive factors can influence autonomic changes "in a remarkable manner." In the same vein, Murray and Jacobson (1971, p. 733) discuss the multiple cognitive factors which can be discerned in traditional aversion therapies. In their view, the effects of aversion therapy may be due in large part to "changes in the individual's beliefs about himself, especially his ability to control his behavior." Certainly, the techniques of covert sensitization and aversion therapy provide much opportunity for repeated cognitive review. Cautela, for example, not only provides imaginal practice during the treatment sessions but also recommends additional practice by a patient at home after each session.

Technique of Repeated Review

Repeated review is a very simple and direct technique for changing unrealistic fears or "phobias." I have used it since 1971 on more than thirty-five cases of avoidance reactions, about half with patients in long-term therapy, the other half with students who came only for treatment of an isolated fear. Three graduate students have also used it successfully. One of them, M. G. Smith

(1974), employed it on a group of test-anxious undergraduates. The experimental group reduced their fear of test taking quite markedly when compared to a control group.

Once the specific avoidance reaction has been isolated, I ask the individual to close his eyes and imagine himself in a concrete situation where he must interact in some fashion with what he fears or avoids. He is also asked to "describe what happens and tell me how you feel." He proceeds at his own pace with little interference from the therapist unless he introduces conditions which would nullify the imaginary interaction. No training in relaxation is given, nor are the imaginary scenes hierarchically graded in terms of estimated threat. If a particular scene appears to be too threatening, the therapist can alter it instantly by changing or deleting some of the details. The client or patient is requested to open his eyes at the conclusion of each recital. If the avoidance reaction has not been satisfactorily dissipated in imagination, he is asked to repeat the task until the imagined avoidance disappears.

To illustrate, a man in his mid-twenties who had been hospitalized for severe anxiety and a depression of several years declared that he would be unable to meet his ex-wife for fear that he would lose control of himself by striking her. Despite his objection that she no longer meant anything to him, he was asked to imagine that he met her on the street. Reluctantly, he described the meeting and discovered to his surprise that when she asked him what he had been doing, he replied and then asked what she had been doing. After two repetitions consuming about fifteen minutes, in each of which he carried on an imaginary conversation with her, he reported that he walked away from the encounter feeling "very good about myself." At the next interview he reported that he believed that many of his conflicts about women had disappeared, and he no longer felt angry with his ex-wife.

The technique has worked successfully with misconceptions or irrational fears of taking tests, viewing one's nude and obese body, speaking in public, talking with one's friends after a mental breakdown, taking an extended trip, and encountering small animals or spiders. The technique contains elements of many other approaches to therapy. Contemplating imaginary scenes is found in systematic desensitization and implosive therapy. Describing one's feelings and carrying on imaginary conversations is found in Gestalt therapy and various forms of role playing. Encouraging the client to work out his own solution to problems is characteristic of client-centered therapy. In fact, the technique seems to be a variant of most forms of therapy, but as a technique it is surprisingly simple. Its main element is the repetition in imagination of the individual's interaction with the object of his misconception. The repetition facilitates the individual's review of the evidence which supports his misconceptions.

The following consistently similar reactions are seen in hospitalized patients and in college students when the technique is employed. There is usually some preliminary skirmishing in which the individual denies that he is able to imagine the situation. Humor is often displayed during these denials. Facial grimacing in the early part of the first recital is usually very prominent. Some somatization of the affective reactions often occurs, as when there are complaints that "My stomach is hurting or upset" or "I'm beginning to develop a headache." The second recital of a specific scene is likely to be far more detailed than the first. This is in accord with the principle that as perceived threat diminishes, the perceptual field broadens and therefore more details are added.

The following brief case of Pete is presented only as an illustration of the procedure. This forty-eight-year-old truck driver was hospitalized at his own request for treatment of arm and shoulder pains which prevented him from working and led to his decision to sell his truck. Because he was also mildly depressed, had little self-confidence, and had suffered a blackout period while driving his truck, he was transferred to a psychiatric ward. No physical disabilities were discovered except for mild arthritis.

During several hours of history taking and general orientation for the therapist, it was discovered that Pete's primary problem seemed to reside in his complete avoidance of anyone but his immediate family. He feared that he had cracked up and was greatly ashamed about a feud which he had carried on with a government agency. His symptoms had persisted for about six weeks before I saw him. He complained of being reduced to watching television outside the hospital, since he could not force himself to visit friends. Previously he had been a very sociable person who greatly enjoyed the company of other men; at one time he had owned a bar.

Since Pete had mentioned one of his former supervisors, Bill, with whom he had been friendly for several years but had not dared visit for six weeks, I asked him to close his eyes and imagine that he was paying a social call on Bill during his next weekend pass. At first he protested that it was impossible; that he had tried to visit Bill several times but had never reached his house. Finally he agreed to try, and closed his eyes while grimacing. As expected, Pete's first reaction was again an avoidance response: he described reaching Bill's house only to find a car parked in front of it; he returned home because he was certain that Bill had visitors. I then assured him that there were no visitors there. Pete started his second attempt by saying that he was taking his wife with him on the visit because her presence would take some of the "spotlight" away from him. This time he managed to ring the bell and entered the house with his wife. Bill greeted him in his usual fashion but "looked carefully at me to see how crazy I am." Pete was so uncomfortable that he left after only a few minutes, feeling very tense. On the third try, Pete again took his wife with him and managed to stay about half an hour; this time Bill did not seem very suspicious of his mental status. Since our time was up, the three scenes having taken about forty minutes, I suggested that he try visiting Bill over the weekend, but Pete shook his head doubtfully.

When I saw him again, on Tuesday of the following week, Pete talked about other things until, looking pleased, he said that he had visited Bill two days ago without his wife. He said that he was quite tense at first but that Bill had treated him as always and he had had a good time. He had not only talked the whole afternoon with Bill, but Bill's brother, whom Pete barely knew, was there for an hour during his visit. After having demonstrated to himself that he could engage in his usual social activities, Pete visited other friends the following day, attended to some business matters in downtown offices, and asked for his discharge before the week was out.

Repeated review is not a complete therapy in itself, but examination of many forms of psychotherapy will reveal that clients and patients spend much of their time in treatment discussing many of the same problems over and over. In the technique of repeated review, the therapist has an opportunity to focus the individual's attention on a particular problem and then to repeat the cognitive review until a different, more satisfactory solution is reached. Neither the limits of the technique nor the extent to which it can be used to facilitate therapy is known at the present time. In any case, repeated review, either in the form of the simple technique described above or in the form of extended discussions, is one of the mainstays of any approach to treatment aimed at changing misconceptions.

Chapter 5

Role of Affect and Insight

A cognitive approach to psychotherapy which tries to change misconceptions emphasizes insight as the most important factor in treatment. Such an approach, however, ignores emotions and feelings at great peril, since inappropriate emotions and feelings are probably the best indicators of the presence of misconceptions. The intimate relationship between misconceptions and affect has produced a long-standing rivalry between the misconception hypothesis and the expression-of-emotion hypothesis. The rivalry appeared as early as 1893, when Breuer and Freud (1957) published their paper on the cathartic method in the treatment of hysteria. A dual explanation of the role of catharsis in treatment is advanced in that paper. On the one hand, according to Breuer and Freud, catharsis brings about "associative correction of pathogenic ideas," which would correspond to our notion of correcting misconceptions; on the other hand, catharsis permits the expressing of "strangulated affect" which is "able to find its way out through speech." This historical rivalry between release of affect and associative correction to explain catharsis continues today in the arguments over the role of affect in psychotherapy. Quite recently the behavior therapists have joined those who would directly focus their psychotherapeutic attack on "emotions," although they advocate counterconditioning or extinction procedures rather than "expression" of emotion or feeling. Other therapists, such as the Adlerians and Ellis, continue to emphasize corrective association but under other names.

The cathartic experience in psychotherapy is usually viewed as being independent of cognition. The events which occur in catharsis are supposed to reduce the emotional charge, or "pent-up affect," which has interfered with the client's functioning. Many current therapies attempt primarily to relieve the client or patient of his pent-up emotion, either in cathartic episodes or over longer periods of time in which emotional release takes place less dramatically. If we examine catharsis more closely, however, we can readily discover several cognitive events which have significant influence on the experience. If these cognitive events do not occur, no amount of "emotional expression" is likely to be helpful.

During catharsis, the client or patient becomes emotional while describing some highly personal and hitherto undisclosed "secrets," which are ordinarily of a shameful nature. Following his recital, he usually reports considerable feeling of relief and a changed attitude toward the content of his emotional recital. In the simplistic explanation, his affect has been "expressed," an ambiguous word which means that he has verbalized his thoughts or has somehow rid himself of their emotional charge. As we have seen, the Breuer-Freud explanation combined both meanings.

Three well-known aspects of the cathartic experience must be added to the skeleton description already given. Each of the three can be regarded as a misconception which is corrected during the recital. In the first place, the individual is fearful that in revealing his secrets he will be shattered or overwhelmed. Yet after the recital he discovers that he is neither shattered nor overwhelmed. Second, he fears that when he tells his "shameful" secrets to the therapist he will be rejected and disgraced. This expectation of rebuff turns out to be an obvious misconception; the therapist remains unruffled. The third misconception concerns the supposedly shameful content of the secrets, often introduced by such statements as "This is so awful I can't even tell you about it" or "I can't even think about it myself." Such statements imply that the client has avoided subjecting his secrets to cognitive review. But as he recites his secrets, he is likely to reevaluate their shamefulness, particularly when he discovers that he is not shattered by the experience or rebuffed by the therapist.

This cognitive analysis of catharsis does not deny that it is a highly emotional experience. The analysis does show, however, that the reduced affect following catharsis is due to the correction of the three misconceptions. The feeling of relief is due to the discovery that the consequences of revealing the secrets were faulty expectations based upon misconceptions.

Cognition and Affect

Bergin (Bergin and Strupp, 1972, p. 451) recently proposed that the central problem in traditional psychotherapy and in the behavior therapies is how to break the bonds between cognition and affect. In the present chapter, we are proposing that affect is largely controlled by cognitions which produce emotional arousal and that changing cognitions will change the affect or eliminate it. In everyday life, we encounter numerous examples of this elementary principle.

Some time ago, I was approached by a graduate student, Tom, who exclaimed in anger that another faculty member had mentioned in a lecture that the student's research was "basically worthless." Since I was interested in the research, I sought out the other faculty member to find out what had happened. I asked what he had against Tom's research. The faculty member was baffled, saying that he had no knowledge of it and had never mentioned it. We puzzled over the incident for a bit until I used Tom's last name, at which the faculty member broke into a smile and said that in the class he had casually mentioned a published report by someone with the same last name. When I gave Tom this new information, he immediately lost his ire and was able to laugh about the whole affair. Most affective reactions which become important in psychotherapy are far more complex than this incident, but their elements may well be similar.

In fairness to other points of view, we should recognize that all theorists are faced with a dilemma in trying to explain how inappropriate affect can be severed from cognition. The same events can be interpreted as cognitive reorganization, as "expression" of affect, or as extinction of a conditioned emotional response by nonreinforcement or counterconditioning. The dilemma is found not only in therapy or in armchair theorizing but also in laboratory research. Subjects in experimental investigations are always awake and thinking; no one has yet discovered how to disconnect cognition in the waking state. The cognitive explanation has a major advantage for psychotherapists in that its referents—the conceptions and misconceptions of the patient—are more accessible to direct observation, whereas "expression" of affect and conditioning are not. In fact, the latter two usually must be inferred from the patient's reported cognitions unless the more laborious procedure of examining behavioral changes *in vivo* is adopted. Complete accuracy of observation is never assured in advance, since patients or subjects can falsely report their cognitions and also act deceptively.

Of particular significance to this basic question of how undesirable affect can be severed from cognition is the widely known work of Schachter and his colleagues. Schachter's research supports the contention that the emotional content of a reaction can be modified or eliminated if the cognitions related to the emotional reaction are changed. Such a contention assumes that emotional experiences always include cognitive aspects. That assumption seems to be well supported, for since 1924 there has been striking evidence that stirred-up autonomic reactions do not in themselves produce recognizable emotional experiences. Marañon (cited in Schachter, 1971) injected adrenaline into 210 human subjects and asked for their subjective reactions. Seventy-one percent reported only physical symptoms, with no recognizable emotional experience. Of the 29 percent who reported an emotional reaction, most described it as a "cold emotion" or an "as if" emotion. Only a very small percentage reported feeling "genuine" emotions. Most of the few cases reporting "genuine" emotional experiences did so only after Marañon had suggested to them a personal memory with strong affective force, thereby supplying them with an appropriate cognition. Injected adrenaline produces the same kind of physiological arousal that occurs in normal emotions accompanied by sympathetic discharges. It thus appears that physiological arousal, produced either by injection of adrenaline or by sympathetic discharge—but without relevant cognitive content—does not result in a recognizable emotional experience.

Schachter and Singer (1962) used Marañon's procedure to produce physiological arousal, but arranged conditions so that some of their subjects were in a situation which induced anger, others in a situation which induced euphoria, and others in a situation which induced amusement. All subjects received the same drug, adrenaline (epinephrine), but were told that they were receiving vitamins. The study was ostensibly an investigation of visual acuity. The results of the study showed that most of the subjects reported emotional experiences appropriate to the cognitions suggested by the experimenter—anger, euphoria, and amusement. Schachter and Singer therefore concluded, "By manipulating the cognitions of an individual in such a state of physiological arousal, we can manipulate his feelings in diverse directions" (p. 395). In a later review of this study, Schachter (1971, p. 59) also concluded that emotions are joint cognitive-physiological experiences: "In nature . . . cognitive or situational factors trigger physiological processes, and the triggering stimulus usually imposes the label we attach to our feelings." The obvious implication for psychotherapists is that if their clients or patients can be induced to perceive differently those situations which produce disruptive feelings or emotions, their affect can be altered in a therapeutic fashion. In other words, the bonds between cognition and a given maladaptive emotion or feeling can be severed if the cognition is changed.

Such a conclusion has been subject to dispute where conditioned emotional responses are concerned. The dispute appears to center around the role played by cognitive factors in the conditioning process in humans. Although the dispute is by no means resolved, laboratory investigators of conditioned responses in humans are becoming more acutely aware of the role of cognitive factors. Much of the material on this subject is summarized in a book edited by Kendler and Spence (1971) entitled *Essays in Neobehaviorism*. The opinion of only one-well known investigator, Maltzman, is mentioned here. His paper deals with cognitive factors in classical conditioning. He argues that conditioning studies of animals cannot be directly applied to the conditioning of humans, because human learning involves "thinking, attention, and emotion." Thus, although the degree to which cognition affects conditioning remains to be discovered, cognition is now recognized as a potent force.

If we abandon the simplistic notion that emotions and feelings are automatic response entities independent of perception and thinking, then emotion and feeling can be seen as enmeshed in cognitions. This point of view is emphasized by Leeper (1970, p. 156): "Emotions are perceptual processes. I mean this, furthermore, not in some odd and marginal sense, but in the full sense of processes that have definite cognitive content, or are rich in informational terms as well as in terms of their motivational properties." We can single out at least two definite cognitive contents of emotion which have considerable importance for psychotherapy. One relates to the cognitive control of emotion; the other relates to the individual's "reflexive awareness," his recall or memory of his emotional reactions.

Schachter is not alone in his conclusion that emotions are controlled by cognitive appraisal, which determines whether a situation is seen as emotional or devoid of affect. Arnold (1970, p. 123), for instance, has commented, "There is hardly a rival in sight for cognitive theory in the field of emotion. . . . Today, most of the newer theories of feeling and emotion assume that [emotional] experiences depend on the interpretation and evaluation of the situation." Arnold terms this interpretation and evaluation process "appraisal." Lazarus, Averill, and Opton (1970, p. 219) describe appraisal as follows: "The individual . . . cognitively filters stimulus information, and the resulting appraisal determines whether the situation is evaluated as relevant, threatening, frustrating, sustaining, etc." They add that cognitive processes "create the emotional response" and shape it into recognizable affect. If cognition creates emotions and feelings, then therapists can use cognitions to modify or eliminate emotions and feelings—mainly by encouraging the client to repeatedly review the misconceptions embedded in a particularly affect-laden topic which interferes with his adjustment.

Reflexive awareness (the memory of feelings and emotions)

is the second cognitive aspect of emotion or feeling which influences the course of therapy as well as the client's conception of himself. One's typical emotional episodes are not only remembered but are also used to characterize and to label the self. Psychotics, for example, frequently think of themselves as criminals because they remember instances of extreme frustration when they have had anger-suffused urges "to kill someone." Individuals who lack assertiveness may think of themselves as "cowards" because they recall instances when they feared and avoided conflicts. The therapist, therefore, when he discusses with a client or patient significant feelings and emotions, is usually dealing with cognitive factors. During such discussions, there may be *redintegrative effects;* that is, as the individual imagines more and more vividly the events leading to his appraisal of the situation which resulted in his affective reaction, additional affect is aroused. The redintegration effect is likely to be highly facilitative of therapy, because the amplified recall also makes more salient the faulty appraisals which led to the emotional reactions. The therapist, as well as his client, is thus enabled to recognize more of the cognitive factors which produced the inappropriate affect.

Both cognitive components—appraisal and reflexive awareness—are subject to misinterpretation and the development of misconceptions. The misconception arising from faulty appraisal can be illustrated by the simple incident described above, in which the graduate student incorrectly inferred that his research had been denigrated by a faculty member. His angry reaction was based upon faulty appraisal of what he had heard. When he was supplied with the correct information, his anger vanished. Reflexive awareness is subject to misinterpretation in the form of mislabeling of an emotion or feeling. For example, a client may describe himself as "hurt" by the way he was treated by someone else; at the same time, although angry feelings usually accompany "hurt" feelings, he may vehemently deny that he feels any anger. Further exploration usually reveals that the anger has been there all along but has been toned down and relabeled as "hurt," so that the client can avoid facing the unpleasant consequences of his anger. In such a case, he is demonstrating a defense or a misconception, rather than his real feeling.

Emotional reactions, then, are of considerable importance in an approach to therapy which emphasizes the locating and changing of misconceptions. Both cognitive components of emotion and feeling—the appraisal and the reflexive awareness—are subject to misinterpretation and can lead to the development of significant misconceptions. Such misconceptions can also be changed by cognitive review.

Appraisal and reflexive awareness of feelings and emotions are not the only aspects of affect which are useful in a cognitive approach to psychotherapy. The mere display of affect during treatment may be of considerable help, because affect frequently is a clue to misconceptions. The graduate student's anger at the other faculty member, for example, instigated my talking to the colleague, which led in turn to the discovery of the misconception. Moreover, emotional episodes in a client indicate that the situations which provoked them were probably of considerable importance. If not, why are affective reactions recalled later in therapy? Emotional episodes are not simply periods of physiological arousal. They also carry with them cognitive content which affects the client. By exploring the cognitive content of these reactions, both therapist and client may find clues to important misconceptions. Such exploration is illustrated below by three commonly encountered clinical problems. The exploration was initially undertaken because of the considerable affect displayed during treatment.

A client described a series of claustrophobic-like episodes which interfered with his normal social life and caused him considerable concern. Claustrophobia in itself implies that a misconception is at work, and the patient's report of his emotional reactions to confined places revealed the misconception. But why did he develop these fears at the age of thirty-four when he had not previously been claustrophobic? Further exploration revealed that he was engaged to a woman who was to become his second wife. She lived in a small apartment and frequently drove him about in her Volkswagen. Unknown to her, he had become seriously disillusioned and wanted to terminate the engagement. He was held back by his desire to keep from hurting her, his own fear that he was messing up his second marital relationship, and the fact that his fiancée was the niece of his employer. When each of these factors was worked through, his symptoms disappeared. The path to them had been marked, how-

ever, by his initial report of his fear of small, enclosed places. The
path to recovery also revealed his misconceptions about the consequences of terminating the engagement.

In another case, a woman who burst into tears whenever she
mentioned her husband ascribed the tears to her failure to be a good
wife. Reluctantly, she revealed that although she had enjoyed sex
during the first years of marriage, she no longer obtained any satisfaction from it. She insisted that she was very much in love with her
husband and that her current lack of sexual responsiveness was due
to her parents' early insistence that sex was immoral. The discrepancy
between her enjoyment of sex early in marriage and her current
negative reaction to it aroused the suspicion that her historical explanation based on early training might be faulty. After a number
of interviews, it turned out that, in her attempt to "save the marriage," she was desperately refusing to recognize her many resentments against her husband. Hence her tears and her insistence that
she was "very much in love" with him. When she recognized clearly
that she probably resented him as much as she liked him, she was
then faced with the problem of what action to take. She again
became highly emotional when I made the conventional suggestion
that she talk her resentments over with him. A flood of tears ushered
in her "I can't possibly do that" misconception. She could and did,
of course, discuss matters with him when her first tentative attempts
were met with his desire to discuss some of his resentments toward her.

What were the misconceptions uncovered in this case? Most
salient was the woman's ascription of her loss of interest in sex to the
early parental training. Second was her blind assertion that she was
very much in love with her husband. Third was her misconception
that she could not discuss with him the many resentments she harbored. The affect she displayed was most useful in detecting a problem of great personal significance to her. When we explored the
misconceptions, her feelings and emotions toward herself and her
marriage underwent considerable modification.

The third case was a twenty-four-year-old graduate student
in engineering who had been seen in therapy for several months. We
discovered that he was an extreme negativist who became markedly
hostile whenever he was asked to do something. His hostility was
ordinarily suppressed; and, until he discovered his negativism in

therapy, he was aware only of feelings of tension and discomfort. Because he was well mannered and got along socially—usually at a distance—he had a number of friends and possessed a lively wit. His negativism, however, was so extreme that he resented being asked to carry a book for a friend or to answer a telephone in someone else's house. He had developed techniques for handling these situations so that he did not provoke hostility among his friends, acquaintances, and coworkers, but at considerable cost to himself. His major complaint upon entering treatment was that he became rapidly exhausted when in social situations and had to withdraw to recuperate.

I wished to work directly upon his negativism and secured his cooperation up to a point. When I asked him to close his eyes and describe a situation in which he was being asked to do something by another person, and then to describe how he felt and what happened, he would close his eyes, describe a few innocuous events, and then block, regardless of what I said. He then revealed that his blocking and irritability were due to my trying to manipulate and control him. I recognized his feelings and asked him to perform a number of actions such as touching his knee, loosening his tie, scratching his cheek, and smoothing his hair—all with his eyes open. He performed the first action but then said he was getting a headache. I persisted, and his complaint of a headache increased. Finally he asked with open irritation, "What are you trying to do, desensitize me?" I explained, as I had before, that I was really trying to maneuver him into performing certain activities upon request to find out what happened in him when he did so.

He recognized the reasonableness of the procedure, but each time I asked him to perform the innocuous activities, he would grudgingly perform a few of them and then would complain that his headache was getting worse; he felt distinctly uncomfortable and very tired. My attempts at obtaining a repeated review of his misconception—that he had to become upset when asked to do something—had failed. The impasse continued for about ten minutes, at the end of which he was becoming openly irritated at himself and hostile toward me.

At that point, I changed tactics and told him that perhaps he was creating many of his own difficulties by his consistent refusal to perform even simple, innocuous actions. Such refusals would often create in other individuals a counterresponse of trying even harder to get him to comply. If he simply complied, he would remain in better control of the situation, since there would be fewer counterpressures exerted upon him, he would be performing the actions of his own volition, and he would not become wearied and distraught by the effort to refrain from compliance and still not offend the other person. He understood the logic but was skeptical of the results.

I then asked him to perform five simple activities, such as touching his knee and smoothing his hair. These he did rapidly and efficiently. I asked how he felt, and he laughed, saying, "No sweat." I then asked him to perform ten activities, which he did without effort. When asked how he felt, he said that his headache had disappeared, he felt no discomfort, and he was generally in fine fettle.

The events in this case seem to illustrate that when the cognitive content of the situation was changed, the client's emotional reactions of tension, headache, discomfort, and fatigue disappeared, despite the fact that he was carrying out exactly the same requests at which he had previously balked. He now perceived that he could retain control by complying, and was in more danger of losing control by negation.

One kind of reported affect is always an important clue to misconceptions of significance. When an individual describes continuing apprehension for which he has no explanation, the term *free-floating anxiety* is usually thought appropriate. Several explanations for this phenomenon have been proposed. One holds that the person is overrun and dominated by his continuing state of fear. Such an explanation is, of course, simply a restatement of the problem. Psychoanalysts propose that the sources of the fear are unconscious and therefore inaccessible for use as explanation. I have found, however, that a client who is supposedly describing his free-floating anxiety is, in fact, invariably describing exactly what he is afraid of. His fear is usually stated in terms such as "I am falling apart" or "I seem to be coming apart at the seams" or "I feel like I'm just disintegrating." The quotations are obviously references to a disintegrating self-concept, produced by long-continued stress or threat. Therefore, a term such as *fear of disintegration* would be more accurate than free-floating anxiety.

If patients with this fear are allowed to tell their stories, even after they have assured the therapist that there is nothing wrong in their lives which could account for their apprehension, they almost always do a fine job of describing one or more threats which account for their continuing stress. Sometimes questioning by the therapist is necessary; in unusual cases, some form of hypnosis or free association may also be required. Even when an array of threats has been uncovered, the therapist may be in a dilemma to sort out causes from effects, but then this is the lot most therapists have voluntarily chosen. In any event, once the fearful threats are exposed, and the misconceptions associated with them corrected, free-floating anxieties, or fears of disintegration, can often be alleviated. The misconception "I am disintegrating" can usually be replaced by "I am not as sick as I thought I was."

In many patients suffering from fears of disintegration, a belief in impending insanity (phrenophobia) may figure prominently. Where phrenophobia is not well entrenched, straightforward explanations of the relationship between continuing stress and symptom formation may change the client's misconception rapidly and dramatically. Where phrenophobia is deeply entrenched, as in patients with histories of previous hospitalization, or those with immediate relatives who have been psychotic, phrenophobia may become the central misconception and may yield only grudgingly to insight.

Insight

Insight is the battered child of psychotherapy. At times it has been endowed with all the magic of successful treatment; at other times it has been cast off as merely epiphenomenal. The compromise position, classically phrased as "Insight is not enough," implies that it has some useful effects but that something else is needed. What seems to be needed is a redefinition of insight that aligns it with a consistent theoretical position so that it can be useful in therapy as well as in research on therapy. Since insight is clearly a term in the cognitive realm, we can attempt to redefine it in accord with the misconception hypothesis.

Lack of insight is commonly ascribed to faulty knowledge—for instance, lack of sufficient information, mistaken ideas about the elements of a situation, or distorted perception of the relationships among the elements. In any case, prior to the obtaining of clear understanding, the situation was falsely or incorrectly interpreted; hence the individual suffered from a misconception. When insight occurs, however, the misinterpretation is eliminated because its falsity is recognized. The core of insight in therapy is thus a recognition by a client or patient that a particular conception of his is faulty and a different conception is required.

On this basis, we can define *insight in psychotherapy* as *the individual's recognition that he suffers from a specific misconception or a cluster of related misconceptions.* By reorganizing his information or by adding new information, he now has a changed perception of the situation; and this changed perception allows him to discard his misconception. (We are, of course, describing insight from the patient's subjective point of view; from the standpoint of external reality, insight may be either correct or false. Thus faulty insights can produce misconceptions.) The patient who exclaims with delight over his newfound insight is either implicitly or explicitly informing the therapist that he "sees things differently," that his new insight is "better than" his former understanding, and that his former understanding was mistaken. The usual course of therapy is made up of a long series of recognitions that one has been mistaken in his previous views of himself and of other persons, as misconception after misconception is located and recognized as such. The process can occur quite rapidly for some insights, but may take many periods of cognitive review for others.

Verbalizing one's insights when the misconceptions are recognized may be extremely difficult. In psychotherapy, we are ordinarily dealing with tenuous, ambiguous data based upon fleeting internal experiences such as "feelings" or even vaguer sensations, or with social experiences which may be just as complex and just as vague. Few of us are gifted with either the vocabulary or the sensitivity of great novelists or great clinicians. Finding words to describe our experiences, even after weeks or months of discussing them, may be a tortured process. If the therapist does not help to phrase and clarify the misconceptions encountered, the client may be at a loss when he tries to describe his changed perceptions.

The following incident exemplifies the attainment of insight in a patient of high verbal ability who was able to put his changed perception of himself into words. Since this patient had shown a lack of confidence when seeking work, I asked him to picture and describe himself applying for a job. Instead of complying, he began to object strenuously on the grounds that "all that psychology is for the birds." Switching tactics, I quickly asked him to repeat exactly what he had said, and with the same intensity, but to listen to himself as he did so. Taken by surprise, he complied. At the end of the second repetition, he launched himself out of his chair and in a wonder-struck tone exclaimed, "My God, I'm really an arrogant bastard!" That self-description would have been accepted by many who knew him, but this was the first time I had heard him reveal such insight.

Prior to his recognition of his misconception about himself, he had described himself as a downtrodden, oppressed person who was trying by sheer will power to return to normal. My efforts at treatment had usually been derided as "all that psychotherapy nonsense." He had been told by others that he had a supercilious attitude, but he had always rationalized this as due to the hostility of others. When his attention was directed to his own repeated acting out of his angry rejection of the therapist's efforts, he was able for the first time to recognize his arrogance. His insight was lacking in historical elements, but he saw clearly that he had had a faulty conception of himself.

Only current misconceptions are influential in behavior, even though they have historical roots. Past misconceptions which are no longer believed are historical events without current influence. Insight must therefore be defined as the recognition of one or more current misconceptions. Such a definition does not, however, imply that explorations of the past are of little help in finding and changing misconceptions. There is, in fact, no unassailable reason to reject the exploration of either the past or the present in helping the client to understand his misconceptions.

The following illustration shows that essentially similar insights can result from either a historical or a contemporaneous approach. A thirty-year-old schoolteacher regarded himself as a "sensitive" person who valued being a "nice guy." Having read widely in psychoanalysis, he invariably explored his past during treatment in an effort to understand his not infrequent current rejections. Although I had suggested to him that some of his behavior might produce rejection by others, he much preferred to believe that his greater sensitivity somehow elicited "envy" in others.

In the course of his historical explorations, he eventually remembered that during the first few years of school he had "been picked on by the other kids." Aloud, I wondered why. He tried to explain that even then he had been very sensitive, to the extent that his peers took advantage of him. At that point, he had another recollection that he had been in many fights during that period. He also remembered the rages which overcame him, so that he himself provoked some of the fights. This recollection made him question his assertion that he had always been a nice guy.

As he continued the exploration, he remembered that in junior high he had decided to imitate an older brother, and to *act* as though he liked everyone to avoid social conflicts. He added that at first he had felt hypocritical but that this feeling had disappeared. His underlying hostilities had not disappeared, but he felt that they were under control.

Armed with the knowledge that he was more hostile than he had surmised, he began to explore his current behavior with others. For the first time, he recognized that despite his own claim to being always a "nice guy," he would occasionally vent his hostilities toward someone who did not appreciate him sufficiently or who interfered with him "too much." Previously he had ascribed these displays of hostility to temporary feelings of fatigue or to the tendency of others to envy his sensitivity. Now he was able to recognize that there were understandable internal sources for his hostility, quite different from those he had assumed.

In the illustration, the client had started his self-examination in the past because of his own predilection for that orientation. He had, however, continued to examine the findings for their implications for the present. If he had started with his present relationships, he undoubtedly would have arrived at the same insight

—that he was often unjustly hostile and that he was not always a nice guy.

A differentiation between "intellectual" and "emotional" insight is automatically invoked by many therapists when a client or patient claims that he now understands something new about himself, but his behavior does not change. *Intellectual insight* is often defined as only verbal, superficial understanding. The vague concept *emotional insight* implies that emotional support has somehow been welded to intellectual understanding. Intellectual insight is often viewed as flabby and unconvincing, whereas emotional insight consists of robust convictions which effectively change behavior. We do not, however, need to make such distinctions in order to account for superficial understanding. The client may simply be verbalizing what the therapist has told him, but without recognition that he suffers from a misconception. Or the verbalized insight may be a valid recognition of a misconception, but the misconception may be unrelated to the problem, even though both therapist and client believe that it is. Understanding of unrelated data is hardly conducive to behavior change. Again, superficial understanding may result from the fragmented nature of the client's insight. Partial understanding is unlikely to produce behavior change. Furthermore, the client may retain unspoken reservations based on contradictory information which he has not revealed to the therapist. If the therapist simply assumes that the client's lack of conviction is based on the failure to link "emotion" to the insight, he forfeits the opportunity to explore additional material which may be crucial in helping the client to recognize his misconceptions.

Even a thorough and valid recognition that one suffers from a misconception may be ineffective in changing behavior if the client still has no good solution to the problem. Recognizing one's mistake does not automatically produce appropriate solutions. More adaptive behavior occurs when the individual not only recognizes his mistake, or his misconception, but also has a more appropriate solution in mind.

Chapter 6

Clustering of Misconceptions

If all of a patient's misconceptions were independent of each other, therapists would face a hopeless task in trying to modify or eliminate them to bring about readjustment. Fortunately, misconceptions have a tendency to be grouped into clusters, with some kind of hierarchical organization. In the case report of Mrs. Bin in Chapter Two we saw that separately identified misconceptions can be arranged into small clusters of misconceptions based upon a common theme.

The clustering of psychological variables is not a novel idea for psychotherapists. *Syndrome,* a well-used term, ordinarily refers to the clustering of signs and symptoms which facilitate diagnosis. The clustering of misconceptions is a significant feature of considerable prominence in two psychotherapies. Berne's (1961) transactional analysis is heavily dependent upon two clusters, the "Child" and the "Parent." Although Berne conceived of them as complex ego states, we saw in Chapter One that each can readily be reinterpreted as clusters of uncorrected misconceptions learned in early childhood. Horney's (1950) notion of the idealized self can also be viewed as a cluster of misconceptions about the self, interwoven with "strands of reality." In Chapter Three, when discussing modeling, I tried to show that minor phobias are controlled by three clustered misconceptions about (1) the harmfulness of the feared object, (2) the probability that one will collapse in the presence of the feared object, and (3) one's inability to change his fear reaction to that object.

Since the clustering of misconceptions is of considerable importance in psychotherapy, this chapter is devoted to a brief exploration of the clustering of misconceptions in diagnostic categories, and a subsequent discussion of two major clusters of misconceptions which are often encountered in a surprisingly large number of persons coming for treatment. Neither of these two clusters—the unwarranted belief that one is about to become insane (phrenophobia) and the belief that one is a special person—has received much attention in the literature. I have, however, found them extremely useful in psychotherapy. Additional clusters of misconceptions proposed by other therapists will be referred to in later chapters.

Misconceptions in Diagnoses

Clustered misconceptions play an important role in a factor-analytic study by Martorano and Nathan (1972) of the signs and symptoms of 924 hospitalized mental patients—mostly psychotics, as well as a few neurotics, drug addicts, and alcoholics. Sixteen experienced residents employed the Boston City Hospital Behavior Checklist to note the presence or absence of one hundred key signs and symptoms derived from a previous systems analysis of traditional diagnostic indicators. Several factor analyses* were carried out to determine how the items could be grouped into diagnostic factors. Only seventy of the most useful items of the check-

* The method used was factor analysis, not cluster analysis. Clustering is used in the present book to refer to any method which divides misconceptions into groups, each with a common theme.

list were used in the final oblique rotation, where thirteen factors were recovered. Each of these thirteen factors could be interpreted as being related to a psychiatric diagnosis.

Of particular interest is the considerable dependence of the checklist upon revealed misconceptions of the patients. Almost half, or thirty-four, of its seventy items are dependent in whole or in part upon patient misconceptions. These thirty-four items will be listed later. As we shall see below, some of the misconceptions are phrased in traditional psychiatric terminology, but they are nonetheless classifiable as misconceptions. For example, the item "disordered form of thought" must refer to misconceptions, since disordered thinking is classified as such because it is illogical or unrealistic. When the disorder is so extreme that it consists of fragmented thoughts without logical connections, the misconceptions are reduced in visibility as the disorganization becomes most salient.

Only two of the Martorano and Nathan factors will be presented here. Each represents an extreme in terms of the usefulness of misconceptions in reaching a diagnosis. Their Factor 5 is labeled *catatonia*. Misconceptions apparently have no part in any of the eight items (with factor loadings ranging from .27 to .82) in this factor; all eight are dependent upon external observation: alteration in the quality of psychomotor activity, catalepsy or waxy flexibility, mannerisms, verbigeration or perseveration, negativism or mutism, compulsions, perseverates, blocking of speech or thought is severe and disabling.

In contrast to catatonia, the diagnosis of paranoid process, Factor 12 in the Martorano and Nathan study, appears to be entirely dependent upon the detection of revealed patient misconceptions. The six items in this factor, with loadings ranging from .31 to .56, are delusions, lacks reality testing, disordered content of thought, delusions of persecution, delusions of persecution the primary symptom, and ideas of reference.

Another way of estimating the possible usefulness of revealed misconceptions in the diagnosis of psychosis is to count the number of items in the Boston City Hospital Behavior Checklist which are dependent upon patient misconceptions. Not all of the thirty-four items listed below are solely dependent upon revealed misconceptions. Clouding of consciousness, for example, can be inferred as a misconception from verbal content, but it can also be inferred without taking misconceptions into account.

Hallucinations
Delusions
Lack of reality testing
Autism
Loose associations
Verbalizes persistent anxiety
Perceptually misinterprets the environment with illusions
Auditory hallucinations
Auditory hallucinations have distinct perceptual quality
Visual hallucinations
Disordered forms of thought
Disordered progression of thought
Obvious logical connections between thoughts (reverse scored)
Thinking circumstantial
Incoherent
Disordered content of thought
Delusions of grandeur
Delusions of persecution

Delusions of persecution the primary symptom
Delusions of self-accusation
Delusions of sin, guilt, impoverishment, or illness
Ideas of reference
Suicidal thoughts
Hypochondriacal thoughts
Obsessional thinking
Phobias, fears, doubts, or indecision
Disordered retention and reproduction of thinking
Amnesic
Confabulation
Irredeemable guilt, profound remorse, despair, and certainty of punishment
Manifests confusion
Clouding of consciousness
Incoherent, apprehensive
Autistic thinking

Most of the items in the preceding list are related to some form of psychosis. That might be expected; the misconceptions of the psychotic are likely to be more bizarre, and therefore more readily perceived as misconceptions, than those of neurotics. But even though the misconceptions in the neuroses are more subtle, current diagnostic syndromes of neurosis depend upon them to a much larger extent than in the psychoses. Illustrations of this assertion are found in the following four common categories of neurosis, which are discussed in terms of the misconceptions frequently associated with such syndromes.

In listing misconceptions under neurotic syndromes, I have

relied to a large extent upon *The Psychiatric Interview in Clinical Practice* by MacKinnon and Michels (1971), although I have supplemented that source with material from my own experience as well as other sources. Since MacKinnon and Michels do not explicitly refer to misconceptions in their discussions of the different neuroses, I have made liberal interpretations of their phrasings in order to make the descriptive material fit the misconception format. The discussions of four common categories of neurosis do not attempt to circumscribe the complete content of each category. They are intended only to illustrate that clusters of misconceptions are already in widespread use as aids to diagnosis. Little attention is paid to the well-known fact that few individuals fit themselves neatly into the classical descriptions of a particular category. That is taken for granted.

Depressive neurosis, or reactive depression, is among those psychological disturbances which are probably most easily identifiable by the revealed misconceptions of the patient. The following list contains at least some of the major misconceptions revealed by most depressives. Not all such patients manifest all of the items on the list, nor is there reason to believe that the list is exhaustive.

1. I am, have been, and will remain hopeless.
2. I am, have been, and will remain helpless.
3. I am, have been, and will remain worthless, a creature of guilt.
4. I shall never recover from whatever ails me.
5. I am unable to engage in normal activities.
6. I have no interest in anything and will never be able to regain interest in anything.
7. I obtain little or no help from others.
8. I am so badly off, so guilty, and so hopeless that suicide is a desirable and probably inevitable solution.
9. I am losing my mind and may become completely "insane."
10. I am not myself and will not be able to regain my former self.
11. I am physically ill and have serious health problems.
12. I am not angry or hostile toward anyone; I alone am responsible for my present condition.

13. I am rejected by others because I am worthless and losing my mind.

14. I must worry all the time, but I can't concentrate.

The misconceptions listed below represent typical misperceptions of *obsessives*. Not all obsessives reveal all of these misconceptions; and the list is certainly not exhaustive, since obsessives display considerable subtlety and refinement in their thinking. For example, even though orderliness and cleanliness are likely to be most frequently characteristic of this group, many obsessives may reverse such behavior and display compulsive disorderliness and compulsive dirtiness. Even in the same individual, opposite kinds of behavior may be found in different places and at different times. When questioned about such apparent contradictions, he is likely to defend it with rationalizations, plus the frequent misconception starting with "I should" or "I must." For that reason, many of the misconceptions listed below are introduced with those words.

1. I must be punctual, conscientious, orderly, and reliable in everything all the time.

2. I can't stand anything that is dirty or germ ridden.

3. I am sure that everyone is competing with me.

4. I need to be first or to win at all costs.

5. I must control everything and everyone if I possibly can, including myself.

6. I should not get angry or hostile, because everything can be solved by reason and intellect.

7. I believe that details are very important and all of them should be attended to or recounted in conversation.

8. I must be efficient at all costs.

9. I must depend upon intellect and logic and ignore my feelings.

10. I should not really trust anyone. People just do things that make me suspicious.

11. I deserve more respect.

12. Being right is more important than anything else.

13. I get along best with others when I can tell them things I know.

14. I make only reasonable demands upon others, who frequently fail to understand that I am only being reasonable.

15. If I am spontaneous I am vulnerable.

Hysterical personalities develop acute symptoms such as anxiety and depression when faced with major threat and frustration. The acute symptomatology often obscures the underlying misconceptions listed below.

1. I am most effective when I am flirtatious, seductive, vivacious, and dramatic.

2. I make things more interesting for others and gain more approval when I exaggerate and bend the truth.

3. I cannot stand disappointments and frustrations.

4. I must constantly have sympathetic attention and approval from others in order to feel comfortable.

5. By acting dependent and helpless I achieve my goals.

6. I am at my best when entertaining and charming others.

7. I am not responsible for my difficulties and problems; I am a victim.

8. I deserve to be given more help and attention by others.

9. Routine and attention to details are unimportant and can best be left to others.

10. I am imaginative, intuitive, and creative—more so than others.

11. When I am just being friendly and warm, others interpret my behavior as sexy.

12. I have relatively little interest in sex.

13. I cannot function in the presence of detached, impersonal others.

14. I have always had many things wrong with my health and suffer much pain.

Phobic reaction is diagnosed almost automatically once an individual has revealed irrational fears of ordinarily harmless objects. (Phobic reactions may, of course, be embedded in other diagnostic categories.) In the introduction to this chapter, we have already shown that clusters of at least three misconceptions can be found even in simple "conditioned" fear responses. When unusual phobias are encountered in clinical practice, many additional misconceptions are also found. Highly incapacitating phobias, in contrast to the simple "conditioned" fear responses, are likely to be related to other clusters of misconceptions which involve nonphobic maladjustments.

Knowledge of the general clusters of misconceptions associated with diagnostic labels is not sufficient for individual diagnosis or for therapy. The general clusters only suggest which misconceptions might be valuable in understanding a particular client or patient. They lack concrete content in regard to the particular persons, situations, and self-concerns which contribute to the individual's psychological difficulties. Thus, diagnosis of the individual case requires considerable knowledge of the concrete and specific misconceptions which interfere with an individual's adjustment.

Phrenophobia

The literature of psychotherapy and psychopathology contains only incidental references to an important cluster of misconceptions which I have found extremely useful in the treatment of hospitalized mental patients as well as students in a university clinic. This cluster, which I have termed *phrenophobia,* has to do with the false belief, and associated fear, that there is something wrong with one's mind which may result in "insanity." As phrenophobia intensifies, a large number of symptoms become salient, most of them anxiety-linked. The lack of systematic reference to phrenophobia in the literature is, I suspect, due to the many and varied ways in which patients reveal, or refuse to divulge, their phrenophobia, as well as the fact that the clinician who does not think in terms of misconceptions has difficulty in viewing such irrational beliefs as having great significance. The significance of these beliefs can be grasped rather vividly, however, if one spends a few minutes imagining how his life would be changed if he were convinced that he is on the threshold of psychosis.

There is still another reason for the lack of attention paid to phrenophobia. If society defends itself against those with mental illness by mechanisms of denial, isolation, and insulation (Cumming and Cumming, 1957), those who fear impending insanity deny, isolate, and insulate themselves against this fear even more intensively. Thus, denial of phrenophobia is constantly encountered in clinical work, even though there are also many patients and clients who reluctantly confess to the fear of "going crazy." The problem of detection is further compounded by the large number of colloquial terms and euphemisms which cloak references to this cluster of misconceptions. In addition to the fairly straightforward concern about "losing one's mind" or "becoming insane" or "going crazy," there are the many other terms richly supplied by our culture— terms such as nervous breakdown, cracking up, breaking down, going around the bend, losing one's marbles. To make matters worse for the clinician, the patient may have highly idiosyncratic meanings for his terms. For example, one thirty-two-year-old college graduate with a severe depression had consistently denied any phrenophobia for several months in the hospital. When I asked him again on the day of his discharge whether he had ever feared insanity, he replied with considerable irritation that such thoughts had never bothered him; his major concern was that he might become so "emotionally unstable that I might be incarcerated for the rest of my life." Most therapists are also familiar with the likelihood that even well-educated patients confuse neurosis with psychosis; "We're all nuts," said one patient with a twenty-year history of occasional hospitalization for severe anxiety.

The prevalence of phrenophobia among persons seeking psychotherapy has not been studied systematically, but Thorne (1961) reports that 78 percent of his patients seen in office practice had "fears of imminent mental breakdown," while 22 percent had "feelings of actual disintegration occurring." In a minor questionnaire study that I supervised, 70 percent of the patients on a psychiatric ward exhibited high phrenophobic concerns. We would probably have found a much larger percentage if we had been able to circumvent the denial phenomenon and used interviews rather than questionnaires.

Even supposedly normal populations of college students show a surprisingly high amount of phrenophobia at some time during their lives. With the help of graduate students, I have conducted questionnaire surveys among undergraduates at the Universities of Colorado and Hawaii. For the six classes queried, the results tended to be similar from class to class in that approximately 20 percent of the males and about 30 percent of the females gave convincing anecdotal accounts of having experienced phrenophobia. Our results were similar to those reported in independent studies by Gurin, Veroff, and Feld (1960), who obtained answers from a stratified sample of the general population for the question "Have you ever felt that you were going to have a nervous breakdown?" Nineteen percent answered in the affirmative, with the percent of women outnumbering the percent of men.

One curious aspect of this cluster is that probably all psychotics (except those with severe brain damage) have intense phrenophobia. This surprising phenomenon has been confirmed by two psychiatrists and one psychologist, who initially doubted it but subsequently confirmed it after querying their own psychotic patients. The intense fear of becoming insane found in those who are already psychotic is probably due to the fact that psychotics are also laymen who have the same stereotype about psychosis as do neurotics, normals, and writers for television, the movies, and the stage. This stereotype almost invariably pictures psychotics as suicidal, homicidal, sexually assaultive, and, most important of all, suffering from complete loss of identity and loss of control. "Better the grave than the asylum" (a dictum of the Swedish writer Strindberg, who was also psychotic at times) is still a fair maxim depicting the layman's conception of psychosis.

The disabling anxiety so widespread among mental patients is largely due to high degrees of phrenophobia. Such patients have unrealistic fears that additional stresses, including the tensions produced by normal social interactions or by well-mastered job activities, will either worsen their condition or precipitate insanity. Severe phrenophobia leads many patients to isolate themselves from others and to avoid most of their normal activities. Reality testing of their actual impairment becomes impossible, and domination by phrenophobic concerns may occur. When patients are dominated by such concerns, we may speak of the autonomy of phrenophobia. In that stage, its intensity may be so great that the threat to existence becomes the vital core around which the patient organizes his life as well as he can, much like patients who face surgery for cancer or like prisoners awaiting execution.

The cluster of misconceptions associated with phrenophobia

varies widely from individual to individual, depending upon his personal experiences with mental illness, his knowledge of his family history, and the culture of which he is a part. Earlier encounters with severe anxiety, referrals to professionals for diagnosis or treatment, and even casual contacts with persons who have become mentally ill help to determine some of the misconceptions. Of greater importance is the knowledge, true or false, that one or more relatives have been hospitalized or treated for mental disturbances. The role of culture is also readily discernible. For example, many patients of Spanish heritage in the western United States still have misconceptions about the role played by *brujas*, or witches, in the development of illness, whereas those of northern European background are more concerned with family inheritance. Regardless of culture, however, misconceptions about "my nerves" are those most commonly reported.

Despite the great variation in misconceptions in this cluster, five related irrational beliefs can usually be found in those suffering from phrenophobia. All five are misinterpretations of the psychological symptoms brought about by prolonged tension. Contrary to the facts, phrenophobics believe (1) that their constant feelings of apprehension or anxiety indicate impending insanity; (2) that any gaps or distortions in their memory, no matter how trivial, are signs that their "minds" are breaking down; (3) that difficulties with concentration are prognosticators of the same fate; (4) that their unaccustomed irritability must signal the onset of severe mental disturbance; and (5) that if the first four symptoms do not precipitate psychosis, their relentless insomnia will do so.

These five misconceptions are, of course, misinterpretations of common anxiety symptoms associated with prolonged tension or stress. All five derive from the patient's preoccupation with his own functioning, often exacerbated by symptom hunting. The immediacy of the evidence for these misconceptions is so great that therapists encounter great difficulties in trying to dispel them, particularly if the phrenophobia is long-standing. A sixth misconception, usually associated with the preceding five, also hampers therapy. This is the patient's belief that because he is in danger of insanity, there is little point in working on other problems.

The treatment of this cluster of misconceptions is beset by

many obstacles, some engendered by the therapist if he fails to recognize the significance accorded phrenophobia by the patient. Such failure usually leads the therapist to offer casual reassurances intended to set the patient's mind at rest. Although the patient may seem to accept the reassurances, he is often utterly unable to understand how symptoms which distort his whole being can be passed off so lightly; remembering the false reassurances given by well-meaning friends and relatives to "cheer him up," he may believe that his therapist shares the same kind of false optimism. Furthermore, patients usually know that their therapists may not be privy to all the facts upon which their fear of insanity is based. They rarely reveal all of the evidence. To do so, they fear, may well lead the therapist to the patient's own conclusion—that he is so ill that he needs long-term incarceration, or at least temporary commitment for observation. Thus, the most disturbing self-observations made by the patient are usually withheld from the therapist.

Simple, direct reassurance is often effective with clients and patients who have lesser degrees of phrenophobia, provided the cluster of misconceptions has not been reinforced over many years, and the patient has considerable faith and trust in the therapist. Direct reassurances are also effective when they help the patient to recognize that the therapist understands the matter from the patient's perspective. Open guessing at the patient's five central misconceptions sometimes has a remarkable impact upon his willingness to listen to the therapist. Many patients also derive much indirect reassurance from the therapist when they are consistently treated as rational human beings who, despite their protests to the contrary, are quite capable of discussing their symptoms and solving their problems. Such indirect reassurance probably accounts for much of the dissipation of phrenophobia without its ever being openly discussed by therapist and patient.

Reassurance is not, however, the most effective treatment for phrenophobia, even though it may often help to reduce anxiety and even panic. The roots of this cluster of misconceptions are often too deep to yield to authoritative statements, especially if the misconceptions have been reinforced by confirmations from others and by the terrifying experiences resulting from severe anxiety. More prolonged treatment by other methods is usually required.

One of my patients, for example, was a forty-year-old severe obsessive-compulsive who had been hospitalized four times over a period of twenty years, sometimes with the diagnosis of anxiety reaction, and sometimes of schizophrenia; I had to work for almost three months during part of each semiweekly hour to persuade this man even to consider the possibility that he might not be a "paranoid schizophrenic," as he preferred to call himself. Another patient was a depressed individual who partially remitted and was seen only once a month; after three years I discovered that this man still harbored the same misconceptions about his sanity that I thought I had dispelled during the first three months of treatment when he was hospitalized.

In my experience, more intensive methods of treating phrenophobia need to be directed at two areas of patient ignorance. One is the patient's lack of knowledge concerning the effects of prolonged anxiety. The other is the patient's ignorance about the relationship between his anxiety and his unsolved personal problems. Individuals who recognize that their anxiety is a product of their unhappy marriages, or their frustrations and rejections in their social lives, do not ordinarily develop phrenophobia. They have adequate explanations for their symptoms; thus, they need not seek another plausible but less accurate explanation, such as phrenophobia or its physiological counterpart, somatophobia. When he examines the patient's anxiety symptoms in detail, and tries to link the anxiety with real-life problems, the therapist is attacking not only the five central misconceptions but also the current problems which have contributed to the phrenophobia. Beliefs in impending insanity cannot be treated in a vacuum devoid of the content supplied by the other misconceptions from which the patient suffers.

In the foregoing discussion there is no intent to assert that phrenophobia is the sole cause of psychological disturbances, or that its eradication will clear up all difficulties. There is an assertion, however, that this particular cluster of misconceptions has major significance in the development of disabling anxiety and in the prolongation of treatment if it is not dealt with. Too little is known about this phenomenon at the present time to write decisively about either its recognition or its treatment. This cluster of misconceptions is, however, of sufficient importance that therapists might routinely bring the matter up with patients who might possibly suffer from such faulty beliefs. There need be no fear that the therapist will be giving the patient "ideas," since most individuals seeking help from professionals in the field of mental health have had those "ideas" about themselves long before they encountered the therapist. Our culture is surprisingly profligate in its use of mental illness as an explanation for almost any kind of psychological distress or deviation.

Special-Person Misconception

The psychological core of the special-person cluster of misconceptions is exaggerated self-importance, which has various names—superiority complex, arrogance, vanity, conceit, egotism, and many others. The number of its verbal referents testifies not only to its prevalence but also to its social significance. Its principal manifestation is found in compulsive attempts to wrest from others confirmation of one's superiority. If that superiority is threatened, vigorous efforts are made to defend it; if it is shattered, serious psychological problems occur. Reducing anyone's self-esteem is usually a hazard to his mental health; reducing the exaggerated self-esteem of the special person is often disastrous.

Perhaps as a result of his self-analysis, Freud (Jones, 1953, p. 5) noted that "the indisputable favorite of his mother keeps for life the feeling of being a conqueror." Although there may be many sources for the cluster of misconceptions found in the special person, being a "favorite" in childhood may well be one of the most important, since favorites tend to be indulged. An oversimplified sketch of adults who display this cluster is "the spoiled or pampered child grown up."

The central misconceptions in the special-person cluster vary with the individual, but most have the following six faulty beliefs about themselves: I must control others; I am superior to others; I should not compromise; I suffer more frustrations than others; I must try to be perfect; and I cannot trust others. In the unsuccessful special person who develops psychological disturbances when he fails to obtain continued affirmation of his self-importance, these six beliefs may be almost impossible to observe during initial therapeutic contacts. The presenting symptoms of anxiety and depression which occupy the center of attention usually obscure misconceptions. Sometimes the therapist can detect these misconceptions in clients and patients only after becoming familiar with their history from other informants.

The first belief, *I must control others*, derives from the special person's mistaken idea that his status and acceptance are dependent upon his success in dominating others. He is unlikely to recognize that a person often receives status and acceptance because he is able to engage in meaningful relationships, rather than as a result of continued domination. Thus, the special person is driven to constant attempts to control by displays of intellectual superiority or by skilled and practiced manipulation or by cultivated charm. Too often, when efforts to control are detected and resented, the special person ends up in self-defeat, usually without insight into his own behavior, which precipitated the rejections and rebuffs.

The second misconception, *I am superior to others*, must usually be inferred, because any direct statement of it carries some social opprobrium. The belief in one's superiority is always in regard to one's reference group. Most special persons are quite content to achieve dominance over their immediate family, friends, and those others with whom they are in constant contact. Only a few special persons find it necessary to achieve superiority over everyone. Some therapists automatically interpret a patient's expressed attitudes of superiority as compensation for his underlying feelings of inferiority. This interpretation was given great impetus by Adler, who emphasized compensation for inferiority feelings as the source of superiority feelings. I believe that Adler's supposition is, at best, only a half-truth. Many attitudes of superiority are genuine aspects of the special person's cluster of misconceptions. They may be found side by side with inferiority feelings, particularly in unsuccessful special persons whose presenting picture is one of depression and anxiety. Vanity can be learned just as directly as humility.

The third misconception, *I should not compromise*, is based on the special person's conclusion that giving in to others, even part way, is to endanger his own superiority. This principle is sometimes willfully violated by sophisticated special persons who have learned the value of giving the appearance of reasonableness; but such temporary yielding is often part of a larger strategy of losing preliminary battles in order to disarm opponents so as to win the war. The inability of the special person to compromise is often referred to clinically as "rigidity," but it is best understood as refusal to compromise. The frequent rejection and rebuffs suffered because of the failure to compromise often lead to great feelings of frustration and consequent hostility.

Thus, the fourth misconception, *I suffer more frustrations than others,* may be partly factual; but the special person usually fails to realize that the frustrations have their source in his own behavior. The hostility produced by the belief thus becomes self-justified. Temper tantrums, one of the most noticeable characteristics of the spoiled child, are often found in special persons as self-justified rage. Peculiar transformations in hostility may occur in that many special persons come to regard any displays of anger and rage as indications of their own weakness, a characteristic as humiliating as inadequacy. Thus, they are unable to recognize their own hostilities, expressing them as sarcasm, justified complaints, or ambiguous condemnations. When their anger is pointed out to them, they insist that they are only being factual.

The rationale behind the fifth misconception, *I must try to be perfect,* derives from the belief that perfectionism is admired by others. Society does, of course, hold out rewards for perfectionism where solid achievement is involved, but society also leavens its regard for perfectionism by making suspect those efforts which do not result in genuine accomplishment. Therapists have long been aware of the implied compulsivity underlying most empty perfectionism. The special person, however, does not ordinarily recognize his own empty strivings as drivenness. Any way in which he can excel helps to reconfirm his self-importance.

The final misconception in this cluster, *I cannot trust others,* again is partly factual, since the special person's own behavior has often led to rejection by others. His constant efforts to control, his attitudes of superiority, his refusal to compromise, his masked hostilities, and his empty perfectionism betray the highly competitive person who must have his own way and must be right at all costs. The failure to trust others is manifested by suspiciousness which may at times verge on the paranoid. In nonpsychotic individuals the suspiciousness is not truly paranoid because it lacks delusional quality. Special persons do not believe that they are victims of plots and conspiracies. They know, however, that they are often rejected or avoided for reasons which they cannot understand. Their lives tend to be filled with tension and guardedness, which inhibits spontaneity. They are at ease only when indulged and admired by others.

McCordick (1973) has added several additional misconceptions which occur in this cluster with regularity. The special person is also likely to be highly critical of others, to have minimum empathy, to have minimum self-insight, and to be unusually self-righteous. These additions are mostly related to the special person's lack of social skills, brought about by his need to wall himself off from the critical reactions of others in order to maintain his high self-esteem. In McCordick's words, the special person's lack of awareness of interpersonal signals protects him from the aversive consequences usually attached to abrasive behavior.

Overindulgence in childhood is not necessarily the only way in which this cluster of misconceptions can originate. Early identification with an illustrious parent, or even with fantasied heroes or heroines in stories, movies, or television, can also produce the same exaggerated belief in one's special significance. The possibility of informal or even formal indoctrination in one's self-worth may also be a fertile ground for learning this cluster of misconceptions about the self. McCordick is independently examining her hypothesis that noncontingent positive reinforcements in early childhood which ignore the appropriateness of the behavior produce the faulty beliefs. Even beyond childhood the cluster may develop in those who receive unusual adulation as leaders, celebrities, or great benefactors. Members of various occupational groups, such as movie stars, political leaders, professors, and physicians, may suffer from this occupational hazard. Knowing no movie stars, I cannot speak personally of them.

There is no reason to believe, however, that this cluster, once implanted, cannot be expunged. Not all overindulged children remain convinced of their self-importance throughout life. One's peers, relatives, and acquaintances often provide punishments and rejections which interfere with the egotist's complacency. If the punishments do not eliminate the misconceptions, the special person may take his misconceptions underground, particularly if he learns early in life that he can obtain his own way and control others much of the time by hiding his vanity and carefully planning his campaigns well in advance. Success, however, is not always assured.

For purposes of convenience we can divide special persons into two broad groups—those who are essentially successful in retaining their special conception of themselves, and those who are unsuccessful. In reality there is a continuum rather than a dichotomy, but the division permits us to avoid burdensome detail when presenting an overview of this cluster. Unless other factors intervene, successful special persons can be well adjusted even though their self-centeredness may be a problem for their families and their intimates. If they are deprived of their special status in their own eyes, however, their adjustment may undergo serious deterioration. Depression is one of the most likely outcomes of deterioration in a hitherto successful special person. It may also be accompanied by anxiety. Obsessive-compulsive trends which had earlier been integrated into the special person's achievements may flower as neurotic symptoms. Jean-Paul Sartre's (1959) novel *Nausea* is a highly detailed and authentic description of the neurotic breakdown of a special person, even though Sartre's avowed purpose was to fictionalize his existentialist philosophy.

Arrogance, egotism, and the insatiable search for public acclaim, combined with sufficient drive, accomplishment, and favorable circumstances, have characterized some of our most notable individuals. These successful special persons may have been recognized as outstanding leaders in various fields, but their private lives were often torn by neurotic conflicts. Their biographies illustrate the chasm between their public accomplishments and their personal maladjustments. The poet Robert Frost is generally regarded as a rugged New Englander whose poetry exemplifies the homely virtues. According to his long-time friend and official biographer (Thompson, 1966, 1970), however, Frost was unable as an adult to overcome his "jealousy, sulking, temper tantrums, and vindictive retaliations" (1966, p. xvi). He had been greatly indulged by his schoolteacher mother. Frost's children detested him when they grew up, and his wife refused to speak to him for twenty years before her death. For those who wonder what happens when two special persons marry, Milford's (1970) biographical account of F. Scott and Zelda Fitzgerald's marriage vividly portrays their efforts to dominate and destroy each other. Both were indulged children. Hitler's early years are still obscure, but various accounts contain considerable evidence that he was greatly indulged by his mother and mostly ignored by his father, who was twenty-five years senior to his wife. Evidence that Hitler suffered from a mental disorder is surprisingly scanty, but the evidence is overwhelming that he displayed all the misconceptions of the special person to an exaggerated degree. One wonders to what extent history has been determined by those who have been slaves to the special-person conception of themselves.

Exaggerated self-importance has not gone unnoticed in the literature of psychotherapy and psychopathology. Adler is particularly remembered for his early emphasis upon the striving for superiority as a universal human motive in reaction to real or imagined feelings of inferiority. As Adler's thinking changed, however, he came to view the striving for personal superiority without regard for others as a neurotic characteristic due to the early "pampering" of the child. Freud's conception of narcissism is also related to the special-person misconception, although narcissism is an energy construct rather than a cognitive construct. For Freud, narcissism develops because of early traumatic injuries to self-esteem, rather than to early learning of the self as being special. Horney dealt extensively with the "idealized self-image," which she initially regarded as the neurotic's unconscious attempt to solve his internal conflicts by creating a highly admired image of himself. Later in her career (Horney, 1950), she decided that the idealized self-image is not a product of neurosis but is responsible for the development of neurosis when the idealized image causes tension with the "real self." Of these three related conceptions, only Adler's notion of the neurotic striving for personal superiority can be clearly translated into the misconception hypothesis, for Adler viewed neurotic behavior as controlled by mistaken opinions.

Treatment of this cluster of misconceptions by psychotherapy is one of the more difficult tasks facing the psychotherapist. The secondary symptoms which result when the special person becomes "unsuccessful" are usually found to be anxiety and depression, with depressive features more common. There is little likelihood that clients or patients will respond to their long-term "characterological difficulties" produced by the special-person cluster as long as they are suffering from anxiety and depression. Thus, treatment of these two sets of symptoms must normally be accomplished before the more difficult task of treating the special-person cluster becomes feasible.

Once the individual is restored to sufficient stability to be willing to consider what might have brought on his anxiety and depression, treatment of the special-person cluster can begin if the therapist believes it worthwhile and if the patient is willing to continue in treatment. Throughout this book we have been insisting that there is no one best way to engage in psychotherapy. Thus, any of the therapeutic approaches which can deal with misconceptions can be adapted to treatment of the special-person cluster.

In treating this cluster of misconceptions, the therapist must be cautious about directly informing the patient that he is a "spoiled child grown up." Some patients interpret any reference to early spoiling or to attitudes of superiority as an accusation of moral deficit. The resulting resentment and hostility seriously impede the speed of treatment. Other patients, those who are more amenable to therapist frankness, are sometimes so intrigued by the diagnosis that they become interested in tracking down the possibility of their having been overindulged as children. When I first encountered this reaction, I was puzzled by it until one individual explained to me that he was tired of having lifelong difficulties and was more than willing to uncover the roots of his problems rather than constantly returning to be patched up. He was, of course, an exception among special persons.

When patients or clients are willing to explore their pasts to determine whether the special-person misconceptions apply to them, their persistence tends to falter. I have therefore found it advisable to ask them to explore in their present relationships the possible manifestations of the six misconceptions commonly found in this cluster. Their explorations often become intensified as they begin to link present behavior with childhood behavior patterns. When clients or patients are unwilling or unable to examine themselves for the spoiled-child syndrome, I usually ask them to consider the current unreasonable demands they make upon others as possible sources of their difficulties. Unreasonable demands can usually be pinpointed in the special person's constant efforts to control. The more concrete and specific the discussion of such demands, the more likely is the client to obtain insight into his misconception that he makes only reasonable requests of others. Once this insight is achieved, there is more likelihood of success with other misconceptions in this cluster.

In my experience, any psychotherapy aimed at helping special persons overcome their long-standing personality difficulties is likely to be long and tedious. The workings of the neurotic paradox seem to be peculiarly intensified in these individuals; they rationalize, intellectualize, avoid thinking about, and justify their faulty social interactions. They are also likely to practice what Phillips (1956) has termed "redundancy." That is, despite frequent failures based upon their misconceptions about themselves, they persist in the same patterns, only with heightened effort and intensity. Their attitude seems to be "If at first you don't succeed, try, try again." And sometimes, of course, persistence does pay off, but failure is met with obtuseness which prevents them from modifying the unsuccessful behavior. Freud had an explanation for the obtuseness of the special person after he himself had been accused of being one by Binswanger (cited by Kohut, 1966). In a letter to Freud, Binswanger wrote that he had been struck by Freud's "enormous will to power . . . to dominate." Freud won the exchange when he replied that he did not trust himself to contradict Binswanger's observation, "but I am not aware of it. I have long surmised that not only the repressed content of the psyche but also the . . . core of our ego is unconscious."

Chapter 7

Direct Approaches to Changing Misconceptions

Among the many therapists whose treatment procedures are openly aimed at trying to change misconceptions, four have been selected to illustrate that markedly divergent practices can be employed in therapy to attain the same goal. The earliest of the four therapists discussed in this chapter, Paul DuBois, published his major work in 1904. The most recent, Albert Ellis, published his in 1962. DuBois was certainly not the first therapist to depend upon the misconception hypothesis; publications by Pierre Janet and Josef Breuer, his contemporaries, preceded his, although there is no known relationship among these three European physicians. Even earlier, however, many hypnotists were attempting to make conscious the "morbid ideas" thought to be responsible for psychological distress. There is also no known relationship among the four therapists under discussion. All seem to have arrived independently at the same general hypothesis concerning psychotherapy. DuBois wanted to change "mistaken ideas," Adler wanted to change "mistaken opin-

ions," Combs and Snygg wish to change "inadequate differentiations," and Ellis tries to change "irrational ideas."

The differences in treatment practices are of considerable
interest. DuBois liked to be the kindly physician who reasoned
calmly with his patients to convince them that they possessed the
moral fiber to overcome their problems by recognizing their mistaken ideas. Without pretentious theory about personality development or psychotherapy, he depended largely upon common sense
and reason. The label he applied to his therapy, "persuasion," is
something of a misnomer if it connotes strenuous efforts to change
his patients' minds. Persuasion, as viewed by DuBois, was directly
opposed to the strenuous efforts of the hypnotists and practitioners
of suggestion, who tried to accomplish their goals with forceful statements and concealed suggestions.

Alfred Adler, on the other hand, was something of a show-
man as a therapist. Treating children in front of groups was one of
his specialties. He developed his own theory of psychological development and a widely recognized approach to psychotherapy.
Despite recent efforts by the Ansbachers (1956) to systematize his
theories, there is still much common-sense flavor to Adler's writings
—so much so that, as Ellenberger (1970) points out, non-Adlerians
are constantly rediscovering many of Adler's basic principles. Adler
also preferred to reason with his patients in order to change their
mistaken opinions, but he depended to a large extent upon his explicit theory.

Combs and Snygg are primarily interested in a perceptual
approach to understanding personality development and therapeutic
change. Their writings on personality theory are the core of a distinct school of personality, but their preferred therapeutic practice
is a variation on the client-centered approach. Whereas DuBois and
Adler reasoned with their patients, Combs and Snygg prefer to
facilitate their clients' self-explorations. Explanation, as the term is
used in this book, was preferred by DuBois and Adler, but Combs
and Snygg largely avoid explanation, at least in the form of interpretation, and instead concentrate upon helping the client to find
and change his own inadequate differentiations. DuBois probably
never heard of group therapy, but Adler and Snygg and Combs

have provided some of the basic thinking for much of modern group therapy.

Albert Ellis, the fourth member of the present group, has not developed a theory of personality development, but he has a theory of therapy. Unlike the other three, he places but little emphasis upon a warm, supportive relationship; instead, he believes that the therapist should act like a "good psychology professor" who strikes immediately at the heart of the matter. He uses any method from rational discussion to exhortation and cajoling to change the irrational ideas which are the target of all his efforts.

DuBois

Paul Charles DuBois (1848–1919) was a Swiss physician and professor of neuropathology at the University of Berne. According to Ellenberger (1970), patients with neurotic problems were referred to him from all over the world because of his considerable reputation. Despite their faith in him, his colleagues could not understand why his methods were successful. Adolf Meyer (1951) suggested that the successes were due to DuBois's dynamic and attractive personality, but DuBois would have disagreed. His approach, called "persuasion," was based upon a cognitive psychology in which "incorrect ideas" are seen as the source of psychological symptoms. The therapist's task, in his view, is to eradicate mistaken ideas from a patient's thinking. So great was DuBois's faith in the power of correct thinking that, like Freud, he would not wait to discharge patients until they had actually demonstrated their improved behavior. That, he claimed, was unnecessary once the misconceptions were changed.

The first edition of his major work, *The Psychic Treatment of Nervous Disorders,* was published in 1904, when he was fifty-six. The book reveals a relaxed, practical thinker who seems to have had a sophisticated grasp of the medical knowledge of his day. Examination of what appears to be a common-sense psychology indicates that he had very definite ideas about psychotherapy. Many of his notions clearly date him, while others are surprisingly modern.

The following passage (1909, p. 329) illustrates his recognition of the role of feminine sexuality in neurosis, as well as his typical Victorian delicacy: "A just respect for feminine modesty prevents the physician from collecting data concerning the erotic life of women. I am led to believe that, consciously or unconsciously, women submit to this yoke more often than they think, and that sensual preoccupations—often very vague, I admit—play a role in the development of their nervousness." Many of his statements about therapy have a modern ring. He recognized, for example, the important role of the family and recommended that the therapist also treat the patient's family in order to obtain lasting results. Skeptical about the effectiveness of the drugs available at the turn of the century, he quoted a distinguished practitioner's advice: "We never take medicine ourselves; we sometimes give it to our friends, and always to our patients." He was distinctly pointed in his criticisms of those physicians who attack psychological problems with drugs, electrotherapy, and diet. DuBois emphasized that rest and diets, which he himself advocated, are only adjuncts to the decisive factor in treatment—psychotherapy.

DuBois made strenuous efforts to differentiate his techniques of rational persuasion from the "suggestive therapeutics" which were popular among the practitioners of his day. He distrusted all deceptions employed by hypnotists and physicians, and he was particularly critical of H. M. Bernheim, leader of the Nancy School of hypnotism; he claimed that Bernheim and his followers eventually dispensed with hypnosis in their treatments and resorted to waking suggestion, which Bernheim in turn insisted was the basis for DuBois's persuasion. Bitingly, for him, DuBois (1909, p. ix) rejected the notion that he used suggestion. Instead, he asserted, "The means men have always adopted in order to come to a mutual conviction is simply called persuasion. It is arrived at by proof, for it is also possible by experience and demonstration to prove things in medicine. Persuasion is practiced by affirmation, pure and simple, which can never come under the head of suggestion if one believes oneself in what one is affirming." Here we have an early emphasis upon the "genuineness" of the therapist, for DuBois disagreed with any attempts to deceive patients in psychotherapy, and regarded suggestion as an "artificial method."

There are interesting parallels between DuBois and Adler, although any direct connection between them is unknown to me. DuBois was the older by twenty-two years. He started practice about 1880 and rapidly developed his rational, persuasive methods. Adler was not born until 1870. Neither man was a systematic theorizer, so that similarities and differences between their approaches are difficult to document. Adler, of course, was a much more prolific writer than DuBois. Although no claim is made here that Adler even knew of DuBois's theory or therapeutic tactics, their basic approaches have considerable similarity. DuBois, like Adler, was a cognitive psychologist who wrote that neurotic symptoms develop as the result of mistaken ideas that have crept into the patient's thinking. In treatment, both advocated a kindly, gentle approach to the patient in order to enlist his help in the rational discussion which could change the faulty ideas and erase the symptoms. They both made a practice of playing down the discussion of specific symptoms in order to deal with disturbances in the patient's pattern of life, which, when corrected, would eliminate the symptoms. Adler labeled a pattern of life as "life style," but DuBois does not seem to have found a label for it. DuBois anticipated Adler's belief in the necessity of encouraging the patient's social interest by advising his patients in a systematic fashion to contribute to the happiness of others in order to alleviate their own sufferings. In so doing, he used words that are far more moralistic in connotation than Adler's, although the underlying principles are the same: "To find inner happiness and health, he [the patient] must turn his attention away from himself and interest himself in others. Altruism must take the place of natural egoism" (DuBois, 1909, p. 461). The reference here to "natural egoism" is not the only such reference in DuBois's book, but I can find no real evidence that he anticipated Adler's notion of the drive for superiority or perfection. In that respect they can be distinguished.

Just as Adler placed his faith in the efficacy of cognitive changes which correct the patient's faulty ideas about himself, Du-Bois also proposed and practiced a cognitive therapy. Although Ellenberger (1970, p. 791) concludes that the reasons for DuBois's therapeutic successes seemed mysterious to his contemporaries and "are not apparent from his writings," his successes may not have been as mysterious as they appeared. If one believes that psycho-therapy is successful only if it makes the unconscious conscious, or redistributes psychic energies, or extinguishes conditioned responses, then DuBois's approach must seem mysterious. If, however, one accepts the notion that neurotic reactions are based upon the patient's misconceptions, and that changing misconceptions is necessary to eliminate neurotic reactions, then DuBois's tactics, like Adler's, do make sense.

DuBois's effectiveness in treating phobias was one of the reasons for the very considerable reputation he gained among his colleagues who referred patients to him. The following statement (DuBois, 1909, p. 368) presents the three principles which he advocated in treating phobias. "First. Give up all fear of the illness itself. . . . Second. Fix the object of your phobia and see more clearly how absurd and irrational is your fear. Third. Finally fight, through self-education, the defects of character which have caused your fears; pusillanimity toward illness, death, susceptibility, fruit of self-love, which creates ideas of persecution and so forth." Despite the hortatory language, which may grate on our modern sensitivities, these three principles of DuBois are actually attacks upon the three misconceptions mentioned at the end of Chapter Three as common to most phobic patients. His injunction to abandon fear of the illness is intended to dissuade patients from believing that they will collapse or become seriously ill as a result of the phobia. His persuading the patient to see how absurd is his fear is intended to dispel the exaggerated belief in the harmfulness of the phobic object. His third exhortation, that the patient fight his weakness of character through self-education, is aimed at the patient's belief that he is incapable of overcoming his fear.

DuBois also reported many successes with cases of anorexia nervosa referred to him by other physicians. Typically, he hospitalized such patients in order to provide them with bed rest and feeding, but he placed his main reliance upon discovering and modifying the personal disturbances which produced the refusal to eat. In his thinking, the failure to eat was brought about by the disappointments, losses, and family conflicts which the patients were currently experiencing. His recitals of the "faulty ideas" which he helped these patients to discover are tantalizingly brief and incomplete.

DuBois, who is now largely forgotten, can hardly be considered a great theorizer about personality, psychopathology, or psychotherapy. He did, however, describe and utilize, apparently with considerable success in the eyes of his colleagues, an approach to treatment aimed at disrupting his patients' relevant misconceptions, which he saw as responsible for the presenting symptoms.

Adler

Of all the psychotherapists who have contributed to the misconception hypothesis, Alfred Adler presents the most comprehensive and elaborate theory based on that doctrine. Although his own writings are largely discursive, his lack of systematic exposition of his views is compensated for by the work of Heinz and Rowena Ansbacher (1956), who have edited Adler's books and papers under the title *The Individual Psychology of Alfred Adler*. The interpretive comments added by the Ansbachers have contributed much to the understanding of Individual Psychology. The following comment, for example, highlights Adler's reliance upon the misconception hypothesis as an explanatory principle in psychopathology: "An individual with a mistaken opinion of himself and the world, that is, with mistaken goals and a mistaken style of life, will resort to various forms of abnormal behavior aimed at safeguarding his opinion of himself when confronted with situations which he feels he cannot meet successfully, due to his mistaken views and the resulting inadequate preparation" (Ansbacher and Ansbacher, 1956, p. 239).

In addition to the Ansbachers, Rudolf Dreikurs, director of the Alfred Adler Institute of Chicago, spent most of his professional life applying and adding his own understanding to Adler's approach to treatment. Dreikurs (1961, p. 79) relied upon the misconception hypothesis without cavil: "He [the patient] needs our help to see what he is doing and to free himself from his false assumptions. In other words, our treatment is not directed toward a change in emotions, but a clarification of cognitive processes, of concepts." Insofar as practitioners of Individual Psychology are in accord with Adler, Dreikurs, and the Ansbachers, they appear to subscribe explicitly to the misconception hypothesis. For that reason, our treatment of this approach is relatively brief. For the present analysis, I have depended primarily upon the book edited by the Ansbachers plus two chapters by Dreikurs (1961).

Adler was an avowed phenomenologist. In 1933 he wrote, "I am convinced that a person's behavior springs from his opinion." A snake perceived as poisonous has the same effect on an individual whether it is poisonous or harmless. For Adler, as for many other personality theorists, the mistaken beliefs acquired in early childhood "dominate the subsequent course of our existence." These mistaken beliefs often remain unavailable to the individual, because they reside on the fringes of awareness, in what Adler referred to as "the unconscious." Adler therefore saw psychotherapy as a procedure directed at rectifying the mistakes or misconceptions of the patient: "We remain convinced that the cure of all mental disorder lies in the . . . process of making the patient understand his own mistakes" ([1929] Ansbacher and Ansbacher, 1956, p. 343). In the rest of the passage he compared his own approach with the work of other schools of therapy, including faith healers. He believed that their successes occurred primarily because of the human relationships they developed with their patients rather than because of the correctness of their therapeutic understandings. For Adler, good human relationships are required to give patients sufficient "courage" to allow them to understand their mistakes. In Adler's well-known doctrine of social interest, courage comes from being a member of a group—or having meaningful human relationships.

Adler saw the ultimate goal of psychotherapy as the patient's acceptance of his need to make his own contributions to social welfare. Each individual, he wrote, feels his existence to be worthwhile only to the extent that he is useful to others. Lack of social interest, in his view, accounts for all psychological failures, including neurotics, psychotics, criminals, drunkards, problem children, suicides, perverts, and prostitutes. In exalting the principle of social interest, Adler was not stating a moral or a philosophical principle; he believed that he was voicing an explicitly psychological principle. Failure to recognize the necessity of contributing to others is, for Adler, the basic mistake which leads to all forms of psychological maladjustment. False strivings for personal superiority are substituted for the making of contributions to the common good.

In their comments on Adler's treatment rationale, the Ansbachers (1956, p. 326) sum up the foregoing as follows: "The rationale of therapy according to Adler is that once the patient has gained in courage, as an accompaniment of the increased social interest, and has gained an understanding of his mistakes, he will no longer make them."

Dreikurs was very much in agreement with Adler about the goals of therapy, but he recast the freeing of the patient from his "false assumptions" into a learning experience. He regarded all psychotherapy as a learning procedure directed at changing concepts about oneself and one's life. Treatment, for Dreikurs (1961, p. 79), should not be aimed at changing emotions, or behavior, or symptoms. Instead, "We are trying to change goals, concepts, and notions. Only such changes can bring about permanent improvement."

Rectifying mistakes and changing false assumptions are both synonyms for correcting misconceptions. The Adlerians have proposed many general and specific misconceptions. Dreikurs wrote engagingly about certain misconceptions which he found in dealing with many patients. In discussing faulty assumptions acquired early in childhood, he wrote, "Unfortunately, children are excellent observers but bad interpreters. They observe keenly what goes on but do not always draw the correct conclusions. . . . Most children who feel rejected are not rejected, but assume that they are because their impressions and interpretations of what they feel are faulty. For instance, a child may assume that mother does not love him if she is not constantly busy with him or does not always do what he wants. Getting constant attention or having his own way are his premises for feeling accepted and having a place and being loved" (p. 69). Dreikurs also found particularly provocative those children who operate on the belief that they can obtain status only by gaining power over others and bringing down in defeat those persons who have authority over them. Such children, he wrote, would be loved and treated differently if they did not base their behavior upon false premises. Another common misconception emphasized by Dreikurs is the belief that emotions are the causes of antisocial and other undesirable actions. When we do not want to blame ourselves, he wrote, we blame our emotions if we have intentions we wish to keep from others. By pretending to be good, we prevent ourselves from recognizing our undesirable intentions, and make our emotions the scapegoat. Dreikurs dealt with guilt feelings in a similar fashion. When we express guilt, he suggested, we demonstrate our good intentions and deceive ourselves about our real intentions; in short, by expressing guilt, we allow ourselves to do what we want without self-incrimination.

Other major misconceptions proposed by Adler are mistaken feelings of inferiority, striving for personal superiority, and mistakes in the life style, including the false goals which individuals set for themselves.

Among the uninitiated, Adler is probably still best known for his early notions concerning the development of inferiority feelings due to constitutional deficits or abnormalities. Although he never abandoned organic anomalies as possible sources for such feelings, he later placed more emphasis on psychological factors, such as unfavorable comparisons with others during childhood, and unfavorable "environments" brought about by pampering or rejection. Later in his career, rather than placing inferiority feelings first among the psychological processes leading to maladjustment, Adler gave the most prominent position to lack of social interest. Nonetheless, the misconceptions upon which inferiority feelings are based lead to the development of many further misconceptions, particularly when unrealistic compensatory strivings for personal superiority occur.

Adler saw the constant striving for personal superiority as characteristic of the life style of the neurotic or other maladjusted individual. Although both normal and abnormal individuals strive for perfection or achievement, there is, according to Adler, a difference in kind between the two. The normal individual is task-centered and motivated by common sense, which includes the welfare of others. The abnormal is motivated primarily by his "private sense," which is lacking in components of social interest; he is dominated by his single-minded striving for personal satisfactions. Among the more likely outcomes of such striving for selfish goals is the tendency to try to control or domineer over others, which leads to hostilities and conflicts. When inevitable rebuffs and rejections occur, the patient does not understand them; he also fails to understand that achievement is possible only with the cooperation of others. Lacking such understanding, the neurotic constantly seeks false goals, such as increased possessions, power over others, and personal influence; at the same time, he disparages others and cheats those persons with whom he is in competition.

In Adler's view, the life style (which he originally referred to as life plan) is a unifying but complex psychological system which all individuals, normal as well as abnormal, construct from their interactions with others. Dreikurs (1961) refers to the life style as the individual's self-concept. Although Adler himself does not seem to have used the term *self-concept,* as a dedicated phenomenologist he would certainly agree that the self-concept encompasses the individual's subjective beliefs about himself. A life style is not necessarily based upon misconceptions; but by examining it, according to Adler, one can frequently detect the mistakes from which the person suffers.

An aspect of the life style, the individual's goals, may also be distorted by mistaken beliefs. Adler is well known for his proposition that all persons set goals for themselves as part of their style of life. These goals are often unconscious and therefore poorly understood. The neurotic, in his striving for personal superiority, sets unattainable goals for himself and rigidly strives for these goals. Two misconceptions are thereby encompassed—the mistaken belief in the value of personal superiority and the belief that only impossibly high goals are worth striving toward. In addition, the so-called "masculine protest" (the fancied superiority of the male role, which is striven for by both male and female neurotics) is based on false goals. In 1913 Adler distinguished two misconceptions which he saw as basic to the masculine protest (Ansbacher and Ansbacher, 1956, p. 250): "As the unconscious assumptions of the neurotic goal striving—in male and female patients alike—we can regularly recognize the following two: (1) Human relations are under all circumstances a struggle for superiority. (2) The feminine sex is inferior and serves in its reaction as a measure of masculine strength."

Like all psychotherapists, Adler preferred a certain kind of therapeutic relationship to facilitate the discovery of misconceptions as well as to bring about changes in them. He advocated strongly that the therapist should establish a friendly, permissive atmosphere in which the patient is expected to take responsibility for himself. Adlerian treatment procedures depend almost entirely upon face-to-face discussions between patient and therapist. Although self-examination is encouraged, the principal tactic of the therapist is explanation directed toward enabling the patient to understand his mistakes and how they can be rectified. Adler's faith in this procedure is well illustrated by the following sentence, written in 1927 (Ansbacher and Ansbacher, 1956, p. 334): "Among my patients, children and adults, I have never found one to whom it would not have been possible to explain his erroneous mechanism." The therapist, then, participates as a coworker who helps the patient to understand himself and his mistakes. Adler was hardly nondirective; he had definite notions about what is good or bad for people. But he believed that patients had to solve their problems for themselves.

We can ask whether this kind of relationship is facilitative in uncovering misconceptions or the mistakes in the life style. Here we are in a realm of mystery, since a variety of approaches seem to be helpful in uncovering misconceptions and bringing about change. The good will of the patient, rather than a particular relationship, seems to be the critical factor; and good will, of course, can be obtained equally well in a variety of relationships. It may be that the coworker relationship is particularly helpful in training the patient to take responsibility for himself, which was one of Adler's explicit goals of treatment.

Although Adler believed that certain rules might be helpful to the therapist in trying to understand the life style, he also believed that "insight into the meaning of [life style] is best acquired through artistic and intuitive empathy with the essential nature of the patient" (Ansbacher and Ansbacher, 1956, p. 328). "Guessing" was also urged by Adler as a procedure for locating a patient's mistakes. He regarded guessing as the offering of tentative hypotheses which could then be verified or discarded as new data become available. In addition, Adler believed that the therapist should analyze the patient's expressive behavior. As one of the early proponents of the unity-of-the-organism doctrine, Adler taught that analyzing a patient's gait, posture, voice characteristics, and other expressive movements provides the therapist with an understanding of the patient's life style. Symptoms are also useful in locating mistakes because symptoms reflect the set-backs encountered in trying to attain one's chosen goals. The patient's mistaken goal is, of course, the attainment of superiority over others. Finally, since a patient's life style is anchored by his early-childhood recollections, early recollections and dreams can illuminate the concrete behaviors by which the patient tries to reach false goals. Such recollections need not be veridical in order to reveal the patient's mistaken beliefs.

For Adler and his followers the patient's understanding of or insight into his mistaken opinions is the principal path toward successful change of faulty conceptions or false assumptions. As cited in Ansbacher and Ansbacher (1956, p. 334), Adler wrote in 1913, "The uncovering of the neurotic system, or life plan, for the patient is the most important component in therapy." As long as the neurotic system remains withdrawn from criticism, it remains intact; but self-scrutiny, with the help of the therapist, leads to changes of a cognitive nature.

Combs and Snygg

The work of Arthur Combs and his early collaborator, the late Donald Snygg, is avowedly phenomenological, concerned with the data of perception and with exploration of the self-concept. This phenomenological theory of personality, for a time at least, formed the theoretical background for client-centered therapy. Their 1949 publication *Individual Behavior* had major influence on the development of psychotherapy and humanistic psychology during the 1950s. It also lent considerable impetus to a perceptual approach to understanding personality. Combs maintained his interest in perceptual psychology and a perceptual approach to psychotherapy, bringing out a revision of *Individual Behavior* in 1959. Most of the following discussion is based on Chapters Nineteen and Twenty of that book.

Human motivation, according to Snygg and Combs, is guided by the basic need to maintain and enhance the self as perceived. Each of the multiple motives of human beings is aimed at making the self "more adequate to cope with life" (Combs and Snygg, 1959, p. 46). Psychological blockings, however, may hinder this striving toward adequacy. Psychotherapy is an attempt to remove these blockings, which "appear to be due to failures of differentiation, particularly those involving the self" (p. 412). Differentiation of perception, in the view of Snygg and Combs, is the major process that permits growth and learning, including personality development and change. Inadequate differentiations may occur for many reasons, such as inappropriate learnings about oneself in childhood, threats which bring about narrowing of perception and defensive behavior, and contradictions arising from conflicting needs.

For Combs and Snygg, the self is an object in the individual's perceptual field; this "phenomenal self" includes everything that the person experiences as "me." At the core of the phenomenal self is the *self-concept,* made up of the most important and enduring perceptions developed by the individual to symbolize or to generalize himself. If the individual's behavior is inadequate, the reason can mostly be found in an inadequately differentiated phenomenal self and related aspects of the total perceptual field. Successful psychotherapy, therefore, depends upon bringing about increased perceptual differentiation of the self. More adequate self-differentiation produces a change in self-definition, which is synonymous with producing new meanings about the self.

If the goal of successful psychotherapy for Combs and Snygg is the bringing about of more adequate differentiations, primarily in the phenomenal self, then we can propose that they are concerned with the modification of misconceptions. That is, an inadequately differentiated perception of an event or object must be a perception that is lacking or distorted in one or more important respects and is, therefore, incorrect. Combs and Snygg (1959, p. 428) themselves refer to inadequate differentiations as "false and misleading" and as providing "no adequate basis for change." Since incorrect perceptions cannot produce appropriate conceptions, misconceptions must occur in the process. Similarly, inadequate self-definitions must be the equivalent of misconceptions about the self, just as inadequate meanings must refer to misconceptions about the self. Although the goal of psychotherapy for Combs and Snygg is to produce appropriate changes in self-definition, or meanings about the self, inappropriate or inadequate self-definitions can readily be translated as misconceptions.

The key concept for understanding inadequate perception (or misconception) is *threat,* or anything that the individual regards as "inconsistent with his existing perceptions of self" (Combs and Snygg, 1959, p. 170). Threat tends to narrow perception to exclude disturbing aspects. Such narrowing of perception renders the individual incapable, at least for the moment, of apprehending all the significant aspects of the situation that he faces. As a result of prolonged defense against threat, the individual's self-concept may become encysted and therefore impervious to change. Defenses render the individual incapable of accepting important aspects of his experience, thereby creating misconceptions. Inadequate self-definitions also arise when the individual is unable to identify with others due to threats which narrow his perception of the available social options.

Combs and Snygg (1959, p. 437) describe a number of the more common sources of threat. They propose that the movement of an individual from one cultural group to another (not only a movement determined by geography or class status but also movement in time from childhood to adolescence or adolescence to adulthood) "may account for the greatest number of cases in which the self is threatened." If the move to a new cultural group is not accompanied by appropriate and necessary changes in the phenomenal self, threat occurs, perception is narrowed, and inadequate self-differentiation is the result. Other common sources of threats are experiences which teach children or adults that they are "unliked, unwanted, unacceptable, or unworthy."

The therapist's primary task, according to Combs and Snygg, is to help the client explore his own psychological field, particularly his self-concept. Such exploration is best facilitated in the therapy situation by "removing the client from threat as much as is practicable" by establishing a particular kind of relationship. Although they recognize that the relationship established varies with the nature and problems of the client as well as with the understanding, skill, and personality of the therapist, they claim that the

therapist can achieve the desired relationship by consistently practicing two attitudes: (1) he tries to avoid being critical or censor-
ious of the client; (2) he manifests positive expressions of his concern, understanding, and compassion for the client. These attitudes
remove the therapist as a source of threat and encourage the client
to lower the defenses he brings with him to the therapy situation.
Self-exploration is thereby facilitated.

The client's task, in exploring his perceptions of himself
and his world, is largely a matter of talking about his deeper feelings—that is, any content related to the inner core of the phenomenal self, the self-concept; since this inner core contains the content
that is most important to the client, it therefore has the most "personal reference or personal meaning" for him. For Combs and
Snygg, the most important aspects of the self which require exploration in therapy are "feelings" that convey a client's inadequacy or
deficiency. When the client is encouraged to talk about his "deeper
feelings" in a nonthreatening situation, he eventually comes face
to face with these perceptions of his inadequacy and deficiency.

The feelings and emotions discussed in therapy, according
to Combs and Snygg, are perceptions that convey the personal
meaning which particular situations or series of events have for the
client. Highly personalized self-perceptions, to be sure, can produce
disorganized, inefficient, and even destructive behavior. The disorganization is not, however, a product of feeling or emotion, but
a product of the threatening perception. By emphasizing the pri-
macy of perception, or meaning, where feelings and emotions are
concerned, Combs and Snygg have no need to try to change affective responses in therapy; instead, they are always concerned with
trying to change perceptions. Helping the client to explore his
deeper feelings means to them that they are helping the client to
examine his most meaningful and personally relevant perceptions
of himself.

Combs and Snygg assert (correctly, of course) that a client
enters treatment with vague and diffuse perceptions of himself and
his world. As he examines these perceptions in the absence of threat
and comes to center his attention upon those perceptions of himself
where he feels most inadequate and ineffective, he recognizes more

clearly and accurately that his self-concept is not aligned with reality. He now recognizes that he needs "to reorganize his self-concept in closer alignment with external reality" in order to maintain and enhance his phenomenal self. "In other words, if it becomes clear that enhancement of the phenomenal self is to be achieved by reorganization, the organism will move in that direction, provided the threat to his present position is dissipated" (Combs and Snygg, 1959, p. 436).

Where do changes in misconceptions fit into the process just described? The answer is not hard to find. If we can accept Combs and Snygg's assertion that the client needs to reorganize his self-concept in closer alignment with external reality, then we can also propose that until this is accomplished the client's self-concept is unaligned with reality because it is inaccurate and mistaken. In other words, the client operates under misconceptions about himself and his relations to the world. When the therapist recognizes and restates the meanings he perceives in the client's reported feelings, the client is enabled to detect the inconsistencies, inaccuracies, and mistakes in what he has been saying and believing about himself. Maintenance and enhancement of the self provides, according to Combs and Snygg, the motive power to bring about change in misconceptions so that more adequate behavior will ensue.

Although self-examination is the preferred therapeutic procedure for Combs and Snygg, in one respect they utilize a self-demonstration procedure in individual therapy. As usually happens, the self-demonstration also includes the presentation of some verbal evidence by the therapist as well as providing the client with opportunities to observe himself in a different kind of social situation over time. They specifically advocate that the therapist should treat the client *"as though he were* lovable, likeable, acceptable, and able" even when the client does not perceive himself in this fashion, which is likely to be the case if clients suffer from feelings of inadequacy and deficiency. Such treatment by the therapist is a self-demonstration procedure clearly aimed at changing the client's misconception that he is *not* lovable, likeable, acceptable, and able. By treating him as though he were, the therapist attempts to change the mis-

conception in the hope that the change will generalize to others outside of the therapy situation.

One of the most direct and active approaches to changing
misconceptions is found in the treatment approach of Albert Ellis,
who was originally trained in and practiced Horneyian psychoanalysis. Dissatisfied with psychoanalysis, he devised his rational-
emotive approach, which emphasizes all forms of *explanation* in the
attempt to modify the patient's "irrational ideas."

For Ellis, man is both a rational and an irrational being
whose psychological disturbances are the product of his irrational
and illogical thinking. The therapist can correct psychological disturbances, then, by helping, forcing, and cajoling patients to re-
order their perceptions and to reorganize their thinking. Although
Ellis's treatment procedures are aggressively cognitive, they are
also intended to control emotional reactions, particularly anxiety
and hostility. Ellis insists that "negative affect," as he labels anxiety and hostility, can be largely controlled and transformed into
normal affect if patients learn to correct their thinking. The second
chapter of his 1962 book, *Reason and Emotion in Psychotherapy,*
contains a full discussion of his theoretical position. Elsewhere, a
chapter on rational-emotive therapy (Ellis, 1967) contains an
abbreviated discussion of his overall approach.

The specific goals of the rational-emotive approach are to
reduce anxiety and hostility to a minimum by changing unrealistic
thinking. Both anxiety and hostility are viewed as unnecessary and
"invariably self-defeating" human reactions. Unlike normal fear,
the cognitive aspect of anxiety includes the irrational conclusion
that one is now and forever unable to deal with the dangers faced.
Unlike normal anger, the cognitive aspect of hostility contains the
false proposition that the objects of the hostility have no right to
exist and should be eliminated.

A more general goal of rational-emotive therapy is to train
patients to observe and evaluate their thinking in order to reduce
anxiety and hostility throughout life. There are also nine more gen-

eral "positive" goals which Ellis includes among his expected outcomes of treatment. He insists that these nine are the products of the reduction of anxiety and hostility, although their attainment also requires active training by the therapist. Of the nine positive goals, self-acceptance appears to be the most fundamental. The therapist actively fosters this goal by teaching the patient that "he has intrinsic value" merely by reason of his existence as a human being. The other eight positive goals can be partially understood from their labels: self-interest, self-direction, tolerance, acceptance of uncertainty, flexibility, scientific thinking, commitment, and risk taking.

With his customary decisiveness, Ellis (1962) lists ten main irrational ideas that are, in his opinion, commonly found in patients. I have paraphrased these ten ideas in the form of misconceptions about the self. I doubt that the paraphrasing alters their content significantly. The first six are supposed to figure prominently in the development of anxiety; the other four allegedly produce hostility.

1. I must be loved or approved of by everyone important to me.
2. I am not worthwhile unless I am completely competent, adequate, and achieving.
3. I am unable to control my own happiness.
4. I am controlled by my history and by my important past experiences.
5. I face disaster if I cannot find the one perfect solution to my problems.
6. I must always be prepared for the worst by constantly agonizing over it.
7. I believe that wicked people should be blamed and punished.
8. I face disaster if my life does not work out just as I would like to have it.
9. I am better off if I avoid difficulties and responsibilities rather than face them.
10. I must become very disturbed over other people's problems.

In order to deal with their misconceptions, Ellis (1967) tries to help his patients attain three kinds of insight. First of all, although he avoids harping upon childhood antecedents of current difficulties, he nonetheless tries to provide patients with some historical insight to vitiate the misconception that their difficulties emerge mysteriously and full-blown without cause from their past experiences. In his second kind of insight Ellis tries to disabuse the patient of the misconception that he is the helpless victim of his past experiences. He insists that it is the patient's reactions to or faulty beliefs about the past which are mistaken and can be modified. The third kind of insight is aimed at the patient's misconception that he is helpless in the face of his difficulties. He fails to recognize that only he can solve his problems by constantly challenging his own irrational ideas and working constantly for better solutions.

Ellis believes that he avoids most of the difficulties created by transference and countertransference by deliberately maintaining a relatively impersonal and not particularly warm relationship with his patients. He explains to them that one of their major problems is the irrational idea that they must be loved by all significant persons. His own attitude toward them in therapy is designed, therefore, to disabuse them of that misconception. He insists that their problems can best be solved if they work them out with the important people in their real lives rather than with the therapist. He also strives to *model* for them the role of a rational person who does not respond with anxiety, hostility, or disappointment when attacked or depreciated by the patient. The relationship which he prefers is thus designed as a series of self-demonstrations in which they can experience directly some of their misconceptions. Acting as a forthright teacher, Ellis combines considerable explanation with these self-demonstrations in therapy.

I was unable to find specific procedures prescribed by Ellis for identifying his patients' irrational ideas. For the clinician, however, the task does not appear to be overly difficult. In rational-emotive therapy, the patient and therapist engage in extended discussions, and the patient is also encouraged to take part in outside activities, which are reported back to the therapist. The therapist thus amasses information on the patient's thinking about himself, his use of logical or illogical reasoning, and his reported or observed emotional reactions. Because Ellis is primarily interested in detecting irrational or illogical thinking, particularly as it is relevant to the patient's problems, he remains constantly alert to pertinent irrationalities in the patient's verbal presentations. The therapist thus uses his own ability and experience to winnow the patient's illogical ideas for further examination. In Ellis's (1962, p. 103) words, "He [the therapist] ruthlessly uncovers the most important elements of irrational thinking."

Patients are also trained to examine their own ideas and logic. Specifically, they are asked to observe and evaluate "the sentences they tell themselves," since Ellis believes that irrational behavior is maintained by the internal statements one makes to oneself about oneself. Patients thus become trained observers of their own faulty logic. Rational-emotive therapy has still other resources for locating misconceptions. According to Ellis, displays of emotion which involve depression, guilt, self-blaming, and particularly anxiety and hostility are always the product of illogical thinking. These negative affects can then be noted as markers which indicate where irrational ideas can be located. Furthermore, the list of ten irrational ideas which Ellis proposes as logical faults in most human beings also serve as probable sources of misconceptions from which most patients suffer in whole or in part.

Ellis is highly consistent and direct in his basic goal of eradicating his patient's irrational ideas. Even in the first interview he may directly confront patients with their "idiotic nonsense" in his sustained effort to train them to analyze their false assumptions and to rid them of their mistaken ideas. Especially at the beginning of treatment, he plays a very active role in confronting, interpreting current misconceptions, persuading, arguing, attacking, and "making mincemeat" of their faulty ideas. The intensity of his activity in this respect is illustrated in his description of how he maneuvers patients into doing "homework assignments," such as dating or seeking employment: "The therapist quite actively tries to persuade, cajole, and, at times, even command the patient to undertake such assignments as an integral part of the therapeutic process" (Ellis, 1967, p. 212). Such assignments outside of therapy can be considered self-demonstrations.

Direct, didactic training on an individual basis is a prominent part of Ellis's attempt to eradicate irrational ideas. He explains the mechanisms of emotional reactions, assigns readings, and otherwise acts "like a good psychology professor." He also teaches patients that they are worthwhile persons "just because they exist."

He directly teaches them the three kinds of insight mentioned above. He also trains them to challenge constantly their own internalized sentences and to work at more constructive thinking and acting. He teaches them to practice disbelieving.

Unlike many other therapists, Ellis is uninterested in having his patients express, abreact, or act out their anxiety and hostility. Instead, he concentrates on getting them to admit that they are self-blaming and angry. As indicated above, he makes little use of transference or countertransference reactions. Although at times he may resort to dream analysis, reflection of feeling, reassurance, and abreaction, his "main emphasis is ordinarily active-directive, confrontational, didactic, and philosophic."

Chapter 8

Contributions by
Psychoanalysis

In examining psychoanalysis in terms of the misconception hypothesis I am not asserting that the misconception hypothesis is an adequate explanation for the successful treatments obtained by analysts. I am suggesting, however, that psychoanalytic procedures and techniques can lend themselves to a cognitive approach to treatment which aims primarily at changing misconceptions. I believe also that psychoanalysis has made major contributions to the misconception hypothesis.

Freud himself was not unaware of the major role played by cognition in psychoanalytic thinking and technique. At the end of his career he was still disturbed that the "underlying realities" (or psychic energies) had always to be translated into the cognitive language of the everyday world. Despite Freud's distaste for cognitive explanations, cognitive analyses are nonetheless necessary to provide analysts with guidelines for observing significant events. Most of these guidelines enable the analyst to identify *faulty think-*

ing when he perceives the patient's slips of the tongue, dream symbols, contradictions in logic, lacunae in memory, inadequate explanations, gaps in logic, and many other major or minor thought disturbances. Without question, a cognitive approach to psychopathology and psychotherapy is anything but foreign to psychoanalysts. Thus, the present exploration of the relations between the misconception hypothesis and psychoanalytic principles and practices is directed toward their use of cognition during treatment. Although Freudians may view this approach as superficial, they make much use of it for their own purposes. In a very recent article, for example, a prominent psychoanalyst, Irving Bieber (1974), describes the irrational belief systems which he believes are involved in virtually every kind of psychopathology. These systems, he believes, need to be delineated and "recognized" by the patient before they can be extinguished. This phrasing corresponds to our definition of insight.

There is no need to question the legitimacy of the energy constructs employed by psychoanalysts. These constructs, however, are—like all constructs—inferred from observations. Observations of patients in treatment are always open to alternative inferences, which need not lead to energy constructs. We are proposing, therefore, that many of the phenomena which interest analysts can also be construed as misconceptions. Although misconceptions must, of course, also be inferred, there are reasons to believe that misconceptions can be inferred more directly than can energy constructs. Analysts translate their observations of faulty or irrational thinking into the hypothesized energy system, but irrational thinking is the very stuff of which misconceptions are made. Therefore, we will here examine the treatment goals of psychoanalysis (in the form of statements rather arbitrarily selected from the writings of Freud, Fenichel, Greenson, and Menninger), as well as four psychoanalytic principles, to show how they produce or depend upon misconceptions of the patient.

Two of the many statements which Freud proposed as treatment goals are presented here. The first is a straightforward description based upon energy constructs. In 1922, Freud (1950b, p. 126) stated, "The aim of the treatment is to remove the patient's resistances and to pass his repressions in review and thus to bring about the most far-reaching unification and strengthening of his ego, to enable him to save the mental energy which he is expending upon internal conflicts." Such a goal leaves little room for the misconception hypothesis; but, as we shall see later, repression is a mechanism which is most influential in producing misconceptions. Also, the removal of repressions is a means of discovering and eliminating or changing misconceptions. Much later—in his 1940 book, *An Outline of Psychoanalysis,* probably written just before his death —Freud (1949, p. 63) presented a cognitively oriented description of the goal of treatment: "Our knowledge shall compensate for his [the patient's] ignorance and shall give his ego more mastery over the lost provinces of his mental life. This pact constitutes the analytic situation." A patient's ignorance can be seen in some fashion as the equivalent of a misconception. Freud here contends that the knowledge of the analyst is aimed at changing patients' misconceptions by dispelling their ignorance. One can generalize further by suggesting that the patient can attain greater mastery over his life if the misconceptions which interfere with his adjustment can be modified or eliminated.

According to Fenichel (1945, p. 569), the goal of psychoanalysis "is achieved by making the patient's ego face what it had previously warded off." That is, when the patient's ego becomes aware of and deals constructively with repressed impulses, the aim of psychoanalysis has been accomplished. This statement is open to at least two interpretations. It can be interpreted traditionally as a strengthening of the psychic energy of the ego by lifting of repression, thereby making energy which was formerly bound in the unconscious available to the conscious ego. It can also be interpreted, however, as referring to the patient's recognition of thoughts or ideas which have been "warded off," or not recognized by the patient as influencing his behavior. The general assumption in psychoanalysis is that there is nothing to be feared or ashamed of in the repressed material. If it can be brought into awareness, it can be dealt with rationally. This second interpretation thus permits the further inference that the correcting of misconceptions which have been brought into awareness is at least one of the goals of psychoanalysis.

According to Greenson (1959), the ultimate aim of psychoanalysis is "to resolve the infantile neurosis, which is the nucleus of the adult neurosis." The infantile neurosis comes about, according to Greenson, when the infant's ego fails to master the demands from the id and from external reality. The failure to master these demands makes them appear dangerous to the ego, which then wards them off (represses them), so that they are unavailable to awareness. "The ego for a long period of time has been using its energy to ward off what it considers to be dangerous and unacceptable instinctual components" (Greenson, 1959, p. 1402). Although Greenson says that the ego uses "its energy . . . to ward off . . . unacceptable instinctual components," the alternative inference of mistaken conceptions would also be plausible. Psychoanalytic procedures, as distinct from analytic energy constructs, usually consist of the patient's engaging in intensive cognitive review of his ongoing experiences, facilitated by training in free association plus interpretations, confrontations, and clarifications by the analyst. Little difficulty is encountered if one conjectures that in the course of these lengthy self-examinations the patient's misconceptions about the dangers of the warded-off components are corrected. When psychoanalysis enables the patient to become aware of the hidden influences on his thinking and to perceive these influences in a more rational fashion, the patient is correcting his misconceptions about himself and his world.

A point of view more directly related to the misconception hypothesis is found in Karl Menninger's (1958, p. xi) discussion of the aims of psychoanalysis: "Psychoanalysis essays to change the structure of the patient's mind, *to change his view of things,* to change his motivations, to strengthen his sincerity" (emphasis added). Although that statement is not entirely clear (since changing the structure of the mind and patient motivations may well refer to energy redistribution), Menninger later emphasizes cognitive changes: "The patient realizes or is told that [his] symptoms are connected with his thinking and feeling—in short, with his psychology. He is prepared, therefore, to accept treatment in psychological terms, *to have certain false ideas taken from him, new ideas given to him, certain other ideas modified.* I have used the word 'ideas' with the understanding, of course, that emotions and behavior are always associated with them" (p. 25; emphasis added).

Although the lines italicized clearly constitute one phrasing of the misconception hypothesis, no claim is made that Menninger is a proponent of that hypothesis. The statement just cited does, however, provide a clear indication from a leading psychoanalyst that analytic procedures can be understood in terms of changing misconceptions.

This very brief review of the complex topic of the goals of psychoanalysis is not intended to prove that psychoanalysts are essentially involved in changing their patient's misconceptions. It does indicate, however, that the misconception hypothesis can be employed as an alternative explanation for the energy constructs which analysts typically employ.

Let us now consider four of the general propositions about human behavior found in psychoanalytic writings: unconscious processes, childhood experiences as later determinants of behavior, the role played by sex, and the role played by aggression. That these four doctrines still receive major emphasis in the main stream of psychoanalysis—despite the addition of other topics, primarily those derived from ego psychology—is attested by Gill (1959). These four doctrines, it should be emphasized, are not themselves regarded as misconceptions held by the analyst or the patient but as four possible major sources of misconceptions held by patients. Whether the misconceptions derived from these four sources are the fundamental misconceptions primarily responsible for neurosis or other abnormal behavior is a different question. Not even analysts claim that these doctrines encompass and exhaust the major psychological impediments to mental health. Most analysts, however, would probably see them as central. The neo-Freudians would for the most part agree, but would also propose other doctrines more directly related to difficulties stemming from cultural patterns and social interactions.

If, as the Freudians insist, man's behavior is dominated by unconscious motives, then the conscious reasons that he gives for his actions must be superficial and inaccurate. Superficial, inaccurate explanations must be misconceptions. Still another source of misconceptions is inherent in the doctrine of the unconscious. Because the patient has falsely evaluated the hypothesized unconscious impulses, considering them something to be feared and rejected, he therefore represses them or seeks to ward them off. If the unconscious impulses can be brought to consciousness and properly evaluated, they will no longer be feared and rejected. The doctrine of the unconscious thus provides a source for two kinds of major misconceptions: the patient's faulty conscious beliefs that he understands his motives, and the faulty beliefs that the warded-off material is dangerous and unacceptable.

In trying to narrow down the kinds of repressed content which are likely to be most disturbing to the patient, the Freudians settled upon early childhood as the period when psychological disturbances are supposedly most influential. Particularly in neurotics, adult behavior is thought to be dominated by unconscious childhood fixations, regressions, and other unresolved remnants of the psychosexual stages of development—most notably the oedipal struggle. In classical analysis, the analyst tries to recover the emotions and other content associated with distorted childhood experiences, in order to help the patient reevaluate the material with the help of his more mature understanding of reality. This process can be viewed as one of cognitive review intended to correct misconceptions. That, at least, is one alternative explanation which is not far removed from analytic statements pertaining to the need to help the ego to reality-test the contents (more properly, their derivatives) of the unconscious.

In addition to specifying that the most important psychological problems are those produced by the process of repression, and that the most significant developmental period for disturbance occurs in early childhood, the Freudians have narrowed the significant content even further by singling out distorted experiences with sex and aggression as the most generally disturbing problems in adjustment. Although the Freudians prefer to write about distorted evaluations of childhood sexual experiences in terms of the vicissitudes of the libidinal drive, the alternative cognitive approach can make use of much of their material, restated in terms of the misconception hypothesis. Examples could be multiplied almost endlessly, since psychoanalysts have collected a mountain of observations on this topic. Only a few will be cited here.

The castration fears of the boy during the oepidal period can be viewed as his misconception that he may be punished by mutilation for his sexual interest in his mother. This fear is even stated as a misconception by analysts when they describe it in such terms as "I may be castrated if I persist in my incestuous desires." Other misconceptions found by analysts in the young boy pertain to such matters as "Masturbation has injured my penis." And when boys observe that girls do not have penises, they often think, "She had one but it was cut off." Some analysts see the girl's castration fear as being contained in such a misconception as "I have been castrated because of my incestuous desires for my father." The much-discussed topic of penis envy seems to center around the female's misconception that "Everything would be much better for me if only I had a penis." In adults, sexual difficulties often arise because the adult patient mistakenly believes that he will be punished if he engages in sexual activities forbidden by his parents when he was a child. In homosexuality, as explained by psychoanalysis, a complex misconception arises when the child fails to identify with the parent of the same sex and identifies instead with the parent of the opposite sex. Identifications can be viewed cognitively as firm convictions that one has basic characteristics similar to those of the person taken as the model. When such identifications are at least relatively in accord with reality, difficulties need not arise. When, however, early identifications cannot be made to fit reality, they then can be viewed as misconceptions.

The adult patient's misconceptions about his sexual interests and inhibitions are multiple, according to psychoanalytic doctrine. They originate in experiences in early childhood, when reality testing is immature. They are likely to be supplemented by faulty information about sex given by embarrassed or punishing parents and uninformed peers. In addition, sexual behavior is governed by unconscious controls, so that the person has only faulty conscious knowledge of his erotic impulses. It is not surprising, therefore, that psychoanalysts find the manifestations of the erotic drive a fertile source of misconceptions, even though they may prefer to speak in terms of distortions of the libido.

Early in his career Freud himself had a misconception about sexuality which he later corrected. He originally believed that hysteria in females resulted from sexual abuses suffered in childhood. When he discovered, however, that many of his patients' stories were based upon fantasy rather than reality, he recast his theory of neurosis to emphasize the etiological influence of fantasy. In 1922, writing about his earlier misconception about the source of female hysteria, Freud (1950b, p. 118) noted, "This misapprehension was corrected when it became possible to appreciate the extraordinarily large part played in the mental life of neurotics by the activities of *fantasy,* which clearly carried more weight in neurosis than did the external world." This Freudian insistence upon the influence of fantasy, which is a cognitive activity, is a direct contribution to the misconception hypothesis. Not all fantasy results in misconceptions; but uncriticized fantasy can be an important source of them.

Few analysts appear to have accepted Freud's supposition that a death instinct lies at the root of all destructive behavior, including that directed toward the self. Instead, most analysts, as well as most psychologists, are likely to agree with Freud's earlier dictum that aggression results from frustration—a proposition that does not invoke a death instinct. The aggressive reaction can also be viewed as a common source for many varied misconceptions. Children learn early that their hostilities, like most of their sexual actions, are not only usually frowned upon but also punished by their parents and their peers. In avoiding punishment for such reactions, the individual may hide his hostility—thereby deceiving others and ultimately himself as well. In hiding his reactions from his conscience as well as from others, he creates for himself enduring misconceptions.

Transference relationships and other social interactions are common situations in which misconceptions arising from aggressive reactions can be detected. Transference itself is a process due to a misidentification of the therapist with past significant persons. "It almost inevitably happens that one day his [the patient's] attitude toward the analyst changes over into a negative and hostile one. This, too, is, as a rule, a repetition of the past" (Freud, 1949, p. 68). Repetitions of the past without regard for current realities must be based upon misconceptions. Freud (1949, p. 69) recognized the misunderstanding component of transference reactions: "The danger of these states of transference evidently consists in the possibility of the patient misunderstanding their nature and taking them for fresh real experiences instead of reflections of the past."

Patients' misconceptions about their attitudes toward others are common topics in psychoanalytic and other therapeutic circles.

Many of the patient's social misconceptions are seen as arising from repressed hostility. They are frequently detected by disguised expressions of hostility, which slip out despite the patient's customary denial that he entertains such feelings. Ambivalence toward the self and others also carries a heavy load of misconceptions, since few people realize that it is normal to have contradictory attitudes toward the same person.

Locating Misconceptions

Although psychoanalysts are unlikely to characterize their therapeutic procedures as methods for locating misconceptions, an examination of them reveals that they are often particularly effective in locating repressed misconceptions about sex and aggression which were acquired in early childhood. We shall concentrate primarily upon the procedures of classical analysis, most of which are employed by psychoanalytically oriented therapists.

The most common procedures in psychoanalysis are the development of a relationship which encourages transference reactions, free association, regression, and dream analysis. All will be discussed as methods for locating patient misconceptions.

Despite considerable variation among analysts as to the optimal therapeutic relationship, they generally agree that the relationship should encourage the development of regression and transference reactions and should facilitate the patient's skill at free association. Because analysts are acutely aware of the many subtle ways in which the analyst's behavior may distort the patient's thinking and his revelations about himself, they avoid too much intimacy and support. Following Freud's admonition, they also avoid the teacher's role: "However much the analyst may be tempted to act as teacher, model, and ideal to other people and to make men in his own image, he should not forget that that is not his task in the analytic relationship" (Freud, 1949, p. 67). The avoidance of both intimacy and the teacher's role is regarded by analysts as desirable not only to prevent distortion in the patient's productions but also to frustrate him in order to encourage regression. When the analyst responds as little as possible to the patient's search for sympathetic understanding, the resulting frustration, according to Menninger (1958, p. 43), "assists the process of self-visualization, objectification, and stabilization." As the regression continues, the patient realizes that he often acts like a child even when he thinks he is performing like an adult. The frustration-induced regression is intended, in our terms, to help the patient to discover his misinterpretation of his own behavior.

Impersonality and extreme abstinence have been questioned by many analysts of note. "There is much evidence that [even Freud] was far from a mirror in his own work" (Stone, 1961, p. 139). Similarly, Fenichel (1941) insisted that the patient should always be able to rely upon the "humanness" of the analyst; and other analysts have spoken with approval "of traits like warmth, decency, reliability, kindness, integrity, as if these are quite naturally and self-evidently reflected in clinical analytic work" (Stone, 1961, p. 41). In exploring patients' memories, therefore, analysts apparently attempt to establish a relationship that is somewhat impersonal but hardly cold and nonresponsive. At the same time, they attempt to keep from being so warm that they encourage the patient to avoid serious self-examination by enjoying the immediate benefits of the relationship itself.

The analyst's somewhat impersonal attitude and his deliberate frustration of the patient are intended not only to produce regression but to intensify transference reactions. Much time is spent on such reactions during treatment to provide the analyst and the patient with opportunities to examine directly some of the patient's distorted perceptions, or misconceptions. To be sure, transference reactions also include the notion of strong feelings and emotions directed toward the analyst; but these affective reactions are viewed here, in accordance with the notion of cognitive control of affect, as the product of the distorted perceptions. Although Freud may not have agreed with that proposal, he has nonetheless described transference in those terms: "The patient sees in his analyst the return—the reincarnation—of some important figure out of his childhood or past, and consequently transfers on to him feelings and reactions that undoubtedly applied to this model. . . . It is the analyst's task to tear the patient away each time from the menacing illusion [that he is embroiled again with a loved and hated parent figure], to show him again and again that what he takes to be new real life is a reflection of the past" (Freud, 1949, pp. 66, 69). Reflections of the past which remain as "menacing illusions" are misconceptions. To correct them, Freud pointed to the need to persuade the patient of the actual nature of transference behavior by substituting a more valid understanding for the illusions. Menninger (1958, p. 77) confirms the idea that transference reactions are misconceptions: "The therapist becomes various someones—a husband, wife, mother, brother, sister, father, grandmother, etc.—in the fantasies and unconscious formulations of the psychoanalytic patient."

Another psychoanalytic procedure, free association, is aimed at training the patient to reveal material about himself which he would not be able to recall under the logical constraints ordinarily governing verbal expression. Since free association is intended to detect unconscious feelings and ideas which are influencing patient behavior, it can readily be interpreted as a means of helping the patient to produce current and past material, which can then be examined by both patient and analyst for its relevant misconceptions.

In addition, as Menninger (1958, p. 75) quite explicitly points out, the psychoanalyst uses the mechanism of regression to locate the patient's misconceptions (italicized terms clearly refer to misconceptions): "Having gone back to the beginnings of all his *misunderstandings* and *misinterpretations* and mismanagements, having conceded his *errors* and forgiven those of others, having recognized the *unrealistic nature of some of his cherished expectations and love objects and methods of procedure,* the patient gradually begins to put away childish things. . . . He works his way back to *reality,* abandoning his *inexpedient goals and techniques and attitudes* for more appropriate ones, *more adult expectations* from more suitable love objects in more effective ways." Menninger (1958, p. 49) also introduced another interpretation of regression, which contrasts with his own: "Some of my colleagues take issue with my model of regression. They hold that what appears to be an increasing regression in the analysis describes rather the increasing accuracy of the patient's awareness of himself, of the infantile nature of his intentions, wishes, needs, moods, and so forth." The unnamed colleagues appear to subscribe even more to the misconception hypothesis. If the process of analysis produces increasing accuracy in self-knowledge, then prior to treatment self-knowledge must have been inaccurate. In other words, patients deceive themselves into thinking that they are mature, when in reality they are infantile.

Dream analysis is another procedure used by analysts in their attempts to locate misconceptions. Even though the manifest content of the dream may be absurd, with little reference to the patient's problems, analysts contend that free associating to aspects of the dream often leads to significant insights—particularly when the beliefs revealed by dream analysis contradict the conscious beliefs of the patient. Two of Freud's dream interpretations (1913, p. 219) are described here to illustrate how he used dreams to locate faulty beliefs of the patient.

The weeping patient was obsessed with the belief that her relatives shuddered at her for unknown reasons. In her dream she saw a fox or lynx walking on a roof. After something fell from the roof, her mother was carried from the house, dead. Freud informed the patient that the dream signified a death wish for her mother, which would explain why the patient felt that her relatives were rejecting her. The woman immediately added confirmatory material, saying that as a small child she had been called "lynx-eye." When she was three, a brick had fallen on her mother's head, producing severe bleeding. The patient's misconception prior to the interpretation of her dream was that her relatives shuddered at her. After the dream was understood, she discovered that she was shuddering at herself because of her death wish for her mother.

In another case, Freud was treating a young woman suffering from agoraphobia. She was particularly fearful of passing men on the street but said that there was no reason for her fear. In her dream she walked by a group of young officers while she was wearing a straw hat that had the middle piece bent upward with the two side pieces hanging down. One of the side pieces was lower than the other. Freud told her that the dream symbolized her belief that if she had a man with virile genitals, like the hat in the dream, she would have no need to fear her own impulses toward young men. Prior to the interpretation, the woman believed, falsely, that she was not sexually attracted to young men.

Changing Misconceptions

Psychoanalysts utilize *self-examination, explanation,* and *self-demonstration* (see Chapter Three) as their preferred methods for treating patients. They attempt to avoid *vicariation,* or serving as models for their patients, because it might lead to identifications with the analyst and therefore interfere with treatment. There is little likelihood that modeling effects can be completely avoided, however, because any long-term, intense therapy relationship is apt to result in the patient's learning new patterns of thought and new methods of reacting to crisis situations. Nonetheless, in the present discussion of how analytic procedures may produce changes in patient misconceptions, we shall concentrate upon explanation, with particular reference to interpretations. Self-demonstration is encountered most directly in the analyst's treatment of transference reactions. The self-examination produced by free association and other methods involving self-report is too well known for comment.

When he refers to the analyst as an "expediter" during periods of impasse in analysis, Menninger (1958, p. 128) is, in essence, describing the goal of interpretation as the correcting of misconceptions: "The analyst [when interpreting] points to the existence or possible existence of connections and implications and meanings which tend to elude the patient. He reminds the patient of forgotten statements or he confronts him with a discrepancy or self-contradiction, a misrepresentation, an obvious but unrecognized omission." In other words, the analyst intervenes when he perceives an opportunity to correct a patient's misconceptions by providing him with information which the patient has failed to take into account in drawing his own conclusions.

Most analysts limit the kinds of self-demonstration which their patients can experience to the analytic interview. Within the typical interview setting, however, analysts make considerable use of transference phenomena as subtle self-demonstrations. Unlike the more obvious demonstrations that can be prearranged by the group therapist or the behavior modifier as a means of helping the patient to recognize his own misconceptions and his ability to correct them, transference reactions occur in analysis with little prearrangement on the part of the therapist. If a patient rebels against the analyst, for example, this reaction can often be shown to depend upon his misidentification of the therapist with a parental figure or with significant others. The skill of the analyst in utilizing transference reactions as self-demonstration lies in his ability to lead the patient to recognize that his distorted perceptions of his analyst are echoes of reactions toward other persons of importance to the patient. Since the analyst is likely to employ verbal interpretations and confrontations in leading the patient to such insights, the use of transference reactions for self-demonstration purposes is mixed with explanation.

What brings about improvement or cure in the patient as a result of a successful psychoanalysis? Later we shall attempt to show that changing patient misconceptions can account for improvement. For the moment, however, we should examine what the analysts have proposed. Menninger (1958) has outlined the following historical developments: (1) Breuer's hypothesis that improvement occurs when the patient is able to recall clearly the pathogenic ideas associated with his traumatic experiences; (2) the notion that improvement depends on abreaction of unhealthy emotions; (3) the belief that improvement results from the self-discipline involved in working through; (4) an emphasis on insight; (5) the proposal that reduction in the strictures of the superego accounts for improvement. Still another explanation for improvement has to do with what Menninger refers to as the "deconditioning process" (later called by Franz Alexander "corrective emotional experience"). That is, when significant unconscious material is made conscious, the boundaries of the ego are extended, so that it then exerts more rational control over id impulses and superego pressures.

There is general agreement that strengthening the ego is one of the expected outcomes of successful psychoanalytic treatment. A strengthened ego is, however, a final product of treatment rather than an explanation of how improvement occurs. Our thesis is, of course, that a patient's rational aspect (or, in psychoanalytic terminology, his ego) is strengthened when important misconceptions, which alienate him from reality, are reduced. In the psychoanalytic explanations mentioned above, only two seem to provide elbow room for the misconception hypothesis—Breuer's notion that conscious recall of pathogenic ideas permits them to be changed by associative correction, and Freud's contention that insight strengthens the ego. We can actually combine the two by suggesting that effective insight is due to the patient's recognition that pathogenic ideas (misconceptions) are invalid.

To illustrate, some years ago I had one interview with a despondent woman who had recently lost her son in the war. During the interview I did little but listen and occasionally comment that she now had no reason to continue her former activities. Toward the end of the hour she began to respond with conventional protests that she was silly to allow her son's death, tragic as it was, to ruin her family. At the end of the interview she remarked with surprise that for the first time in weeks she felt much better but did not know why. A follow-up telephone call a week later revealed that she had resumed most of her former activities, sad but energetic. We can surmise that the woman came to the interview dominated by the misconception that life could hold no interest for her now that her son was dead. That misconception may be regarded as a pathogenic idea, which she had not previously questioned. In the course of the interview, and perhaps because of my frequently making the misconception salient without criticizing her, she herself developed insight when she recognized it as invalid. An alternative constructive conception, to resume her normal activities, was immediately at hand.

How can we explain her lack of apparent recognition that a pathogenic idea, or a misconception, had been replaced by a more satisfying alternative? The most direct answer might well be that, despite its simplicity, the idea that she had corrected a misconception would seem to her an inadequate explanation for her change in behavior. Most people, in fact, are probably unwilling to recognize a change in conceptions as a valid reason for major behavior change. Complex problems are ordinarily thought to require complex answers. In short, one cannot report an explanation of which one is unaware. The doctrine of insight, as suggested here, happily does not require that patients become aware of and accept the theoretical abstractions which their therapists utilize.

Chapter 9

Indirect Contributions
to the Hypothesis

The first three therapies discussed here, transactional analysis, Gestalt therapy, and direct psychoanalysis, have little in common besides the fact that the originator of each was initially trained in psychoanalysis. The fourth contributor, Albert Bandura, is a research and clinical psychologist who has been very influential in the development of the behavior therapies; from his interest in observational learning he abstracted a technique called "modeling," a technique with many therapeutic applications. The theoretical foundations and the methods of these four therapies are quite distinct except for the ubiquitous interview, which can be structured in many different ways. As might be expected, the contributions which each can make to the misconception approach to treatment are also independent. None of the four adheres to a cognitive explanation for psychotherapy, although Bandura includes cognitive (or symbolic) factors in his general system.

Transactional Analysis

At first glance, transactional analysis appears far removed from a cognitive approach to treatment. Berne's (1966, p. 364) fundamental construct, ego state, "A consistent pattern of feeling and experience directly related to a corresponding consistent pattern of behavior," is only tantalizingly reminiscent of a cognitive orientation. Experiences may be cognitive, but feelings are not. Berne, of course, had no reason to face the issue of the role of cognition in his treatment approach; he was quite content to deal with his system in his own frame of reference. One can, however, reinterpret his system in the cognitive realm without committing too grave an injustice. Before doing so, we should first look at some of the major aspects of his system.

Liberally adapting Freud's division of the mind into superego, ego, and id, Berne posited three "psychic organs," each with its own ego states. The three organs are referred to colloquially as Parent, Adult, and Child. Parent ego states, much like the superego, are supposedly derived from early identifications with parents or parent surrogates. Adult ego states are essentially data-processing activities; like the Freudian ego, they function as the reality-oriented, intellectual apparatus of the mind. Child ego states are the psychological residuals of childhood. Unlike the id, which is composed of chaotic drives without organization, the Child, according to Berne, is an organized, albeit frivolous, entity. Berne insisted that Parent, Adult, and Child are "phenomenological realities" because they can be directly observed, a claim open to question. Many practicing transactional analysts ignore or give lip service to ego states, evidently preferring to speak only of the Parent, the Adult, and the Child. Berne, however, retained ego states in his system to give substance to his theory.

The goal of transactional analysis, according to Berne, is to strengthen the Adult ego states to help the patient understand himself so that he can control his behavior. When the Adult is not sufficiently in control of Parent and Child, confusion occurs. As commonly used, confusion connotes multiple misconceptions resulting in bewilderment and inability to think clearly. Its resolution, according to Berne, can be accomplished in a variety of ways, including the correction of distorted "feelings or viewpoints." That is, the patient is helped to clarify his understanding of himself so as to reorient him "to what some reasonable consensus would regard as more constructive" (Berne, 1966, p. 213). In essence, Berne seems to have been interested in correcting distorted viewpoints to provide the patient with more realistic understandings. Although Berne avoided the terms *reality* and *reality testing* after his 1961 book, probably because of the knotty problems encountered when one tries to define reality, it appears that reality—in the form of "some reasonable consensus"—slipped in through the back door. Moreover, if distorted viewpoints are to be corrected and patients' understandings of themselves are to be reoriented, Berne must have been concerned with modifying or eliminating misconceptions.

Further support for a cognitive interpretation of transactional analysis can be found in the constructs labeled Parent and Child, which, almost as a matter of definition, can be regarded as clusters of misconceptions. The Parent, according to Berne, is directly acquired from the parents without adequate evaluation; this state, then, may have little relation to the patient's current reality. According to Berne (1961), the Parent is made up of "imitative judgments" and "borrowed standards" which distort feelings, emotions, and behavior unless the patient is able to recognize these judgments and standards for what they are. Such foreign ego states are either themselves misconceptions, if they are defined as persisting distorted perceptions learned in childhood, or they produce misconceptions, if ego states are defined as dynamic processes. The Child is made up of "prelogical, poorly differentiated, distorted perceptions" which motivate the individual (Berne, 1961, p. 37). By definition, if perceptions are accepted as cognitive processes, distorted perceptions are the equivalent of misconceptions. The feelings and behaviors motivated by the Child must therefore be based upon misconceptions. Berne also referred to the Child as "a relic of the past," which, when active, controls feelings and behavior. Since relics do not include data from the individual's current situation, they are irrational.

Berne also made liberal reference to three psychological processes which inevitably produce misconceptions and consequent maladjustment if they are permitted to persist by a weakened Adult. The three processes are exclusion, contamination, and crossed transactions.

Exclusion prohibits activity on the part of any two of Berne's three clusters of ego states. For example, an individual who completely inhibits his Parent and Adult, leaving only the Child in control, is a victim of exclusion. When this occurs, according to Berne, there is manifest psychosis. Or the individual's Parent and Child may be inhibited, leaving only the rational, prosaic Adult in control. Such a person lacks all spontaneity derived from the Child and must examine all choices he makes without the automatic help given by the Parent. An individual who excludes the Adult and Child, leaving the Parent in sole control, may be severely neurotic or psychotic; in any case, he is a bore who is concerned only with doing what is right. The healthy individual, according to Berne, is controlled primarily by his Adult but still makes allowance for the necessary activities of the Parent and Child. When exclusion occurs, the individual is ignorant of the appropriate activities of the excluded parts of himself. Such ignorance leads to severe maladjustment or psychosis. Exclusion cannot help but produce major misconceptions for the patient.

Contamination, another pathological process according to Berne, is in some respects the obverse of exclusion. Contamination occurs when there are unrecognized intrusions of the Parent or the Child into the Adult. The contaminating ego states are incorrectly perceived by the Adult as being genuine aspects of the Adult rather than as intrusions. This failure to recognize archaic and foreign elements for what they are leads the Adult to engage in illogical behavior in the belief that he is being mature. Two examples of contamination cited by Berne are prejudices and delusions. By definition, prejudices and delusions are irrational and are therefore misconceptions. More generally, we can say that contamination always produces misconceptions, since the Adult believes that he is behaving rationally when, in fact, he is not.

A third construct, *crossed transactions,* may produce communication difficulties rather than pathology. If individual X's Adult addresses a comment to individual Y's Adult, but is answered by Y's Child addressed to X's Parent, a crossed transaction has occurred. Both parties in the transaction are unaware of the failure in communication; X believes that he is talking to Y as an adult, but Y's Child responds to X as a Parent. On the basis of such mixed-up communication subtle and more obvious misunderstandings (misconceptions) can occur for both parties. Treatment in transactional analysis for crossed transactions consists in clearing up the misconceptions which occur.

Transference, for Berne (1961), is a particular kind of crossed transaction. It occurs when the therapist's Adult addresses a comment to the patient's Adult, but the response comes from the patient's Child. In such a transaction, neither therapist nor patient may be aware that the patient's response comes from the childlike aspects of the patient rather than from his rational adult aspects. This misconception Berne regarded as "the chief problem of psychoanalytic technique." Extending this kind of crossed transaction to situations other than therapy, Berne added that it probably causes frequent "misunderstandings" in marriage, work, and other social interactions. We ordinarily do not expect to be answered by a child when we converse with another mature individual.

A brief example of a crossed transaction in a group conducted by Berne (1961, p. 91ff) illustrates how the misconceptions involved may produce persisting social maladjustment. One day Camellia announced to the group that she was no longer intending to have intercourse with her husband. When Rosita asked why, Camellia burst into tears, saying, "I tried so hard and then you criticize me." Here Rosita thought she was asking a question of a rational adult, only to be met with a childlike flood of tears and an unjust criticism. Berne's comment on this interchange is significant: "This sort of thing happened regularly to Camellia. As she saw it, people were always misunderstanding her and criticizing her. In reality, it was she who made a practice of misunderstanding people and criticizing them." When patients misunderstand their own motives and behavior, they are controlled by their misconceptions.

Two other devices widely applied by transactional analysts

are games and scripts. For Berne, a *game* is a social transaction in which the ulterior motives of any participant go unrecognized by all. Although a game may vary in time from a few minutes to several hours, the same game may be played incessantly by the same individual under many different guises. Berne regarded games as so ubiquitous that he devoted a separate book (Berne, 1964) to them. One of his favorite games can be used to illustrate the role played by misconceptions. "Wooden leg," which can be played in or out of therapy, is used by a patient to defend himself against requests he regards as unreasonable. The patient can counter any such request by aggrievedly asking, "How can you expect a man with a wooden leg (or poor sick me) to do such a thing?" Since the emphasis is placed on the patient's incapability, both therapist and patient are likely to be unaware that the patient's ulterior motive is to avoid engaging in normal behavior. Thus, games contain concealed motives which lead to the development of misconceptions. Game analysis, as Berne termed treatment directed at game playing, is largely a matter of helping patients to discover their misconceptions.

Scripts, as described by Berne, are similar to Adler's notion of the life style, a long-term plan for controlling one's interactions with others. Unhealthy scripts, derived from inadequately evaluated childhood experiences, are the product of elaborate and frequently irrational fantasies. They are (Berne, 1961, p. 116) "adaptations of infantile reactions and experiences." Scripts also are treated by helping patients to understand the underlying misconceptions.

Berne's general approach to psychotherapy is based upon the role of the therapist as a very active teacher, confronter, and sensitive clinician. In order to facilitate reality orientation, Berne advocated that the therapist's Adult should ordinarily address the patient's Adult. Therapy thus is conducted in the form of two or more rational individuals talking together. Berne believed that the patient should be helped to understand everything going on in therapy in much the same fashion that a student therapist is kept informed when he is supervised. Patients individually or in groups are taught the general principles and terms employed in transactional analysis in order to engage their rational capacities. The patient is listened to, but the therapist can intervene to correct misconceptions about the nature and aims of the therapeutic program or to correct faulty

ideas about the social transactions in which he is engaged in or out
of therapy.

Patient misconceptions can be discovered by therapists, according to Berne, by the use of observational skill, intuitive sensitivity, and the understanding of symptoms. Symptoms are externally
observable exhibitions of "disruptive ego states of the Parent or
Child." For example, Berne viewed hallucinations as "exhibitions"
of Parent ego states; delusions, in his view, are Child ego states that
contaminate the Adult when they are accepted as rational. One of
the most important skills of the therapist is his ability to recognize
when the two clusters of irrational misconceptions, the Parent and
the Child, are interfering with the rational Adult. This skill is also
routinely taught to patients.

Berne employed many of the usual techniques used by therapists in individual and group therapy, but he stressed that all therapeutic activities in transactional analysis are intended to strengthen
the patient's reality testing, or, in other words, to strengthen the
Adult. Berne strongly advocated the giving of information to help
the patient analyze his own reactions and behavior. Information
giving can be categorized in our terms as explanation (see Chapter
Three). Berne believed that the Adult is strengthened when the
patient is taught to recognize the three sets of ego states—Parent,
Adult, and Child—as sources of his feelings and behavior. In other
words, reality testing is improved if the patient understands that
early distorted experiences are the source of at least some of his maladjusted feelings and behavior. The process of treatment seems
clearly intended to correct the patient's misconceptions about himself.

Although transactional analysis, according to Berne, is
heavily involved with "feelings" and other experiences, he specifically rejected the "expression of feelings" as being therapeutically
useful. In fact, he coined two names for games played by therapists
who subscribe to the expression-of-emotion hypothesis: *Critique*
is a game "in which the patient describes her feelings in various situations and the therapist tells her what is wrong with them"; *Self-
Expression* is "a common game in some therapy groups, and is based
on the dogma 'Feelings are good' " (Berne, 1964, p. 156).

Despite the lack of a cognitive language, transactional analysis can be readily understood as a method for helping patients to

correct their misconceptions. Its constructs and procedures provide
the therapist with a number of practical advantages in trying to
change patient misconceptions. Perhaps the greatest advantage is its
systematic framework, which can be readily and rapidly taught to
the patient as a logical and presumably authoritative explanation
of how his difficulties developed and how they can be alleviated.
The simplicity of the theory is a great practical advantage; its elements require no special vocabulary or difficult conceptions, and
the common-sense language can be grasped by almost anyone. Three
circles representing the Parent, the Adult, and the Child lend themselves to simple, graphic representations of psychological events
within the self as well as in social interactions. The theory also
clearly segregates the major clusters of misconceptions which supposedly account for maladjustments. It is also sufficiently flexible
to provide quick understanding of minor as well as major disturbances, ranging from psychotic behavior to uncomplicated misunderstandings between husband and wife. Even though many
psychologists and psychiatrists may have difficulty accepting some
of the basic propositions of transactional analysis, the typical layman
who comes as patient is not ordinarily beset with such doubts. Instead, he finds a plausible explanation for his difficulties within his
range of understanding as well as a set of procedures for locating
and trying to change his misconceptions.

Gestalt Therapy

One of the outstanding features of Gestalt therapy, as practiced by its originator, Fritz Perls, is the active search for misconceptions in the immediate present. Although Perls would have been
horrified and indignant at such an assertion, for in his later years
he decried anything that smacked of the intellect, careful examination of his actual procedures reveals that Gestalt therapy includes
many subtle and complex techniques for detecting misconceptions
and for modifying them. Perls himself claimed that his approach
was governed by one therapeutic principle, which he stated in diverse fashions. One phrasing of that principle appears in "Four
Lectures" (Perls, 1970, p. 26): "The incredible thing is that experi-

ence, awareness of the now, is sufficient to solve all . . . neurotic difficulties." By "awareness of the now," Perls meant sensory input from internal and external sense receptors. Allegedly drawing upon Gestalt psychology, psychoanalysis, and the early work of Wilhelm Reich, Perls devised a method whereby the therapist attempts to help the patient become vividly aware of his sensory experiencing. The theoretical goal is to integrate the patient's "sensory awareness" with those situations to which his organism is "attending" or oriented. To achieve this goal, some Gestalt therapists emphasize professional techniques, and some emphasize "spontaneous human responses" (Enright, 1970, p. 122). Perls, who frequently inveighed against imposing external controls on patients, was highly directive, confrontative, and manipulative when treating patients, even though he practiced these procedures with disarming charm, humor, wit, and great clinical sensitivity. A single-minded intention to expand sensory awareness appears to take precedence over all other principles for the Gestalt therapist.

In theory, Perls posited one basic misconception which accounts for neurosis: the mistaken emphasis on intellectual problem solving instead of sensory awareness. When patients are taught to expand their sensory awareness through individual or group therapy, according to Perls, they learn to allow their organisms to be guided by natural integrating functions. Their problems can then be solved without interference from internal disruptions caused by irrelevant intellectualizing, which narrows sensory input.

Early in the history of Gestalt therapy, the misconception hypothesis played a role, but Perls evidently abandoned it because it smacked too much of the intellectual. In an early book originally published in 1951, *Gestalt Therapy* (Perls, Hefferline, and Goodman, 1965, p. 382), the authors wrote, "When interpersonal behavior is neurotic, the personality consists of a *number of mistaken concepts of oneself,* introjects, ego ideals, masks, and so forth. But when therapy is concluded (any method of therapy), the personality is a kind of framework of attitudes understood by oneself" (italics added). In his later theorizing, Perls (1969, p. 19) made strenuous efforts to eliminate cognitive activities in favor of sensory experiencing. He decried any reference to "concepts of the self." He emphasized his disdain for the cognitive, insisting that we should "do away with concepts and work on the awareness principle" (p. 16). "Intuition is the intelligence of the organism, intelligence is the whole, and intellect is the whore of intelligence—the computer. . . . If you are busy with your computer, your energy goes into your thinking and you don't see and hear anymore" (p. 22). As a consequence of such forthright rejection of the intellectual, Gestalt therapists usually avoid theorizing about their treatment procedures; in their view, the experiences themselves are effective, whereas the analysis of experiences is not.

In the face of such rejection of the cognitive, it would seem the greatest presumption to attempt to find relationships between Gestalt therapy and the misconception hypothesis. Examination of Gestalt therapy protocols reveals, however, that strenuous efforts are made to find and change misconceptions by means of a large number of somewhat novel techniques. We have already mentioned that Perls viewed the patient's substitution of intellectual processes for awareness of sensory input as a major mistake, which can also be regarded as a misconception. Perls also identified another important class of misconceptions: the patient's convictions that he should do certain things or that he should be better than he is; in allowing himself to be guided by moral imperatives, he is mistakenly following intellectual principles and thus contracting his awareness.

Again, according to Perls and other Gestalt therapists, four specific "blockings" prevent patients from becoming aware of their feelings. Two of these blockings, retroflection and desensitization, are difficult to interpret as misconceptions, since they allegedly occur at motor or sensory levels. The other two, introjection and projection, are evidently cognitive processes based upon misconceptions. In *introjection* the individual adopts wholesale the complex patterns of behavior of others without integrating them into himself. Even though unintegrated, these patterns are perceived by the individual as valid aspects of himself. Mistaken perception breeds misconceptions. The concept of *projection* is employed by Gestalt therapists just as it is ordinarily employed in psychopathology. The individual projects or perceives in others those aspects of himself which he denies or rejects. In projection, therefore, one suffers from a misconception, since he mistakenly believes that disliked or disowned aspects of himself are actually characteristic of others,

If we examine some of the characteristic procedures and techniques employed by Gestalt therapists—most notably their emphasis on patients' postural behavior, gestures, voice qualities, and dreams, and the events in group sessions—we can also discover that these practices are helpful in locating misconceptions.

Although other approaches to therapy deal with posture and motor behavior, the Gestalt therapist claims, and probably rightfully so, that he deals with them more often and accords them greater significance than do other therapists. Gestalt therapists usually also claim that their approach is essentially nonverbal, or at least only incidentally concerned with patient verbalizations. Their transcribed interviews and their tapes, however, reveal that the verbal productions of their patients are very influential in treatment, even though posture, gesture, and voice quality also produce changes in therapist behavior. When faulty beliefs are revealed in either verbal or nonverbal behavior, the Gestalt therapist is likely to engage in various endeavors intended to change patient misconceptions—despite his claim that the treatment is aimed only at helping the patient repair "splits" between his awareness and his attending. For example, upon observing a particular posture in the patient, such as subtle cringing movements, the therapist may suspect that the cringing is related to a psychological problem. He may then directly instruct the patient to exaggerate the motor behavior and to report how he feels. The patient may thereby discover that he has been cringing away from his difficulties. If, prior to this incident, he believed that he was attacking his problems head on, a misconception has been discovered. Thus, feelings detected during the therapist's examination of postural behavior often reveal significant misconceptions.

An example of therapist-induced postural stress which helped the patient to discover a misconception is found in the case of "Mary," reported by her therapist, James Simkin (1970). Mary was struggling with her dependence upon the therapist—a dependence that he regarded as typical of her relations with others. While Mary was following Simkin's instruction to "squeeze yourself in and out," she reported that when squeezing in she felt frightened and in the dark; she wanted to scream but could not. The therapist informed her that when squeezing in she also brought her feet up from the floor. He asked her to repeat the movement, thus inducing postural stress. While complying, Mary reported in a scared voice that her hands were tied. Emotionally, she added that she remembered being tied to a post and left alone when she was little. The recall of this event helped Mary to recognize that she was no longer "tied up" and that she could be independent. The recall also helped her to obtain insight into the misconception that she still needed to be dependent. The incident, moreover, illustrates the use of a presumably buried memory from the past in Gestalt therapy.

Gestalt therapists also believe that voice qualities reveal much about patient attitudes. Without disagreeing with that contention, one can show that the attention paid to voice qualities by Gestalt therapists also helps patients to recognize misconceptions. The following incident is taken from a case of family therapy reported by Kempler (1970). During one of Kempler's sessions with this family, the father reported that he was unable to deal with the children because his wife stopped him whenever he tried to discipline them. Noticing that the father complained in a whining voice when his wife argued with him, Kempler called the whining to the father's attention by a sarcastic attack. The father then whined at the therapist, who subtly induced a self-demonstration by returning to the attack until the father responded angrily and aggressively. The father thereby demonstrated to himself, and to the others present, that he could assert himself and therefore could keep his wife from interfering with his handling of the children. His misconception about his ability to deal with his wife became apparent when the therapist used the whining voice as a cue for self-demonstration.

Dreams were also used by Perls to reveal patient misconceptions. Unlike other approaches to dream interpretation, Perls had the patient play the role of any significant aspect of the reported dream on the supposition that all dream contents are related to aspects of the patient's self. In acting out or describing one or more aspects of the dream, according to Perls, the patient often reveals some significant but hitherto unrecognized aspect of himself. These unrecognized aspects of the self are treated by the therapist as misconceptions under which the patient is laboring. The following brief verbatim report of "Linda's Dream" (Perls, 1969) illustrates how Perls used dreams to reveal patient misconceptions. Linda told a dream about porpoise-like people in a lake which was drying up. When the water was gone, only an outdated and useless license plate was found on the bottom. Perls had her play the role of the license plate. Linda identified with it, saying that she did not like to be useless and outdated. She went on to say that she was useless because she could no longer reproduce (bear children). Perls then had her play the role of the disappearing water. Linda reported that she saw herself sinking into the ground, watering the earth so that flowers and other living things could grow. She then concluded that because she could still paint and create beauty she could continue to play a creative part in life without having to obtain a license from anyone. Perls ended the session by pointing out how she had corrected her misconception that she was useless because she could no longer bear children.

In the Gestalt approach, groups provide an efficient procedure for training in sensory awareness. Sensory reporting, as we have seen, is also a fertile ground for detecting misconceptions. Group activities also facilitate self-demonstration experiences for group members, since they can observe themselves while interacting with others. Gestalt group therapists also encourage group members to provide verbal feedback to other members. Such feedback calls attention to one member's possible misconceptions, and other group members may recognize their own similar misconceptions.

Group sessions also provide Gestalt therapists with opportunities to help patients change misconceptions as well as discover them. Once a significant misconception has been located and brought to light, the therapist either rests content with the patient's insight; or, if insight does not occur, the therapist tries to modify the misconception—often through confrontative techniques and persuasion. The therapist may openly approve of constructive alternatives tentatively offered by the patient. He may enlist the help of the group to reinforce the desired alternative by urging the group to voice open approval. The therapist may encourage the patient to continue acting out constructive roles in treatment and sometimes destructive roles to emphasize their undesirable aspects. Insight, confrontation, persuasion, reward, group reinforcement, and role playing are only some of the techniques employed by Gestalt therapists, either in groups or in individual treatment, to change misconceptions. Chapter Four contains a brief analysis of Perls's determined attempt to change one patient's misconception about herself by using all of these techniques plus others.

One of the major theses of this book should be repeated here. There is no one best way to discover and to change misconceptions in psychotherapy. Analyzing therapists' activities in terms of a misconception approach is not intended to detract from the effectiveness of the approach or to belittle the strategy and tactics they employ. The Gestalt approach has certainly enriched the repertoire of tactics which can be employed by therapists of any persuasion who wish to emphasize at one time or another the finding and changing of misconceptions by detailed attention to nonverbal behavior or by having patients act out aspects of their dreams or engage in other forms of role playing so heavily emphasized by Perls.

Direct Psychoanalysis

Relatively little attention has been paid to psychosis and the misconception hypothesis by psychotherapists. Most therapists have theorized about and treated neurotics, character disturbances, and the lesser maladjustments. Despite the obvious application of the misconception hypothesis to the delusions, hallucinations, and other distortions of reality typically found in psychotics, the etiological riddle of psychosis has hindered the search for psychological explanations. As a result, most psychotics are now treated with antipsychotic drugs, which at least control their most disruptive behaviors.

Only a small number of intrepid souls still cling to psychotherapy as the treatment of choice for psychosis. Among the most successful on the public record is John N. Rosen, whose treatment procedures but not his theory appear to be encompassed by the misconception hypothesis. Although current evaluations of Rosen's work hardly indicate that a panacea has been discovered for schizophrenia, there is little doubt that he has been almost uniquely effective in producing rapid remission of acute psychosis by psychological methods alone. Reports of Rosen's work appear in a small series of books from Temple University's Department of Psychiatry, where foundation grants provided a number of psychiatrists and other professionals with opportunities to observe and evaluate Rosen's treatment of acute psychotics. Treated without drugs, the patients were selected independently by two psychiatrists and one psychologist. The most detailed description of this extraordinary investigation, unparalleled in psychotherapy research, can be found in an excellent book by Scheflen (1961). Less detailed but highly informative reports by other psychiatrist observers have been published as books by Brody (1959) and by English, Hampe, Bacon, and Settlage (1961).

In commenting on the results of Rosen's treatment of the eight cases he observed, Scheflen (1961, p. 230) stated, "In each of these eight cases, whenever Rosen personally and regularly saw the patient, there was evident improvement in psychotic systems within a few days or weeks. Six cases went on to remission. Of the others, one committed suicide; the other is usually psychotic but shows periods of remission." In reporting on a larger sample of twelve cases, English and his associates (1961, p. 2) reported that "all but two . . . recovered from psychosis sufficiently to return to the community." The extraordinary ability of Rosen to gain rapport with acute psychotics was also noted by Scheflen (1961, p. 68): "Rosen often established rapport in the early minutes of a first interview even with very evasive or withdrawn patients. We have repeatedly seen him succeed with patients who had not responded to other therapists over a period of days and weeks."

Although other therapists have employed Rosen's procedures, there are few good reports on their successes. An exception is B. P. Karon, who spent some time working with Rosen. He recently reported considerable success with acute schizophrenics, although he does not appear to subscribe to all of Rosen's theories and procedures. Karon (Karon and Vanderbos, 1972) describes his approach as "a psychoanalytic psychotherapy of an active variety, *without* medication, stressing oral dynamics and utilizing so-called 'direct' interpretation."

The theoretical significance of Rosen's work in treating acute schizophrenics is considerable, even though for practical purposes treatment with antipsychotic drugs may be the treatment of choice. Rosen eschews all drugs, but in a relatively short period of time he restores a respectable percentage of his patients to relative normality.

Although the long-term results of his work have been disputed (Horwitz and others, 1958), his work suggests that remission of the acute stage of psychosis can be brought about by psychological methods only. The implications of such results for the psychological understanding of schizophrenia are obvious provided Rosen's results can be substantiated. Furthermore, if his procedures can be shown to be based upon his correction of patient misconceptions, which I believe to be the case, then the misconception hypothesis may have direct application to the treatment of psychotics.

Before suggesting how the misconception hypothesis can be applied to direct psychoanalysis, we should first look at Rosen's (1968) own theory. In a chapter entitled "Direct Analysis: A Summary Statement," Rosen contends that his approach attempts to recreate and revise the patient's "relationship with his early maternal environment." That environment includes not only the real or foster mother but the maternal environment "in general." A malevolent early maternal environment, according to Rosen, dominates the schizophrenic's psychosexual development and becomes internalized as his superego. When schizophrenics undergo acute illness, they regress to the malevolent relationships of the early maternal environment and project its malevolent qualities upon persons and objects in their current environment.

Rosen proposes that during treatment the direct psychoanalyst "fosters" and "nourishes" the patient psychologically, in accordance with the parental role which the patient thrusts upon the therapist. Thus, the primary therapeutic agent is the "complex, emotionally charged parent-child relationship," in which "the psychiatrist must be a loving, omnipotent protector and provider." Rosen asserts that recall of childhood traumas, insight, and abreaction are of little importance or "not enough." Instead, through direct interpretations, questions, and demonstrations, the therapist helps the patient to understand the unconscious meanings of his behavior. In order to communicate with the psychotic, who understands only highly concrete terminology, the therapist talks specifically about the patient's "mother."

The expert observers who wrote evaluations after lengthy observation of Rosen's work at the Temple Institute question most of Rosen's theory and also deny that his approach is psychoanalytic. They specifically deny that Rosen makes interpretations during therapy, insisting instead that he constantly confronts his patients with content which is similar from patient to patient. With this Rosen concurs, stating that acute schizophrenics are as alike as "peas in a pod"; thus, the direct analyst need not wait for the patient to reveal traces of his unconscious but can directly interpret unconscious material from the therapist's prior knowledge—hence the name "direct psychoanalysis."

Despite Rosen's recognized effectiveness in dealing with acute psychotics, the question of how he accomplishes his results is a matter of considerable controversy. Rosen's own explanations receive short shrift from his highly experienced observers. In fact, if Rosen's writings are scripture, the three books from the Temple studies are apocryphal. But when a mercurial and kaleidoscopic therapy such as Rosen's obtains results so rapidly that our expectations are jolted, a variety of theoretical explanations are offered. After studying Rosen's writings, the reports of the observers from the Temple studies, and several tape recordings, and after attempting to apply Rosen's procedures under very limited conditions, I offer the following explanation, based upon the misconception hypothesis.

As a preamble, I must emphasize an earlier observation on phrenophobia (elaborated in Chapter Six)—namely, that acutely psychotic patients are petrified by the possibility that they may lose all control of themselves and become homicidal, suicidal, and sexually assaultive. They also fear complete loss of personal identity. In other words, the psychotic patient perceives himself in imminent danger of psychological death, which in his confusion he also perceives as physical death. This cluster of mistaken beliefs can produce disabling anxiety. From that standpoint, many of the puzzling aspects of schizophrenic behavior as well as the procedures of direct psychoanalysis take on a new perspective. Many of Rosen's procedures are attempts to correct his patients' misconceptions that they are being thrust with accelerating speed down the steep path which leads only to death.

The treatment atmosphere is one of intense concern for curing the patient's psychosis. Rosen tries untiringly to distract the patient from his inner preoccupations by unusual and even bizarre behavior. What the external observers view as criticism and abuse by the therapist are intended as evidence of concern for the patient and efforts to fasten the patient's attention upon the direct psychoanalyst. By means of explanations and self-demonstrations, Rosen tirelessly presents evidence to the patient designed to counteract his misconceptions about his mental condition, particularly the misconception that he suffers from incurable and irreversible insanity. All of these procedures are intermingled in time, but Rosen emphasizes some of them more at the beginning of treatment and others closer to termination. The basic aspects of Rosen's treatment during his therapeutic interviews are continued by his assistants during all of the patient's waking hours.

From the paragraph above, we can extract five interrelated principles employed by Rosen in reducing or eliminating psychotic behavior in acute schizophrenics. The first three principles essentially outline the treatment atmosphere; the last two outline Rosen's procedures in changing misconceptions.

1. *Warm support.* The therapeutic atmosphere in the interviews and in the patient's daily life with Rosen's assistants must be perceived by the patient as warm and supportive and designed to help him recover from his psychosis. Aggression or punishment by the therapist will not retard treatment if the patient perceives the overall process as one intended to help him recover.

The emotional reactions of psychotics include many hostile feelings, which originate in their frustrations about their condition as well as in perceived rejection by others. Many psychotics, in addition to their phrenophobia, perceive themselves as criminals because of their stereotype that the insane are completely out of control. Warm support, if faithfully administered, may therefore have a major role in changing the patient's misconception that he is an object of scorn and rejection. Rosen's warm support can best be characterized by his "governing principle": "The therapist must be a loving, omnipotent protector and provider for the patient." Rosen thus sees himself as "the good mother," although his observers are more likely to see him enacting the strict father's role.

The support shown by Rosen during his own interviews is carried on by his assistants, who are specially trained to treat the patient with warm, friendly, and tireless devotion but without allowing the patient to wallow in regressive behavior. Adult performance is constantly stressed. "Rosen's own dramatic and sometimes punitive behavior with his patients has received more attention in the literature than his gentleness, sympathy, and support" (Scheflen, 1961, p. 183). But although Rosen may be critical, abusive, and rejecting at times, his observers agree that most patients become strongly attached to him very rapidly. The same phenomenon is often observed in the patients of surgeons, physicians, and dentists, who inflict far more physical pain on their patients than does Rosen. Clearly, the patients understand that the infliction of pain is intended to benefit them in the long run.

2. *Distraction.* By forceful psychological or physiological stimuli, the patient is distracted from his emotional panic and inner preoccupations. For purposes of distraction, Rosen uses such unconventional devices as forceful language, dramatic statements, rapid changes in interview topic, shocking accusations, occasional physical assault, praise and punishment, and the arousing of patient curiosity. Brody (1959, p. 71) surmises that many of Rosen's therapeutic activities are attempts to "awaken" the patient: "Rosen overthrows restraint and uses a primal language. . . . He tries literally to awaken the patient from a state of sleep. His language is strong, loud, and forceful; the patient is forced to listen to him." According to Scheflen (1961), Rosen's rapid changes in mood, attitude, and stance are initially "a most striking and bewildering" aspect of Rosen's treatment. He may change with great rapidity from violent denunciations of the patient to a show of soft, gentle concern. Such changes seem to fascinate his observers as much as the patient.

Rosen usually treats his patients in front of an audience composed of assistants and professionals interested in his procedures. Therefore, when Rosen makes sexual offers and accusations, the shock value is a distraction device which is hard to parallel. Although Rosen claims that his verbal sexual confrontations are direct interpretations of the patient's sexual problems, his observers question the claim because he pays little if any attention to patient responses. Praise and punishment can also serve as powerful distractors. Neither is neglected by Rosen in his tireless efforts to keep the patient from concentrating upon his inner preoccupations. A more subtle distraction device is Rosen's curious procedure of ignoring the patient from time to time, either by turning to discuss the case with his observers or by simply ignoring the patient without excuse. The patient's curiosity is undoubtedly aroused by such tactics, for who could possibly ignore the opportunity to hear his case discussed with doctors?

Distraction devices of a less dramatic nature are employed by the assistants who live with the patient. Their interventions are as tireless as Rosen's but are more matter of fact as they correct and guide the patient in normal behavior during all his waking hours.

3. *Attention maintaining.* The patient's attention must be continually directed toward the therapist, who must be perceived as a prestigeful person able to help the patient recover from his psychosis. Since something more than simple distraction is required to offset the rapidly fluctuating attention of psychotics, Rosen has developed a large number of attention-maintaining devices, such as the expectation of cure, the continued use of assistants to reinforce the therapist's treatment, and training the patient to expect criticism or even punishment if his attention wanders from the therapist. Acute psychotics are not only intensely interested in recovering from psychosis but are also terrified by the thought of becoming worse. Rosen's recognition of these overwhelming needs results in his frequent assertions about his intention to cure them of their insanity. Even in the beginning of treatment Rosen emphasizes his purpose not only to the patient but also to the observers. The expectation of cure can be one of the most powerful attention-maintaining devices whether the patient's problem is medical or psychological. Once the therapist believes that the patient is at least partially distracted from his inner preoccupations and ruminations, and that his attention is focused on the therapist, other treatment techniques can be utilized.

4. *Explanations: Verbal correction of misconceptions.* Rosen strenuously tries to correct his patients' misconceptions about their condition by means of specific, concrete, and often-repeated verbal reassurances that they will recover from psychosis. The primary therapeutic content of direct psychoanalysis may well reside in the correcting of misconceptions and the reexperiencing of normal behavior rather than in the pathological themes, such as sexuality and dependence, which Rosen emphasizes. The observers from the

Temple Institute agree that Rosen does not employ an interpretive, uncovering type of therapy. It is possible, of course, that Rosen's confrontations may be brilliant maneuvers which illuminate and resolve unconscious conflicts, but the evidence for such is scanty. He pays but little attention to specific etiological events; his continuous emphasis is on the present and the future rather than the past.

As an integral aspect of his effort to force the psychotic to correct his misconception that he is hopelessly insane, Rosen relentlessly tries to force the patient to publicly admit his psychotic condition. The apparent paradox lies in the psychotic's tendency to deny reality, even to deny his knowledge that he is psychotic. (The denial of illness is, of course, a common phenomenon found in medical as well as mental patients.) Once the psychotic is able to admit to his psychotic condition publicly, the therapist can deal with the reality which both therapist and patient now openly accept.

Rosen also tries to break patients' identifications with their parents, particularly the mother. Maternal rejection by a "malevolent mother" whose "milk poisons" the child is one of Rosen's favorite metaphorical themes in explaining the cause of schizophrenia. Concretely and literally he attempts to indoctrinate his patients with that point of view. In doing so, he employs a variety of techniques aimed at clearing up what he considers the misconceptions which the patient still retains about his relationships with his parents. This procedure can be described in another way. Rosen's patients perceive themselves as being strongly influenced by the "ghosts" of their parents, whether they are living or dead. This influence is often unwitting or unverbalized by the patients but is nonetheless very strong. In his shocking attacks upon the parents during treatment, Rosen "exorcizes" the ghosts by helping the patients realize by means of repeated cognitive review that they have been irrationally influenced by one or both parents or other parental surrogates. Thus, their misconceptions about themselves in relation to their parents become at least partially modified or eliminated.

5. *Self-demonstrations of normality.* Mental patients need not only warm support and verbal reassurances but also the reassurance obtained from observing themselves performing ordinary activities in a normal fashion. Whereas the normal individual places implicit trust in the functioning of his mental apparatus, the psy-

chotic distrusts his. The normal can be amused by and ignore minor distortions in his cognitive-affective functioning because he knows that these lapses are temporary and unimportant. The psychotic, however, cannot ignore even minor distortions because of his fears that his mind is shattered. Therefore, Rosen and his assistants give endless verbal reassurances that the patient is recovering and can behave normally; they also make ceaseless efforts to force or cajole the patient to show himself that he can behave normally. Forcing normal behavior is generally regarded as useless by most therapists; but Rosen and his assistants use any available methods to motivate or prod patients into normal behavior. Once the desired behavior has been performed, patients are rewarded. They are rewarded, for instance, for conforming to Rosen's prescribed role for patients, for the disappearance of a symptom, for expressing attachment to the therapist, for proper behavior outside the residential unit, and for gaining an insight (Scheflen, 1961). "Sane thinking and behavior is rewarded and conversely reward is withheld when the patient does not think and behave sanely" (English and others, 1961, p. 36).

The demands made on patients for normal behavior are perhaps best illustrated by the activities of the assistants, who do not permit the patient to withdraw into himself. House rules are rigidly enforced in the residential units. The patient's daily routine is similar to that of a normal person, except that patients do not leave the house to work. Patients are not allowed to stay in bed in the daytime or to dally in the bathroom. Washing, shaving, and dressing are required in the morning. If the patient does not care for himself voluntarily, the assistants do it by force. Withdrawal into autism, listening to voices, and infantile behavior are all prohibited. Patients are not babied but are cajoled or forced into normal behavior.

One of Rosen's most unusual techniques is his forcing patients to reenact earlier psychotic behavior as they recover from the acute psychosis. Patients are deliberately instructed to imitate their most psychotic behavior until, in Rosen's words, they can demonstrate their "return to reality." This technique is probably as much a therapeutic as a testing device. An acute psychosis is a highly traumatic experience, which recovered patients ordinarily avoid thinking about. If, however, the recovered psychotic denies or re-presses his earlier traumas, he is likely to believe that he is con-stantly at the mercy of accidental recall and possible redintegration of the acute phase of his illness.

Rosen's desensitization technique of having the patient imi-tate his earlier disorganized behavior appears similar to the prin-ciple of repeated review discussed in Chapter Four. When Rosen systematically rehearses his patients in recalling and reenacting psychotic experiences, he is helping them to review repeatedly the misconception that they are so fragile that psychological collapse will recur if they accidentally recall previous psychotic episodes. By so doing, they gain a reasonable and rational perspective on them-selves rather than being constantly beset by their fear of recall.

Rosen would undoubtedly disagree that his treatment of acute schizophrenics is successful because he has applied the mis-conception hypothesis. Nonetheless, as we have seen, there is con-siderable evidence that his treatment goal is to change the miscon-ceptions which maintain psychosis. His warmth and support, his distraction devices, and his maintaining the patient's attention upon the therapist are necessary preludes for bringing the patient to the point where verbal corrections of his misconceptions and guided self-demonstrations of normality can be successfully applied.

Modeling

Recent years have seen a quickening of interest in cognitive explanations of treatment, not only among traditional therapists but also among the more recently arrived behavior therapists. Although most of the latter prefer to explain the effects of treatment as the result of learning based upon principles of classical and operant conditioning, Albert Bandura (1969, 1971) has combined con-ditioning and cognitive principles in his analysis. With his students and coworkers, he has been instrumental in developing a new method of treatment called *modeling*.

In Chapter Three modeling is discussed as one of the four methods whereby the therapist presents evidence to clients or patients to bring about changes in their misconceptions. Bandura also refers to modeling as imitation or observational learning. Modeling consists of inducing the client to observe a real or an artificial model performing behavior feared by the client. Under favorable circumstances, after one or more exposures to the previously avoided activity the client is able to show that he, too, can perform the same behavior without fear. The method has been applied most frequently to common phobic reactions, such as fears of small animals. Bandura suggests that it is most useful for treatment of problem behaviors, such as fears, that are "inspectional" or open to direct observation. There are, however, many other uses for the procedure, although they have not been exploited very systematically.

Bandura's emphasis upon behavior and his skillful use of learning terminology might at first glance appear to preclude any major role for misconceptions in explaining modeling. He does, however, place considerable emphasis upon cognitive variables, which he usually refers to as "symbolic" variables. When cognitive principles are employed in a theory of behavior change, then—since misconceptions are incorrect cognitions—the misconception hypothesis might find a place. And Bandura, when discussing the control of psychotic behavior, has made at least two felicitous contributions to the language of the misconception hypothesis: his references to "fictitious contingencies" and "fantasied reinforcements" (terms that can be applied also to the behavior of nonpsychotic individuals). In order for contingencies and reinforcements to be effective, whether they are correctly or incorrectly perceived, the individual must be aware of them. The same is true of misconceptions. Although some of the early learning theorists, and more currently the Skinnerians, ignore awareness as a factor in learning, Bandura (1969) explicitly includes awareness as an important factor in the acquisition and control of behavior. Citing many research studies, he concludes that minimal learning may occur without awareness; but when understanding (awareness) develops, learning speed and efficiency increase dramatically. Even greater learning occurs, he says, when motivational factors in the form of incentives are introduced. Both understanding and incentives are cognitive factors in the subject's awareness. Bandura (1969, p. 572) also asserts that awareness "under some conditions can exert a more powerful discriminative control over behavior than reinforcement variables."

That is, under certain conditions cognitions can override the external reinforcements in a given situation. Bandura accounts for the powerful role of awareness by proposing, with considerable research support, that awareness in problem solving produces hypotheses or rules about the correct solution. Hypotheses or rules are cognitions; some of these cognitions are correct, while others are incorrect. Incorrect cognitions are also misconceptions.

In Bandura's system, then, cognitive or symbolic behavior may produce misconceptions, which under certain conditions can account for maladjusted behavior. But Bandura's system attempts to integrate cognitive learning with classical and operant conditioning. Thus, we cannot conclude that for him misconceptions alone can explain the learning of maladjusted behavior or that just the correction of misconceptions can account for successful treatment. But despite his basic reliance upon all three kinds of learning, Bandura does lean in some respects toward a more cognitive explanation of treatment, particularly where older children and adults are concerned. That is, although he recognizes the influence of conditioning, he accords cognitive processes, referred to as "central mediational processes," their due in the regulation of the behavior of the more mature individual: "In many respects, the most influential regulatory mechanism operates through central mediational processes" (Bandura, 1969, p. 63).

Bandura's recognition of cognitive control of behavior is also evident in his discussion of self-evaluating and self-regulating processes. One of the consequences of behavior, according to Bandura, is that the person obtains information about the possible outcomes of his responses. The person then forms hypotheses about future outcomes. When a hypothesis is confirmed, the person is likely to establish a rule or conclusion as to how the problem can best be solved. When there is sufficient confirmation to validate the rule, it then guides future behavior. Therefore, although the behaviorists insist that "behavior is largely governed by its consequences," behavior which is governed by rules of this kind is at least partially controlled by *antecedent* conditions, the rules, rather than by consequences. Misconceptions, which can be regarded as mistaken or invalid rules, may thus control much maladjusted behavior even within Bandura's system.

When modeling is used to treat maladjustments such as common phobic reactions, subjects who are fearful of specific objects, such as dogs or rats, are repeatedly shown a fearless model handling the feared objects without being harmed. According to Bandura, both the conditioned fear responses and the maladaptive cognitions associated with the feared object disappear when the modeling has been successful. Certain variations in this basic pattern of treatment have been found to increase its effectiveness. Bandura states that *graduated modeling* is an important adjunct. In graduated modeling, the feared object is first presented so as to arouse low levels of fear or threat, after which increasingly threatening scenes can be presented. By starting with low levels of threat, the therapist reduces the risk of increasing fear to an undesirable level and has greater control over the treatment. In *multiple modeling,* another variation of the basic procedure, more than one fearless model is shown to the subject. Another variation is the use of *symbolic models,* portrayed in motion pictures or videotapes; Bandura finds, however, that symbolic models are somewhat less effective than live models. In still another variation, *guided participation,* the subject and the therapist simultaneously handle the feared object, under the guidance of the therapist.

In extensive studies of modeling, Bandura (1969, 1971) has successfully eliminated a variety of phobic reactions in both children and adults, whereas his control subjects have shown no change in their avoidant behavior. The treatment appears to be relatively rapid and generally effective. In one study, live modeling with guided participation was compared with systematic desensitization for snake-phobic adolescents and adults; live modeling was found more effective. Other studies have shown that there is generalization of the fear reduction from the modeled object to a variety of social events and other feared objects. One might say that self-confidence is increased after successful treatment of this kind. Bandura (1969, p. 187), in fact, infers that two different processes are at work in producing such generalization: "generalization of extinction effects" and "positive reinforcement of a sense of capability through success." The second inference introduces a new cognitive factor, "sense of capability."

In explaining how modeling eliminates fears, Bandura (1971,

p. 672) assigns an important role to cognition. Again, however, he infers that two processes are involved. One is the noncognitive extinction of conditioned emotional fear responses; the other is the elimination of fear-arousing cognitions associated with the phobic object. His most succinct explanation for the elimination of the of the noncognitive and cognitive fear responses reads as follows (Bandura, 1971, p. 688): "The process of change associated with the powerful procedure involving modeling combined with guided participation may be conceptualized as follows. Repeated modeling of approach responses, *mainly through its informative function,* decreases the arousal potential of aversive stimuli below the threshold for activating avoidance responses, thus enabling persons to engage, albeit somewhat anxiously, in approach behavior." Since the italicized phrase did not appear in an earlier, almost identical paragraph (Bandura, 1969, p. 192), one might conclude that in the later writing Bandura assigns more weight to the cognitive or informative function of the modeling procedure. He has not, however, abandoned his two-factory theory.

What does he mean by "informative function," which seems to carry the burden of accounting for the success of modeling? The semantic problem is considerable, and Bandura has not escaped it. In his 1971 chapter, for example, he writes, "Apparently giving information to severely phobic people may, if anything, increase their fearfulness." Yet one page later, as we have seen, he writes that modeling works "mainly through its informative function." Despite the apparent contradiction, he appears to be distinguishing between information supplied verbally and information acquired by observing a model in action. Such a distinction may, however, be superficial. The essential distinction may rest on the fact that in certain situations verbal information may be more helpful to the subject, that is, may have a larger informative function, than visual information and vice versa. For example, a therapist would have considerable difficulty trying to describe verbally a modeling scene intended to overcome a fear of dogs because of the highly complex character of the components of the scene—the actual appearance and movements of the dog, the appearance and actions of the model, and the feelings and behavior of the client. But, in Kelly's fixed-role therapy, which

Bandura (1969, p. 163) claims relies "almost exclusively upon [verbal] modeling procedures," the therapist can more readily instruct the client in the general principles of the role to be followed in a variety of social situations. Preparing opportunities for direct visual observation of the different social situations the client might encounter would be exceedingly difficult if not impossible. Thus the information most helpful to the client, visual or verbal, depends upon the problem being treated and the resources of the therapist.

If modeling works "mainly through its informative function," as Bandura claims, is a dual-process theory, which includes change in both conditioning and cognitive (informational) factors, truly necessary? Or can cognitive changes alone explain the effects of modeling? Final answers to these questions are impossible to give at the present time because even in the laboratory it is extremely difficult to disentangle cognitive from conditioning variables. We can, however, join Bandura in pointing to the accumulating evidence from laboratory investigations of conditioned fear responses that cognitive variables play an unexpectedly large role. Bandura (1969) himself cites an investigation by Dawson (1966), who found that the experimental subject's belief in whether shock will follow a conditioned stimulus is an important determinant in acquiring the fear response. Other investigators cited by Bandura have also shown experimentally the influence of cognitive factors in fear conditioning (Dawson and Grings, 1968; Grings, 1965; Bridger and Mandel, 1965). Cognitive factors have also been shown to have great influence in the extinction of already learned fear responses (see Bandura, 1969, p. 671). Simply informing subjects that no shock will follow the conditioned stimulus may eliminate the fear response. In such demonstrations, information alone overrides the fear response. Bandura explicitly recognizes that such overriding takes place in the laboratory situation when the subject knows that the experimenter has control of the feared or noxious object. But in real life, Bandura asserts, complete control is uncertain, and information provided a subject is unlikely to override the conditioned response; therefore, according to Bandura, extinction procedures based upon information alone cannot explain the effects of modeling. But when modeling is conducted as a treatment procedure, it is essentially the same as a laboratory situation in that the therapist must be assumed to have complete control over the feared objects, at least to the extent that they will not be able to harm the clients being treated.

Thus, it is possible to explain the effectiveness of modeling on the basis of cognitive restructuring alone. Graduated approaches controlled by the therapist allow the client to obtain information through direct observation that the objects are truly harmless. At the same time, he perceives that he is not responding as fearfully as anticipated. His changed perception of the formerly fearful object has facilitated cognitive reorganization. In this formulation, which depends upon cognitive review to produce cognitive reorganization, the evidence which is acted upon by the client is presented to him in words as well as in his direct observation. Modeling, from this point of view, is a cognitive procedure designed to change the client's misconceptions about the objects of his fears as well as his misconceptions about how he behaves in the presence of the feared object. This formulation depends upon the assumption that conditioned responses can be overridden by cognitive factors, as has been shown in the laboratory under conditions similar to modeling.

Admittedly, the cognitive formulation of modeling presented here is based on inference, just as is Bandura's dual-process explanation. The investigations which would determine whether extinction must be accounted for by processes other than cognitive overriding are exceedingly difficult to design. In any case, how important is the argument over a dual-process theory versus cognitive reorganization in guiding the therapist when he employs modeling procedures? Would a therapist employ different methods in modeling if he preferred one of the two explanations over the other? I have difficulty in finding differences in application apart from the language of the description. Both cognitive reorganization and the extinction of conditioned responses depend upon repeated presentation of the corrective evidence—the actual modeling by the fearless model. Furthermore, the behavior required by the model during treatment would be identical for both theories. In both, for example, a fearless model would be necessary; a fearful model would increase rather than reduce the client's fears. One might argue that there are heuristic advantages for the therapist who bases his approach upon conditioning theory in that the large amount of research on conditioning provides many guidelines for regulating modeling procedures. But the heuristic advantage of the misconception hypothesis is that therapists can use their own self-concepts when devising and administering modeling procedures. They can temporarily empathize with the client's fears in order to understand how the client might react during treatment. The therapist can imagine that he has the same fear as the client and speculate on how he would be affected by the components of the modeling procedure he is about to employ. Such imagining may be less specific than some conditioning principles, but it is likely to have richer content. There is considerable likelihood, in fact, that conditioning advocates frequently use their imagination in this fashion when engaged in modeling. Tolman's dictum "to think like a rat" when designing research on the learning of rats may have major implications for therapists interested in modeling as well as in other kinds of therapy.

Although Bandura's modeling is the only behavioral approach considered here in detail for its relevance to the misconception hypothesis, other behavioral approaches are also helpful in providing opportunities to change misconceptions. For example, the research literature on Wolpe's systematic desensitization has been examined by Wilkins (1971), who concludes: "Neither training in muscle relaxation nor the construction of a graded hierarchy of fear-relevant scenes nor the concomitance of instructed imagination to muscle relaxation are necessary conditions for treatment success. . . . Instructed imagination by itself is the only necessary element of the desensitization procedure" (p. 311). Even more explicitly, Wilkins asserts that systematic desensitization is effective because of social variables in the therapeutic relationship and "cognitive variables involving expectancy of therapeutic gain, information feedback of success, training in the control of attention, and vicarious learning . . . through instructed imagination" (p. 331).

Wilkins' analysis provides a straightforward cognitive explanation for the effectiveness of systematic desensitization as a means of changing misconceptions. In fact, his conclusion that instructed imagination is the only necessary element in Wolpe's procedure is strikingly reminiscent of the technique of repeated review (discussed in Chapter Four). Although Wilkins does not specify the need for repetition of instructed imagining, Wolpe's system typically requires a large number of repetitions of the scenes presented by the therapist.

Wilkins is not alone in his interpretation of systematic de-sensitization as a cognitive procedure. When asked by Bergin and Strupp (1972, p. 285) about the role of cognition in behavior-ism, "Bandura replied: 'What could be more cognitive than desensitization?' "

Other behavioral approaches that use instructed imagining can also be reinterpreted as cognitive procedures. Under this head-ing would fall Stampfl's implosive therapy; assertiveness training, which inevitably involves the subject's imagining himself engaging in more assertive behavior; and the various role-playing or role-taking techniques which have recently come into favor with behavior therapists. Most behavioral approaches to treatment include so many cognitive procedures that the temptation to label them as cognitive methods useful in changing misconceptions is difficult to resist.

Chapter 10

Major Principles in Retrospect

This final chapter is devoted to a condensed discussion of the principles of the misconception hypothesis, which have been described and illustrated in greater detail in the earlier chapters of this book. The numbering of the major principles is only for the convenience of the reader and for ready reference. There is no implication that these principles provide a tightly defined and organized system of psychotherapy. In fact, these same principles can be used within the context of any of our general approaches to psychotherapy, provided the therapist thinks that faulty beliefs should be major targets for treatment. The principles can also be used independently of other systems of psychotherapy, provided the therapist has a working knowledge of the techniques and procedures offered by a variety of our current approaches. The principles provide general guidelines for therapy. As always, success in treatment is dependent upon the clinical knowledge and skills of the therapist.

1. Learned misconceptions (or faulty beliefs or mistaken ideas) are the crucial variables which must be modified or eliminated before psychotherapy can be successful. This is a pragmatic principle in that valid or invalid conceptions are viewed as the end product of various psychological processes, not all of which are cognitive. Regardless of how misconceptions are learned, however, their detection and modification is the central task of psychotherapy. Thus, arguments over how learning takes place are of little importance in this approach to therapy. Of most importance is the recognition that misconceptions are the keys to the control of maladjusted behavior. They may be only the observable end products of other processes; but when they are modified or eliminated, the associated behavior is also modified or eliminated. This principle places the misconception hypothesis squarely in a cognitive orientation to understanding human behavior, even though it does not rule out other psychological processes which contribute to the development and alteration of misconceptions.

2. Misconceptions are specific and concrete when properly identified. Proper identification sometimes requires the therapist to rephrase the jumbled verbalizations of his client or patient. The specificity and concreteness of a misconception is illustrated in the following excerpt from the case of a 250-pound dominating husband who was hospitalized for depression. He explained that his wife was neurotic because she claimed that he frightened her and therefore she could not talk with him. He insisted that he was blameless and had always tried to help her to reason calmly; his intentions were always of the best. Whenever a point of dispute arose in our interviews, however, he spoke loudly, forcefully, dogmatically, and with great persistence. His eagerness to win all battles was one of his outstanding characteristics. Nonetheless, his misconception that he had done nothing to bring about his wife's refusal to talk was sincere. This misconception, "I have done nothing to frighten my wife; her fear of me is irrational," is specific and concrete. Only after repeated discussions of this patient's ingrained habit of overwhelming others, illustrated by instances from our interviews, did he begin to recognize that for years he had frightened and wearied his wife by his domineering manner and tactics. Although he had other misconceptions about himself in relation to his wife, and she had

some about him, his behavior toward her altered remarkably when he recognized that he frightened her by his attacks, not all of which were motivated by the best of intentions.

This discussion of the specificity of misconceptions should not mislead one into thinking that psychotherapy is a simple process of pointing out to clients their faulty understandings of themselves and their relationships with others. Even though misconceptions can eventually be discovered, the process of discovery may be long and tortuous.

3. Misconceptions are often obscured by defensive misconceptions; thus, psychotherapy rather than simple reeducation is ordinarily required. Normal persons often will correct a faulty belief when they are shown that they have been misled by their own thinking. The neurotic or otherwise maladjusted, however, have been given corrective evidence over long periods of time with little or no effect. In those who come for treatment, ordinary methods of education have failed. Therapy based upon the misconception hypothesis is not, therefore, a naive rationalism which holds that misconceptions can be corrected simply by providing more accurate information. Another principle, the neurotic paradox (see Chapter One), is required to account for the failure of reeducation. Psychoanalysts generally explain this paradox—the neurotic's tendency to cling to beliefs even after they have been shown to be irrational and self-defeating—by invoking the doctrine of repression or other defense mechanisms. By the use of these mechanisms, the neurotic is able to avoid making a thorough evaluation of his beliefs since the mechanisms render the beliefs inaccessible to conscious, rational consideration. There are other explanations for the avoidance phenomenon, but in general they all imply that somehow the individual prevents himself from close consideration of the validity of his beliefs.

4. Therapy based upon the misconception hypothesis provides the therapist with constant, specific goals throughout treatment: to find and change the misconceptions which control undesirable behavior. Relevant misconceptions which impede recovery may be detected at any stage of treatment. Even in the opening interview, the therapist may be faced with the patient's misconceptions about the process of treatment itself. If these faulty beliefs about therapy can be corrected, its course proceeds more smoothly.

If a history is taken, it can be most helpful in indicating the pattern of self-defeating misconceptions which lie behind the client's difficulties. As treatment progresses, the therapist, with the help of the patient, tries to detect the misconceptions which guide and control the patient's maladjusted behavior. In the course of treatment, the patient's distorted perceptions of the therapist—his transference reactions—provide both therapist and patient with invaluable knowledge about the characteristic misconceptions the patient relies upon in other social interactions. Finally, the termination of treatment may reveal further misconceptions about the patient's ability to live comfortably without psychotherapy.

5. There are many procedures available to the therapist for discovering relevant misconceptions. The most widely used technique is the interview in which therapist and client discuss the individual's problems. The initial discussions may not, of course, reveal either the client's central problems or the misconceptions underlying them. Many additional interviews, sometimes employing specialized techniques, may be required before the most significant misconceptions are uncovered. Only some of the specialized techniques will be mentioned here.

Client-centered therapy makes extensive use of self-examination procedures, in which the therapist facilitates the client's examination of his difficulties in the hope that he will himself discover his basic misconceptions. Psychoanalysts have devised a number of techniques for this purpose. Free association is the best known of these techniques; analysts also make extensive use of patient behavior within the interview, particularly transference reactions. Some therapists use hypnosis with susceptible subjects in the hope of finding content which has not been accessible to ordinary interview techniques. Systematic behavioral analyses are practiced by behavior therapists, who hope that examination of the fine details of the individual's problem behaviors will help to specify his difficulties more exactly. Although behavioral analysis is supposedly limited to observable behavior, the procedure often reveals the faulty beliefs underlying the external behavior. Gestalt therapists emphasize the usefulness of postural, gestural, and vocal characteristics of the individual as a means for discovering his primary difficulties with himself and his social interactions. Transactional analysis differentiates among the patient's Parent, Adult, and Child ego states in attempting to determine when irrational Parent and Child ego states (which can be viewed as clusters of misconceptions) are controlling undesirable behavior. Although psychological tests have not been formally used for discovering misconceptions, many of their results, particularly for the Thematic Apperception Test, can be directly viewed as indicators of misconceptions.

6. Misconceptions are often clustered in groups of related misconceptions. Although a client or patient may have a large number of misconceptions, therapists need not find and change all of them. For the clusters tend to be loosely organized into dominant or superordinate misconceptions which subsume related but subordinate ones. If the central or significant ones which control disturbed psychological functioning can be discovered and changed, the associated maladjustments are reduced or eliminated without the necessity of dealing painfully with each and every subordinate misconception. (The clustering of misconceptions is discussed in Chapters Two and Six.) Not all misconceptions, moreover, need to be modified or eliminated. Many are benign in that they have little if any influence on the individual's adjustment. Both the clustering of misconceptions and the innocuous nature of those which are benign reduce the task of therapy.

7. When the therapist diagnoses the central problems of a particular individual for purposes of therapy, his major task, according to the misconception hypothesis, is to ascertain the crucial clusters of misconceptions which govern the disturbed behavior. Although there has been no systematic use of misconceptions for diagnostic purposes, the logic of individual diagnosis within this system is clear. If, as hypothesized, psychological disturbances are due to the faulty beliefs which control them, then detecting these clusters serves as a means for specifying the problems which need to be dealt with in treatment. At the present time, however, we do not have adequate instruments for detecting the crucial clusters. We are usually forced to engage in long periods of intensive interviewing in the hope that the significant clusters will be uncovered. In addition, there is little general agreement on the misconceptions which are likely to be most influential for particular syndromes of disturbed behavior. A number of therapeutic approaches which ex-

plicitly attempt to specify central misconceptions are discussed in Chapters Seven, Eight, and Nine. Chapter Six also includes a description of two basic clusters which I have found particularly useful but which are not dealt with at great length in the literature: the misconception that one is on the verge of insanity because of persisting anxiety symptoms, and the misconception that one is a special person who must have his own way at all costs.

Despite the large number of significant misconceptions known to most psychotherapists, clinical judgment must still be employed in determining which faulty beliefs in a given individual are most in need of treatment. One of the greatest problems of the therapist is to determine early in treatment which misconceptions are most relevant to the patient's difficulties. This problem is also the one which might profit the most from systematic research. The variety of techniques for discovering relevant misconceptions, briefly discussed under principle 5 above, all provide at least tentative leads for such research. For just one example, thematic apperception tests are in widespread use for detecting some of the themes that are important in a client's or patient's psychopathology. Such themes can be interpreted rather directly as being due to faulty beliefs held by the individual. When, for example, a thematic apperception protocol contains the theme that the subject consistently becomes anxious over sexual topics, that theme can be viewed as a result of his misconceptions about himself in relation to sex. There are good reasons to suspect that a systematic method for discovering basic misconceptions early in treatment would forward the process of therapy more than almost any other discovery. Therapists and their patients can spend many weeks and months struggling to uncover the misconceptions which are most central. Failure to uncover them can lead to unproductive treatment strung out over years. Once the misconceptions are detected, there are many methods for trying to change them.

8. Clustered misconceptions can be used to classify patients in diagnostic categories. Therapists have not ordinarily found current classifications of help, although all therapists probably assign some rough diagnostic label to each person they see in treatment. The nonsystematic classification procedures which have dominated formal diagnosis since the time of Kraepelin add little to the thera-

pist's knowledge of the patient or the specific goals of treatment. On the other hand, the misconception hypothesis can provide a systematic procedure, whereby an individual is classified according to the most prominent clusters displayed by him. Even when current diagnostic labels are at issue, the patient's self-report of his misconceptions constitutes much of the basis for the diagnosis. For example, reported irrational beliefs about persecution or grandiosity are elementary indicators of paranoid reactions. Reported irrational beliefs about the harmfulness of ordinarily harmless objects or situations are the accepted basis for diagnosing phobic reaction. Similarly, other psychoses and neuroses can be shown to depend for their diagnosis upon revealed misconceptions. Diagnostic labeling based upon clusters of observed misconceptions would be far more meaningful to the therapist, since it would specify some of the significant goals of treatment—the changing of key misconceptions associated with that diagnostic label. (See Chapter Six.)

9. Misconceptions are vulnerable to many different therapeutic procedures or techniques. Just as there is no one best way to teach a foreign language or to teach surgery or any other higher-order skill, so there is no one best way to correct mistaken ideas. For misconceptions are faulty beliefs or convictions. Those of most importance in therapy are the misunderstandings of the self and of one's relations with others. Chapter Three discusses four general methods used by therapists to present evidence to their clients and patients in order to bring about changes in their misconceptions. Not surprisingly, these four tools are not the property of psychotherapists alone; they have been used throughout history whenever efforts have been made to change mistaken ideas. The four general methods are self-examination, explanation, self-demonstration, and vicariation or modeling. Certain of these methods are typically employed in given approaches to therapy, but some therapists may use all four. At least traces of all four may be found in all therapies. These methods, it should be emphasized, merely describe the ways in which therapists attempt to bring about changes in misconceptions. What happens within the patient may be a different story, for there are no infallible means for changing faulty beliefs.

In self-examination the therapist tries to encourage the client or patient to consider and evaluate the assumptions or beliefs related to his problems. In the accepting atmosphere of the therapeutic interview, he may perceive hitherto overlooked relationships, faulty conclusions based upon misinterpreted evidence, corrective evidence hitherto obscured by the vivid demand characteristics of his emotional reactions, or new orientations which had been blocked by defensive misconceptions. The process of self-examination is often facilitated by helpful reflections from the therapist as practiced so consistently in the client-centered approach. If interpretations and confrontations are also employed to supply the client with information not previously available to him, there is a blending of self-examination with explanation.

Explanation is probably the most widely used of all therapeutic methods to change misconceptions. When using explanation, the therapist provides the individual with verbal evidence intended to change the misconception at issue. Most therapists have learned that an obvious teaching approach is rarely of help to the patient unless the problem itself is a lack of information. Thus, the therapist is usually forced to work step by step, hoping to find openings in the patient's private logic by encouraging him to discuss in great detail his intimate thoughts about himself and others. Psychoanalysts have developed these methods over many years in the context of free association and dream interpretation. They have also paid particular attention to the timing of interpretations and confrontations. Although ordinarily eschewed, informal teaching is sometimes employed, particularly for informing the client of therapeutic frames of reference designed to instruct him about the therapist's preferred approach to treatment. For example, in transactional analysis the therapist teaches each patient the tripartite conception of personality involved in the notion of Parent, Adult, and Child ego states. Fortified with this knowledge, the patient can then apply this formula when trying to identify his inappropriate childlike behaviors or his unevaluated beliefs learned in early childhood. The formula can also be viewed as a means of distinguishing clusters of misconceptions attributed to the Child or the Parent from the more rational activities of the Adult.

In self-demonstration, therapists maneuver their clients and patients into situations where they can see for themselves that they have been laboring under false assumptions. Self-demonstration in everyday life is nothing more than trying oneself out to see what happens. The evidence collected in such real-life experiments may, of course, either contradict or confirm the misconceptions. For that reason therapists usually proceed cautiously when preparing self-demonstrations. They might, for instance, use trial discussions during therapy, or role playing under protected circumstances, before carrying out the self-demonstration. If the preliminary trials appear to predict successful outcome, the self-demonstrations are then assigned as homework.

Self-demonstration can also be carried out within the therapy interviews without prearrangement by the therapist. Naturally occurring transference reactions, in which the patient displays distorted attitudes toward the therapist, can be used as self-demonstrations. When such behavior is interpreted by the therapist or when the patient spontaneously develops insight into his transference reactions, self-demonstration has occurred. If the transference reactions are characteristic of the patient in his relationships with others, such self-demonstrations may have considerable influence in changing his misconceptions and the associated maladjusted behavior.

The fourth general method of changing misconceptions may be called *vicariation,* although *modeling* is a term now in much wider use. In modeling, the client or patient observes one or more models performing activities which he believes he is incapable of performing or which he regards as too dangerous. There are many variations on this basic procedure, but in all of them the individual supposedly obtains evidence that when he imagines himself performing the previously avoided activity he no longer finds himself overwhelmed by fear or forebodings of incapability. When his misconception changes to a more rational belief, he is encouraged to attempt the avoided activity in reality rather than just in imagination. Modeling has its limits in that relatively few avoided or feared activities can be reenacted within a therapeutic setting. So-called verbal modeling, however, may be employed to encourage clients to play new roles by providing them with a set of verbal instructions. In trying out new roles in accord with the instructions, clients may discover that their old conceptions of themselves were faulty. When verbal instructions are employed in this fashion, modeling becomes very difficult to distinguish from explanation.

Modeling may also be thought of more broadly, inasmuch as some kind of imitation may occur whenever one individual interacts intensively with another. The intensive interactions with the therapist are likely to produce such imitation in many patients. Such identifications in psychotherapy are usually unintentional and widespread.

These four methods of presenting evidence to change misconceptions are interchangeable to a large extent. That is, what self-examination accomplishes is also likely to be accomplished by explanation or by self-demonstration or by modeling. The method chosen by a particular therapist for a given patient at a particular time depends upon a variety of factors, the most important of which is likely to be the therapist's predilections based upon his previous training and experience. Most approaches to therapy, however, are likely to specify certain techniques thought to be especially appropriate by that particular school of therapy. As used here, *technique* refers to such procedures as free association, dream interpretation, the empty chair in Gestalt therapy, psychodrama, or any of the other procedures associated with a given approach. Such techniques may combine two or more of the four general methods. For example, in transactional analysis patients are likely to be given informal instruction (explanation) in the definitions of Parent, Adult, and Child behaviors. Once they have learned how to apply the concepts to their own behavior, they may then participate in therapy groups, where they can be maneuvered into self-demonstrations to determine whether their understandings of themselves are in accord with the observations of others. In the course of group therapy they may covertly or overtly engage in self-examination, which is often facilitated by further explanations by the therapist or other group members. Modeling may occur if other members of the group provide the patient with helpful examples of how to deal with problems, or more extended identifications may occur if group members or the therapist are taken as more general models. The more specific techniques of the various therapies are thus variations upon or combinations of the four general methods.

This rather lengthy recapitulation of the four methods for marshaling evidence to change misconceptions has been presented here because they are the primary tools used to encourage clients and patients to engage in cognitive review of their misconceptions.

10. Misconceptions are modified or eliminated as a result of repeated cognitive review. This principle, elaborated in Chapter Four, is the core of the patient's task in psychotherapy once he and the therapist have reached at least a tentative understanding of the misconceptions which may be relevant to his problems. Most current methods of psychotherapy provide ample opportunity for repeated cognitive review, although a different terminology may be employed. The psychoanalytic term *working through* refers to the tendency of patients to discuss their central concepts repeatedly; patients thus have many opportunities to reconsider their false beliefs in many contexts. The behavior therapists systematically arrange opportunities for repeated cognitive review by repeatedly presenting real or imagined situations intended to produce new learning or the extinction of old responses. Although some behavior therapists would probably insist that these repetitions have little to do with cognition, their clients are always awake during treatment and are therefore aware of its purpose each time the therapist repeats his instructions. Although most approaches to treatment do not have explicit requirements for repeated cognitive review, all of them practice it. Chapter Four provides a number of illustrations of such practices, including a detailed presentation of the use of repeated review in Gestalt therapy. Since repeated discussion of bothersome topics is found in all therapies, repeated cognitive review on a systematic or on a nonsystematic basis is common to all of them.

Some years ago I devised a very simple method of overcoming isolated fears and other circumscribed misconceptions. The details of the procedure, which is based upon the principle of repeated review, and a case illustration are found at the end of Chapter Four. In this procedure the individual repeatedly describes aloud to the therapist the disturbing situation he is imagining. It has worked successfully with over fifty individuals, about half of whom were also in treatment for more extensive problems. Its simplicity permits its use in almost any therapeutic approach, since it requires no elaborate training or preparation by either therapist or client. The client is asked only to perform the very simple task of reporting what he is imagining and how he feels.

11. Cognitions control emotions and feelings; disruptive affect is the result of faulty perceptions, beliefs, and convictions.

Therefore, if the misconceptions which control disruptive affect can be changed, it can be eliminated or brought under the individual's control. Although much of the literature on psychotherapy implies that treatment should be directly aimed at changing undesirable feelings and emotions, the currently accepted understanding of emotion (see Chapter Five) holds that affective reactions are triggered by cognitions and can be modified by cognitions. The alternative point of view, that emotion or affect is somehow an independent entity which can be modified or eliminated only by "expressing" it, is an outmoded doctrine given enormous impetus by the early publications on catharsis by Breuer and Freud. The currently accepted doctrine, that emotions and feelings are instigated and controlled largely by cognitions, calls for a radical reassessment of those therapeutic techniques which supposedly depend upon catharsis for their success.

If inappropriate emotions, such as anxiety, hostility, and depression, are controlled by faulty beliefs and convictions, then changing these misconceptions should bring about reduction in the undesirable affect. Therapy based upon the misconception hypothesis consistently attempts to discover the misconceptions which trigger and control inappropriate affect. Many of the misconceptions may be deeply ingrained if they have persisted over long periods of time. As long as the therapist is unaware that misconceptions control persistent emotional outbursts, he is likely to be impressed with the strength of the passions. Once the misconceptions which govern emotional reactions are recognized, the power of misconceptions in controlling affect becomes far more impressive. Despite the priority accorded cognition in this point of view, there is no intention here of overlooking the great importance of the emotional reactions and feelings so often observed during treatment. Instead of their being viewed as the ultimate targets of treatment, however, they are viewed as extremely useful signals of the presence of faulty beliefs and convictions.

12. Undesirable emotional reactions and feelings displayed during therapy are indicators of underlying misconceptions which may require modification or elimination. Such affective displays should alert the therapist to difficulties which the patient has not

resolved because he has not been able to clear up his underlying misconceptions. When these misconceptions are revealed and challenged by the therapist—a challenge usually directed at fundamental assumptions—the patient may well undergo intensified emotional reaction; challenging anyone's assumptions about himself and his relations with others is only too likely to raise storms of emotion. Therefore, even though therapy guided by the misconception hypothesis is based upon cognitive principles, the events during such therapy are rarely cold and rational. Chapter Five deals in more detail with the role of emotion and feeling in a cognitive approach to psychotherapy.

13. Insight is defined in this book as the individual's recognition that he suffers from one or more misconceptions (see Chapter Five). Whereas most other definitions of insight depend upon the person's organizing rather large numbers of abstract events into some coherent pattern, the present definition is not only more narrow but also more specific and concrete. When defined as recognition of a misconception, the concept of insight can be applied to a specific event—the patient's recognition that he has been acting on a faulty assumption.

When a patient obtains insight into a cluster of misconceptions, he is likely to become oriented to many of his related problems. For example, one young woman recognized that she had been using sex in her relations with males to obtain total control over them. Prior to this insight, she had believed that she was merely playing the usual social games with them. When she recognized that she was actually using sexual favors as a means of control, she was then able to understand why she encountered so many rejections from the males with whom she tried to trade sex for domination. She was also able to give up, grudgingly to be sure, her constant efforts to control. Consequently, her relationships with men changed radically.

14. Progress in therapy can be gauged by the number and quality of insights gained during therapy. Once therapists have an approximate knowledge of the basic misconceptions from which the individual suffers, then progress can be assessed by the changing of misconceptions. The absolute number of misconceptions which are

altered may, of course, have little relationship to actual progress. Peripheral misconceptions may influence only isolated aspects of behavior; thus, insight into these minor faulty beliefs may produce little readjustment. When, however, insight occurs for the more central clusters of misconceptions which control large areas of maladjustment, progress is far more noticeable. The young woman referred to above who used sex to gain control over men had spent several months discussing her dating behavior before she recognized her central problem. In the early weeks of therapy she discovered that she pursued men too actively, that she expected to have the undivided attention at all times of the man she was currently dating, and that she felt quite justified in dating other men who struck her fancy. These preliminary peripheral insights improved her social skills, but they had little influence on her overall relationships with men. When, however, she became aware of her expectation that sexual favors conferred on a man should automatically make him her slave, the entire texture of her relationships changed. In a few additional interviews she discovered that her needs to dominate were so strong that even with females she kept books to decide when she had given enough so that she could expect constant help and admiration from them. After she gained insight into her trading of favors for control over others, her relationships with girls also underwent considerable improvement.

Insight into peripheral or central misconceptions may not, of course, result in the automatic acquisition of alternative conceptions which will produce more adjusted behavior. Nonetheless, recognition of error provides one with the necessary foundation for trying to find more constructive beliefs. The woman discussed above was young, bright, highly motivated, and very unhappy about her social relationships. For her, the finding of more constructive solutions was largely a matter of combing through alternative ways of interacting socially. For those who lack her resources, the search for better conceptions may be far more difficult. Thus, the gaining of insight is only a partial gauge of progress in treatment, but perhaps the most important one. For the person who lacks insight into the specific sources of his difficulties lacks all guidelines for finding his way out. If he can resolve his confusion by finding the misconceptions that have created his difficulties, he can seek better solutions with some hope of success.

Contributions to the misconception hypothesis from many different sources have facilitated the present formulation of this cognitive approach to psychotherapy. After over a hundred years of concern with the problem of expunging faulty ideas from the mind, psychotherapists are becoming increasingly aware of methods for discovering and changing them. Perhaps the most useful contribution of the hypothesis to the practicing therapist is that it frees him from the tyranny of technique. While therapists were seeking magic formulas which would specify how psychological treatments could be made more exact and efficient, other therapists were finding still other techniques which seemed to accomplish the same purpose. We are obviously more proficient with our current storehouse of techniques, but general principles can better point the way to better treatment. General principles which can be applied with the help of many different techniques are more congruent with the known flexibility and complex nature of man.

References

ALEXANDER, F. *The Scope of Psychoanalysis.* New York: Basic Books, 1961.

ALEXANDER, F., and FRENCH, T. M. *Psychoanalytic Therapy.* New York: Ronald Press, 1946.

ANSBACHER, H. L. "Sensus Privatus Versus Sensus Communis." *Journal of Individual Psychology,* 1965, *21,* 48–50.

ANSBACHER, H. L., and ANSBACHER, R. R. (Eds.) *The Individual Psychology of Alfred Adler.* New York: Harper and Row, 1956.

ARNOLD, M. (Ed.) *Feelings and Emotions: The Loyola Symposium.* New York: Academic Press, 1970.

BANDURA, A. *Principles of Behavior Modification.* New York: Holt, Rinehart, and Winston, 1969.

BANDURA, A. "Psychotherapy Based Upon Modeling Principles." In A. E. Bergin and S. L. Garfield (Eds.), *Handbook of Psychotherapy and Behavior Change: An Empirical Analysis.* New York: Wiley, 1971.

BERGIN, A. E., and STRUPP, H. H. *Changing Frontiers in the Science of Psychotherapy.* Chicago: Aldine-Atherton, 1972.

BERNE, E. *Transactional Analysis in Psychotherapy: A Systematic Individual and Social Psychiatry.* New York: Grove Press, 1961.

BERNE, E. *Games People Play.* New York: Grove Press, 1964.

BERNE, E. *Principles of Group Treatment.* New York: Oxford University Press, 1966.

BIEBER, I. "The Concept of Irrational Belief Systems as Primary Elements of Psychopathology." *Journal of the American Academy of Psychoanalysts*, 1974, *2*, 91–100.

BREUER, J., and FREUD, S. *Studies on Hysteria*. New York: Basic Books, 1957. Originally published in 1895.

BRIDGER, W. A., and MANDEL, I. J. "Abolition of the PRE by Instructions in GSR Conditioning." *Journal of Experimental Psychology*, 1965, *69*, 476–482.

BRODY, M. W. *Observations on "Direct Analysis": The Therapeutic Technique of Dr. John N. Rosen*. New York: Vantage Press, 1959.

CAUTELA, J. R. "Treatment of Compulsive Behavior by Covert Sensitization." *Psychological Record*, 1966, *16*, 33–41.

COLBY, K. M. "Psychotherapeutic Processes." In P. R. Farnsworth (Ed.), *Annual Review of Psychology*. Palo Alto, Calif.: Annual Reviews, 1964.

COMBS, A. W., and SNYGG, D. *Individual Behavior, A Perceptual Approach to Behavior*. (Rev. ed.) New York: Harper, 1959.

CUMMING, E., and CUMMING, J. *Closed Ranks*. Cambridge, Mass.: Harvard University Press, 1957.

DAWSON, M. E. "Comparison of Classical Conditioning and Relational Learning." Unpublished master's thesis, University of Southern California, 1966.

DAWSON, M. E., and GRINGS, W. W. "Comparison of Classical Conditioning and Relational Learning." *Journal of Experimental Psychology*, 1968, *76*, 227–231.

DREIKURS, R. "The Adlerian Approach to Psychodynamics" and "The Adlerian Approach to Psychotherapy." In M. I. Stein (Ed.), *Contemporary Psychotherapies*. New York: Free Press, 1961.

DUBOIS, P. C. *The Psychic Treatment of Nervous Disorders*. New York: Funk and Wagnalls, 1909. First published in 1904.

ELLENBERGER, H. E. *The Discovery of the Unconscious*. New York: Basic Books, 1970.

ELLIS, A. *Reason and Emotion in Psychotherapy*. New York: Lyle Stuart, 1962.

ELLIS, A. "Goals of Psychotherapy." In A. R. Mahrer (Ed.), *The Goals of Psychotherapy*. New York: Appleton-Century-Crofts, 1967.

ENGLISH, H. B. Personal communication, 1960.

ENGLISH, H. B., and ENGLISH, A. *A Comprehensive Dictionary of Psychological and Psychoanalytical Terms*. New York: Longmans, Green, 1958.

References 203

ENGLISH, O. S., HAMPE, W. W. JR., BACON, C. L., and SETTLAGE, C. F. *Direct Analysis and Schizophrenia.* New York: Grune and Stratton, 1961.

ENRIGHT, J. B. "An Introduction to Gestalt Techniques:" In J. Fagan and I. L. Shepherd (Eds.), *Gestalt Therapy Now: Theory, Techniques, Application.* Palo Alto, Calif.: Science and Behavior Books, 1970.

FENICHEL, O. *Problems of Psychoanalytic Technique.* Albany, N.Y.: Psychoanalytic Quarterly, 1941.

FENICHEL, O. *The Psychoanalytic Theory of Neuroses.* New York: Norton, 1945.

FERENCZI, S., and RANK, O. *The Development of Psychoanalysis.* New York: Dover, 1956. Originally published in 1923.

FRANK, J. *Persuasion and Healing: A Comparative Study of Psychotherapy.* Baltimore: Johns Hopkins Press, 1961. (Revised 1973)

FRANKL, V. *Psychotherapy and Existentialism.* New York: Simon and Schuster, 1967.

FREUD, S. *The Interpretation of Dreams.* (3rd ed.) New York: Macmillan, 1913.

FREUD, S. *An Outline of Psychoanalysis.* New York: Norton, 1949. First published in 1940.

FREUD, S. "Further Recommendations in the Technique of Psychoanalysis: Recollection, Repetition and Working Through (1914). In *Collected Papers.* Vol. 2. London: Hogarth Press, 1950a.

FREUD, S. "Psychoanalysis" (1922). In *Collected Papers.* Vol. 5. London: Hogarth Press, 1950b.

FROMM-REICHMANN, F. *Principles of Intensive Psychotherapy.* Chicago: University of Chicago Press, 1950.

GILL, M. "The Present State of Psychoanalytic Theory." *Journal of Abnormal and Social Psychology,* 1959, *58,* 1–8.

GREENSON, R. R. "The Classic Psychoanalytic Approach." In S. Arieti (Ed.), *American Handbook of Psychiatry.* Vol. 2. New York: Basic Books, 1959.

GRINGS, W. W. "Verbal-Perceptual Factors in the Conditioning of Autonomic Responses." In W. F. Prokasy (Ed.), *Classical Conditioning: A Symposium.* New York: Appleton-Century-Crofts, 1965. Pp. 71–89.

GURIN, G., VEROFF, J., and FELD, S. *Americans View Their Mental Health.* New York: Basic Books, 1960.

HARPER, R. A. *Psychoanalysis and Psychotherapy, 36 Systems.* Englewood Cliffs, N.J.: Prentice-Hall, 1959.

HORNEY, K. *Neurosis and Human Growth.* New York: Norton, 1950.

HOROWITZ, L. L. "Strategies Within Hypnosis for Reducing Phobic Behavior." *Journal of Abnormal Psychology,* 1970, *75,* 104–112.

HORWITZ, W. A., POLATIN, P., KOLB, L. C., and HOCH, P. H. "A Study of Cases of Schizophrenia Treated by 'Direct Analysis' (1957)." *American Journal of Psychiatry,* 1958, *114,* 780–783.

JAMES, W. *The Principles of Psychology.* New York: Holt, 1890.

JANET, P. *The Major Symptoms of Hysteria.* London: Macmillan, 1907.

JONES, E. *The Life and Work of Sigmund Freud.* Vol. 1. New York: Basic Books, 1953.

JURJEVICH, R. *Direct Psychotherapy.* Coral Gables, Fla.: University of Miami Press, 1973.

KARON, B. P., and VANDERBOS, G. R. "The Consequences of Psychotherapy for Schizophrenic Patients." *Psychotherapy: Theory, Research and Practice,* 1972, *9,* 111–119.

KELLY, G. A. *The Psychology of Personal Constructs.* Vols. 1 and 2. New York: Norton, 1955.

KEMPLER, W. "Experiential Psychotherapy with Families." In J. Fagan and I. L. Shepherd (Eds.), *Gestalt Therapy Now: Theory, Techniques, Application.* Palo Alto, Calif.: Science and Behavior Books, 1970.

KENDLER, H., and SPENCE, J. (Eds.) *Essays in Neobehaviorism.* New York: Appleton-Century-Crofts, 1971.

KOHUT, H. "Forms and Transformations of Narcissism." *Journal of the American Psychoanalytic Association,* 1966, *14,* 243–272.

LAZARUS, A. A. "Behavior Rehearsal Versus Nondirective Therapy Versus Advice in Effecting Behavior Change." *Journal of Behavior Research and Therapy,* 1966, *4,* 209–212.

LAZARUS, A. A. *Behavior Therapy and Beyond.* New York: McGraw-Hill, 1971.

LAZARUS, R. S., AVERILL, J. R., and OPTON, E. M. "Toward a Cognitive Theory of Emotion." In M. Arnold (Ed.), *Feelings and Emotions: The Loyola Symposium.* New York: Academic Press, 1970.

LEEPER, R. S. "The Motivational and Perceptual Properties of Emotions as Indicating Their Fundamental Character and Role." In M. Arnold (Ed.), *Feelings and Emotions: The Loyola Symposium.* New York: Academic Press, 1970.

LOCKE, E. A. "Is 'Behavior Therapy' Behavioristic?" *Psychological Bulletin,* 1971, *76,* 318–327.

MACKINNON, R. A., and MICHELS, R. *The Psychiatric Interview in Clinical Practice.* Philadelphia: Saunders, 1971.

MALTZMAN, I. M. "The Orienting Reflex and Thinking as Determiners of Conditioning and Generalization to Words." In H. H. Kendler and J. Spence (Eds.), *Essays in Neobehaviorism: A Memorial Volume to Kenneth Spence*. New York: Appleton-Century-Crofts, 1971.

MARTORANO, R. D., and NATHAN, P. E. "Syndromes of Psychosis and Nonpsychosis: Factor Analysis of a Systems Analysis." *Journal of Abnormal Psychology*, 1972, *80*, 1–10.

MC CORDICK, S. Unpublished manuscript, 1973.

MC FALL, R. M., and TWENTYMAN, C. T. "Four Experiments on the Relative Contributions of Rehearsal, Modeling, and Coaching to Assertion Training." *Journal of Abnormal Psychology*, 1973, *81*, 199–218.

MENNINGER, K. *Theory of Psychoanalytic Technique*. New York: Basic Books, 1958.

MEYER, A. *Collected Works of Adolf Meyer*. Vol. 2. Baltimore: Johns Hopkins Press, 1951.

MILFORD, N. *Zelda*. New York: Avon Books, 1970.

MOWRER, O. H. "Learning Theory and the Neurotic Paradox." *American Journal of Orthopsychiatry*, 1948, *18*, 571–610.

MURRAY, E. J., and JACOBSON, L. I. "The Nature of Learning in Traditional and Behavioral Psychotherapy." In A. E. Bergin and S. L. Garfield (Eds.), *Handbook of Psychotherapy and Behavior Change*. New York: Wiley, 1971.

PERLS, F. S. *Gestalt Therapy Verbatim*. Lafayette, Calif.: Real People Press, 1969.

PERLS, F. S. "Four Lectures." In J. Fagan and I. L. Shepherd (Eds.), *Gestalt Therapy Now: Theory, Techniques, Application*. Palo Alto, Calif.: Science and Behavior Books, 1970.

PERLS, F. S., HEFFERLINE, R. E., and GOODMAN, P. *Gestalt Therapy: Excitement and Growth in Human Personality*. New York: Dell, 1965. Originally published in 1951.

PERRY, H. S., and GAWEL, M. L. (Eds.) *The Interpersonal Theory of Psychiatry*. New York: Norton, 1953.

PETERSON, D. R., and LONDON, P. "A Role for Cognition in the Behavioral Treatment of a Child's Elimination Disturbance." In L. P. Ullmann and L. Krasner (Eds.), *Case Studies in Behavior Modification*. New York: Holt, 1965.

PHILLIPS, E. L. *Psychotherapy: A Modern Theory and Practice*. Englewood Cliffs, N.J.: Prentice-Hall, 1956.

POTTER, S. *Lifemanship*. New York: Holt, 1950.

RACHMAN, S. "The Role of Muscular Relaxation in Desensitization Therapy." *Behavior Research and Therapy*, 1968, *6*, 159–166.

RACHMAN, S., and TEASDALE, J. D. "Aversion Therapy: An Appraisal." In C. M. Franks (Ed.), *Behavior Therapy: Appraisal and Status*. New York: McGraw-Hill, 1969.

RAIMY, V. "The Self-Concept as a Factor in Counseling and Personality Organization." Unpublished doctoral dissertation, Ohio State University, 1943. Published under the same title by Ohio State University Libraries, Columbus, Ohio, 1971.

RAIMY, V. "Self-Reference in Counseling Interviews." *Journal of Consulting Psychology*, 1948, *12*, 153–163.

ROSEN, J. N. *Selected Papers on Direct Psychoanalysis*. Vol. 2. New York: Grune and Stratton, 1968.

ROSENZWEIG, S. "Some Implicit Common Factors in Diverse Methods of Psychotherapy." *American Journal of Orthopsychiatry*, 1936, *6*, 412–415.

ROTTER, J. B. *Social Learning and Clinical Psychology*. Englewood Cliffs, N.J.: Prentice-Hall, 1954.

ROTTER, J. B. "Some Implications of Social Learning Theory for the Practice of Psychotherapy." In D. J. Levis (Ed.), *Learning Approaches to Therapeutic Behavior Change*. Chicago: Aldine-Atherton, 1970.

SALTER, A. *Conditioned Reflex Therapy*. New York: Farrar, Straus, 1949.

SARTRE, J.-P. *Nausea*. New York: New Directions, 1959.

SCHACHTER, S. *Emotion, Obesity, and Crime*. New York: Academic Press, 1971.

SCHACHTER, S., and SINGER, J. E. "Cognitive, Social, and Physiological Determinants of Emotional States." *Psychological Review*, 1962, *69*, 377–399.

SCHEFLEN, A. E. *A Psychotherapy of Schizophrenia: Direct Analysis*. Springfield, Ill.: Thomas, 1961.

SIMKIN, J. "Mary: A Session with a Passive Patient." In J. Fagan and I. L. Shepherd (Eds.), *Gestalt Therapy Now: Theory, Techniques, Application*. Palo Alto, Calif.: Science and Behavior Books, 1970.

SMITH, M. G. "Cognitive Rehearsal: A Systematic Investigation of a Psychotherapeutic Innovation." Unpublished doctoral dissertation, University of Colorado, 1974.

SNYGG, D., and COMBS, A. W. *Individual Behavior*. New York: Harper, 1949.

STAMPFL, T. G. "Implosive Therapy: An Emphasis on Covert Stimula-lation." In D. J. Levis (Ed.), *Learning Approaches to Thera-peutic Behavior Change.* Chicago: Aldine-Atherton, 1970.

STONE, L. *The Psychoanalytic Situation.* New York: International Uni-versities Press, 1961.

THOMPSON, L. *Robert Frost, the Early Years, 1874–1915.* New York: Holt, 1966.

THOMPSON, L. *Robert Frost, the Years of Triumph, 1915–1938.* New York: Holt, 1970.

THORNE, F. C. *Personality: A Clinical Eclectic Viewpoint.* Brandon, Vt.: Journal of Clinical Psychology, 1961.

WHITE, R. W. *The Abnormal Personality.* (3rd ed.) New York: Ronald, 1964.

WILKINS, W. "Desensitization: Social and Cognitive Factors Under-lying the Effectiveness of Wolpe's Procedure." *Psychological Bulletin,* 1971, *76,* 311–317.

WOLPE, J. *The Practice of Behavior Therapy.* New York: Pergamon Press, 1969.

Index